AMERICA'S ARTS AND SKILLS

"America's Arts and Skills" series appeared in LIFE at intervals of approximately six weeks from April 18, 1955 to May 21, 1956.

TIME INCORPORATED

Editor-in-Chief
Henry R. Luce

President
Roy E. Larsen

Edward K. Thompson, *Managing Editor*
Robert T. Elson, *Deputy Managing Editor*
Philip H. Wootton Jr., *Assistant Managing Editor*
Joseph Kastner, *Copy Editor*
Marian A. MacPhail, *Chief of Research*

by the following editorial staff:

Editor
Margit Varga

Art Director
Charles Tudor

Writer
Roger Butterfield

Editorial Assistants
Margaret Bassett, Barbara Briller,
Vivian Campbell, Helen Deuell,
Robin Hinsdale, Sheila O'Connor

Photographs by
Eliot Elisofon, Andreas Feininger, Fritz Goro,
Gjon Mili, Arnold Newman, Bradley Smith

Publisher
Andrew Heiskell

Assistant Publisher
Arthur R. Murphy Jr.

Book Manager
Robert L. Blackmore

AMERICA'S

ARTS and SKILLS

By the Editors of LIFE

With an Introduction by
CHARLES F. MONTGOMERY, *Director*
The Henry Francis du Pont Winterthur Museum

New York   *1957*   E. P. DUTTON & CO., Inc.

Copyright 1955, 1956, 1957 by Time, Inc.

No part of this book may be reproduced in any form without permission in writing from the publisher, except by a reviewer who wishes to quote brief passages in connection with a review written for inclusion in a magazine or newspaper or broadcast.

Library of Congress Catalog Card Number: 57-8994

Acknowledgments

LIFE is indebted to the following individuals and institutions for their generous assistance in the preparation of the "America's Arts and Skills" series:

General assistance on the entire series:

Edward Alexander, *Colonial Williamsburg Inc., Williamsburg, Va.*
Paul M. Angle, *Chicago Historical Society, Chicago, Ill.*
Turpin C. Bannister, *University of Illinois, Urbana, Ill.*
E. O. Christensen, *National Gallery of Art, Washington, D. C.*
Thomas D. Clark, *University of Kentucky, Lexington, Ky.*
Marshall B. Davidson, *Metropolitan Museum of Art, New York, N. Y.*
Leon DeValinger, Jr., *Delaware State Museum, Dover, Del.*
James M. Fitch, *Columbia University, New York, N. Y.*
James T. Flexner, *New York, N. Y.*
Henry C. Forman, *Baltimore, Md.*
Anthony N. B. Garvan, *University of Pennsylvania, Philadelphia, Pa.*
Samuel M. Green II, *Wesleyan University, Middletown, Conn.*
Walter J. Heacock, *Eleutherian Mills-Hagley Foundation, Wilmington, Del.*
Louis C. Jones, *New York State Historical Association, Cooperstown, N. Y.*
Howard Mumford Jones, *Harvard University, Cambridge, Mass.*
Michael Kraus, *College of the City of New York, New York, N. Y.*
Ronald F. Lee, *National Park Service, Washington, D. C.*
Charles F. Montgomery, *The Henry Francis du Pont Winterthur Museum, Winterthur, Del.*
John A. Munroe, *University of Delaware, Newark, Del.*
John A. Perkins, *University of Delaware, Newark, Del.*
Earl H. Reed, *Chicago, Ill.*
Meyric R. Rogers, *Art Institute of Chicago, Chicago, Ill.*
Donald A. Shelley, *Henry Ford Museum, Dearborn, Mich.*
Robert C. Smith, *University of Pennsylvania, Philadelphia, Pa.*
Frank H. Sommer III, *University of Delaware, Newark, Del.*
Robert D. Starrett, *Indiana State Parks, Indianapolis, Ind.*
Paul Vanderbilt, *Wisconsin State Historical Society, Madison, Wis.*
Roger Van Bolt, *Henry Ford Museum, Dearborn, Mich.*
Charles Van Ravenswaay, *Missouri Historical Society, St. Louis, Mo.*
Louis B. Wright, *Folger Shakespeare Library, Washington, D. C.*

Special Assistance

(Roman numerals after each name indicate the particular chapters on which the assistance was given.)

Bart Anderson—*Chester County (Pa.) Historical Society* V
Wayne Andrews—*New York Historical Society, New York, N. Y.* III, V
Paul M. Angle—*Chicago Historical Society, Chicago, Ill.* VI, VIII
John A. Aubuchon—*Canyon de Chelly National Monument, Ariz.* VII
Kurt Baer—*University of California at Santa Barbara, Calif.* VII
Turpin C. Bannister—*University of Illinois, Urbana, Ill.* IV
Mrs. Florence Bittner—*Prairie du Chien, Wis.* VIII
Mrs. Peter Bolhouse—*Newport Historical Society, Newport, R. I.* VIII
Frederick A. Bonsal—*First Ironworks Association, Saugus, Mass.* I
E. Boyd—*The Museum of New Mexico at Santa Fe, N. M.* VII
Clarence S. Brigham—*American Antiquarian Society,* author of *Paul Revere's Engravings* II
James M. Brown—*Corning Glass Center, Corning, N. Y.* III
Charles E. Buckley—*Wadsworth Atheneum, Hartford, Conn.* I

Mrs. Kathryn C. Buhler—*Boston Museum of Fine Arts, Boston, Mass.* I, II
Helen D. Bullock—*National Trust for Historic Preservation, Washington, D. C.* I, IV
Arthur B. Carlson—*New York Historical Society, New York, N. Y.* I
Carl Carmer—*Irvington-on-Hudson, N. Y.* V
Harold Dean Cater—*Sleepy Hollow Restorations, Inc., Tarrytown, N. Y.* VIII
Father Donald Cheetham—*Eltingville, N. Y.* V
Thomas D. Clark—*University of Kentucky, Lexington, Ky.* VI
Captain David M. Cook—*U. S. Corps of Engineers, Memphis, Tenn.* VI
Charles H. P. Copeland—*Peabody Museum of Salem, Mass.* II
Abbott Cummings—*Metropolitan Museum of Art, New York, N. Y.* I, IV
Colonel John C. Cummings—*Bucks County Historical Society, Doylestown, Pa.* I, V
Carl Cutler, *Mystic, Conn.* V
William Distin—*Henry Ford Museum, Dearborn, Mich.* VIII
Ernest S. Dodge—*Peabody Museum of Salem, Mass.* II
Mrs. Marjory Douglas—*Missouri Historical Society, St. Louis, Mo.* VI
Harry J. Downie—*Carmel, Calif.* VII
Mrs. Antoinette F. Downing—*Providence, R. I.* VIII
Paul H. Downing—*Staten Island, N. Y.* V, VI
Carl W. Drepperd—*Pennsylvania Farm Museum of Landis Valley, Pa.* II, VI
Howard Duncan—*U. S. Corps of Engineers, Memphis, Tenn.* VI
B. T. Ellis—*Laboratory of Anthropology at Santa Fe, N. M.* VII
Betty J. Ezequelle—*New York Historical Society, New York, N. Y.* I
Dean A. Fales, Jr.—*The Henry Francis du Pont Winterthur Museum, Winterthur, Del.* I, II, III, IV
Reginald Fisher—*The Museum of New Mexico at Santa Fe, N. M.* VII
James M. Fitch—*Columbia University, New York, N. Y.* V
Joseph T. Fraser, Jr.—*Pennsylvania Academy of the Fine Arts, Philadelphia, Pa.* IV
Robert P. L. Frick—*Kenmore Association, Fredericksburg, Va.* II
Martha Lou Gandy—*The Henry Francis du Pont Winterthur Museum, Winterthur, Del.* I
Samuel M. Green II—*Wesleyan University, Middletown, Conn.* IV, V
Talbot Hamlin—*Columbia University, New York, N. Y.* IV
M. R. Harrington—*Southwest Museum, Los Angeles, Calif.* VII
Lee M. Hartwell, Jr.—*Kansas City, Mo.* VII
Walter J. Heacock—*Eleutherian Mills-Hagley Foundation, Wilmington, Del.* III
Robert L. Hoke—*Colonial Williamsburg, Inc., Williamsburg, Va.* II
Colonel C. C. Holbrook—*U. S. Corps of Engineers, Memphis, Tenn.* VI
H. Maxson Holloway—*Chicago Historical Society, Chicago, Ill.* VI
Dr. Thomas Hoopes—*City Art Museum, St. Louis, Mo.* VI
Horace L. Hotchkiss, Jr.—*Cooper Union, New York, N. Y.* IV
Louis C. Jones—*New York State Historical Association, Cooperstown, N. Y.* III, IV
Edgar Kaufmann, Jr.—*New York, N. Y.* VIII
John D. Kilbourne—*Historical Society of York County, Pa.* III
Joe Kindig, Jr.—*York, Pa.* II
James Kiryakakis—*Independence National Historic Park, Philadelphia, Pa.* IV
Robert Koch—*Yale University, New Haven, Conn.* VIII
Richard J. Koke—*New York Historical Society, New York, N. Y.* IV
Marjorie Lambert—*The Museum of New Mexico at Santa Fe, N. M.* VII
Oliver Larkin—*Smith College, Northampton, Mass.* V
Bertram K. Little—*Society for the Preservation of New England Antiquities, Boston, Mass.* I
Carl L. Lokke—*National Archives and Records Service, Washington D. C.* II
Janet R. MacFarlane—*New York State Historical Association, Cooperstown, N. Y.* III, IV
C. Boone McClure—*Panhandle-Plains Historical Museum, Canyon, Tex.* VII
Malcom D. McGregor—*Marine Historical Association, Mystic, Conn.* V
Jean McNiece—*New York City Public Library* III

5

John Maxon—*Rhode Island School of Design, Providence, R. I. VIII*
Grace M. Mayer—*Museum of the City of New York, New York, N. Y. IV*
Mr. and Mrs. Ward Melville—*Suffolk Museum, Stony Brook, N. Y. V*
Walter M. Merrill—*Essex Institute, Salem, Mass. II*
V. Isabelle Miller—*Museum of the City of New York, New York, N. Y. IV, V*
George Mills—*The Taylor Museum of the Colorado Springs Fine Arts Center, Colo. VII*
Clifford P. Monahon—*Rhode Island Historical Society, Providence, R. I. II*
Charles F. Montgomery—*The Henry Francis du Pont Winterthur Museum, Winterthur, Del. I, II, III, IV*
Lamont Moore—*Yale University Art Gallery, New Haven, Conn. I, IV*
Reginald C. Morrell—*Bristol Clock Museum, Bristol, Conn. III*
Margaret Munier—*Old Sturbridge Village, Sturbridge, Mass. I*
John W. Myer—*Museum of the City of New York, New York, N. Y. IV*
Murray H. Nelligan—*Independence National Historic Park, Philadelphia, Pa. IV*
Professor David T. Nelson—*Luther College, Decorah, Iowa VI*
Frederick D. Nichols—*University of Virginia, Charlottesville, Va. IV*
William H. Noble, Jr.—*Fairmount Park Art Association, Philadelphia, Pa. IV*
Mrs. Inga B. Norstog—*Norwegian-American Historical Museum, Decorah, Iowa VI*
Thomas H. Ormsbee—*Pound Ridge, N. Y. VIII*
Brooks Palmer—Author of *The Book of American Clocks III*
Mrs. Monique Panaggio—*Preservation Society of Newport County, Newport, R. I. VIII*
Virginia Parslow—*New York State Historical Association, Cooperstown, N. Y. III*
Paul Perrot—*Corning Glass Museum, Corning, N. Y. III*
Harold L. Peterson—*National Park Service, Washington, D. C. II*
M. L. Peterson—*Smithsonian Institution, Washington, D. C. VI*
Lydia Bond Powel—*Metropolitan Museum of Art, New York, N. Y. I, IV*
Frederick L. Rath, Jr.—*National Trust for Historic Preservation, Washington, D. C. I*
Donald O. Reichert—*Yale University Art Gallery, New Haven, Conn. I, V*
William Ricciuti—*New Orleans, La. VI*

Lawrence P. Riddle—*Henry Ford Museum, Dearborn, Mich. IV, VI*
Stephen T. Riley—*Massachusetts Historical Society, Boston, Mass. I*
Edsel Rintala—*Henry Ford Museum, Dearborn, Mich. VIII*
Elizabeth Roth—*New York City Public Library III*
Hugh Grant Rowell—*Sleepy Hollow Restorations, Inc., Irvington, N. Y. V*
Alice M. Runyon—*Sleepy Hollow Restorations, Inc., Irvington, N. Y. V*
Carolyn Scoon—*New York Historical Society, New York, N. Y. III, IV, VIII*
Vincent J. Scully, Jr.—*Yale University, New Haven, Conn. VIII*
Josephine Setze—*Yale University Art Gallery, New Haven, Conn I*
Donald A. Shelley—*Henry Ford Museum, Dearborn, Mich. IV, VI*
Frank O. Spinney—*Old Sturbridge Village, Sturbridge, Mass. I*
Edouard A. Stackpole—*Marine Historical Association, Mystic, Conn. V*
Alice E. Starner—*Historical Society of York County, Pa. III*
Robert D. Starrett—*Indiana State Parks, Indianapolis, Ind. IV, VI*
Stanley Stubbs—*Laboratory of Anthropology at Santa Fe, N. M. VII*
John A. H. Sweeney—*The Henry Francis du Pont Winterthur Museum, Winterthur, Del. I*
Holman J. Swinney—*Old Sturbridge Village, Sturbridge, Mass. I*
Alan Symonds—*Henry Ford Museum, Dearborn, Mich. VIII*
Mrs. Catherine Thornton—*Sleepy Hollow Restorations, Inc., Tarrytown, N. Y. VIII*
John Kent Tilton—*Scalamandré Museum of Textiles, New York, N. Y. V*
Karl L. Trever—*National Archives and Records Service, Washington, D. C. II*
Everard Upjohn—*Columbia University, New York, N. Y. V*
Roger Van Bolt—*Henry Ford Museum, Dearborn, Mich. IV, VI, VIII*
Paul Vanderbilt—*Wisconsin State Historical Society, Madison, Wis. VI, VIII*
Charles van Ravenswaay—*Missouri Historical Society, St. Louis, Mo. VI*
Axel von Saldern—*Corning Glass Museum, Corning, N. Y. III*
Margaret V. Wall—*Suffolk Museum, Stony Brook, N. Y. V*
Samuel Wilson, Jr.—*Louisiana Landmarks Society VI*
Myron Wood—*The Taylor Museum of the Colorado Springs Fine Arts Center, Colo. VII*
Arthur Woodward—*Altadena, Calif. VII*
Harry Woodward, Jr.—*Eltingville, N. Y. V*

Table of Contents

Introduction	Charles F. Montgomery, Director, The Henry Francis du Pont Winterthur Museum	*9*
I	The Practical World of the Colonists	*11*
II	The Look of Liberty in Craftsmanship	*37*
III	The Sturdy Age of Homespun	*55*
IV	The Magnificent Greek Revival	*69*
V	The Romantic Decades	*81*
VI	The Fabulous Frontier	*97*
VII	The Timeless Southwest	*113*
VIII	An Age of Gilded Opulence	*129*
IX	Beauty in the Tools of Today	*145*
	Picture Sources	*165*
	Index	*169*

Introduction

CHARLES F. MONTGOMERY

Director, Henry Francis du Pont
Winterthur Museum, Winterthur, Delaware

"The true character of the Americans is mirrored in their homes," said Moreau de Saint-Méry, a perceptive French émigré who came to the United States not long after our Revolution. His remark suggests that a reflection of the inner spirit and genius of the young nation could be glimpsed in the way Americans lived, and in the arts that enriched—indeed were part of—their lives.

Such an insight has come most often from an outsider. Art historians have long recognized the importance of historical background as a necessity for the understanding of any art, but historians in America, with notable exceptions, have been slow to utilize our arts in the study of our history. The Editors of *Life*, in exploring this rich field, have vividly illustrated the truth of Moreau's statement. For this survey reveals not only the development of a distinct pattern of American tradition in the arts, but also brings forth intimate clues to the American character.

The first group of settlers, while maintaining close cultural ties with their various mother countries, were nevertheless—from the moment of their landing—a new kind of people. Here was endless land to be owned by anyone who could transform it from wilderness. Here were refuge and plenty—often even comfort after a few years—for anyone who could fashion for himself the tools for living; it was to the fulfillment of his immediate practical needs that the early colonist applied his ingenuity and craftsmanship, and from self-reliance gained in meeting challenge after challenge sprang the free and imaginative spirit that was to assert itself over the years in a thousand different directions.

Our colonial forebears were busily engaged with the problems of everyday life. First, they were deeply involved in the conquest of a new land, and then in the establishment of a new government. But while they were doing these things, craftsmen and artisans erected public buildings, built houses, and made furniture and furnishings for those houses. That these things were considered too important to be left to chance is illustrated by this comment of Gouverneur Morris in a letter to Washington:

> ... I think it of very great importance to fix the taste of our country properly, and I think your example will go very far in that respect. It is therefore my wish that everything about you should be substantially good and majestically plain, made to endure ...

Such simplification of ornament as well as emphasis on line and proportion are keynotes of American craftsmanship. Seldom did the most ornate native product approach the European in embellishment and lavishness. Americans utilized the styles and ideas which were current in their time by simplifying and adapting patterns from abroad to their needs. However, in New England, the Middle Colonies, and the South problems were divergent, and materials at hand different. As might be expected, a study of forms in both furniture and architecture reveals that the solutions also were different. Unquestionably the different Old World backgrounds of the settlers in different sections contributed to the development of the regional vernacular. In Pennsylvania German crafts we see German custom, design, and motifs grafted to an English stock to evoke American designs of a new and different sort.

We have never as a nation adopted the doctrine of "art for art's sake." Until recent years our strongest aesthetic impulse has been manifested in the direction of the utilitarian arts, in the work of the craftsman rather than that of the professional "artist." It is especially significant, therefore, that the editors of *Life* magazine have traced the development of the American cultural tradition in the things our people have used in their daily living—in the home and at work—their trestle tables and Philadelphia highboys; their clipper ships, prairie schooners, and Model T's; their cotton gins and computing machines; their salt-box houses, Greek temples, and modern research centers. In them we see the broad sweep of achievement in the arts for living, from the first resourceful make-do to today's unparalleled know-how. Furthermore, these functional objects represent not only the aesthetic values of a free people, but also are a reflection of evolving social and economic forces at work.

But *America's Arts and Skills* also illustrates America's growing awareness of the beautiful—and this too is significant. We know that our forebears were conscious of the value of building not only well, but handsomely. Jefferson pointed out, "Architecture is among the most important arts and it is desirable to introduce taste into an art that shows so much." John Adams expressed his high esteem for the arts when he wrote in 1780:

> I must study politics and war, that my sons may have liberty to study mathematics and philosophy. My sons ought to study mathematics and philosophy, geography, natural history and naval architecture, navigation, commerce, and agriculture in order to give their children a right to study painting, poetry, music, architecture, statuary, tapestry, and porcelain.

Interest in art and in history is at a high pitch in America today. Annually both art museums and history museums report ever-increasing attendance. Vast expansion programs to improve exhibits, increase educational facilities, and better accommodate larger crowds are under way at Colonial Williamsburg, the Metropolitan Museum of Art, the Smithsonian Institution, the National Park Service, the Henry Francis du Pont Winterthur Museum, and a host of other places. Membership in the young [American] National Trust for Historic Preservation is booming; and its staff is hard pressed to furnish advice and direction to the myriad preservation projects scattered over the land. But interest is not restricted, by any means, to the arts of the past. No other museum enjoys a healthier growth or greater enthusiasm on the part of its public than the Museum of Modern Art. No other art thrills, delights, or enthralls more than our modern architecture.

America's Arts and Skills is thus a significant and timely book. Its text and superb photography relate and illustrate the resources of our museums, national shrines, historic houses, private collections, and public buildings from the early 1600's through 1956. It opens our eyes to a national tradition of artistic accomplishment that began in the seventeenth century and continues unbroken today. This tradition is part of our history, part of the American story. It is marked by one quality above all others: a vitality born out of optimism, freedom, and belief in the dignity of man. Perhaps that is the reason it is so necessary that we relate ourselves to the past as a part of a continuing tradition, for out of a greater familiarity with our heritage will come increased awareness of the integrity of our people.

Part I

THE PRACTICAL WORLD OF THE COLONISTS

OLD STURBRIDGE VILLAGE, MASS.

EARLY AMERICAN TOOLS are, from left: clamp, broadax used for shaping logs into house timbers, carpenter's square, compass, sickle, flail, wooden

Americans, proud of their achievements in government, industry and science, have had less confidence in their art—perhaps because they are inhibited by a limited use of the word. But Webster defines art first as "skill in the adaptation of things in the natural world to the uses of human life." Another definition is "the production of beauty." It is with these meanings in mind that LIFE presents "America's Arts and Skills," which in a number of essays displays the traditions of American taste and design and the great history of American skill in fashioning beautiful, useful things. The book starts with the tools above, which are not only handsome themselves but were used to make handsome objects, like those shown on following pages.

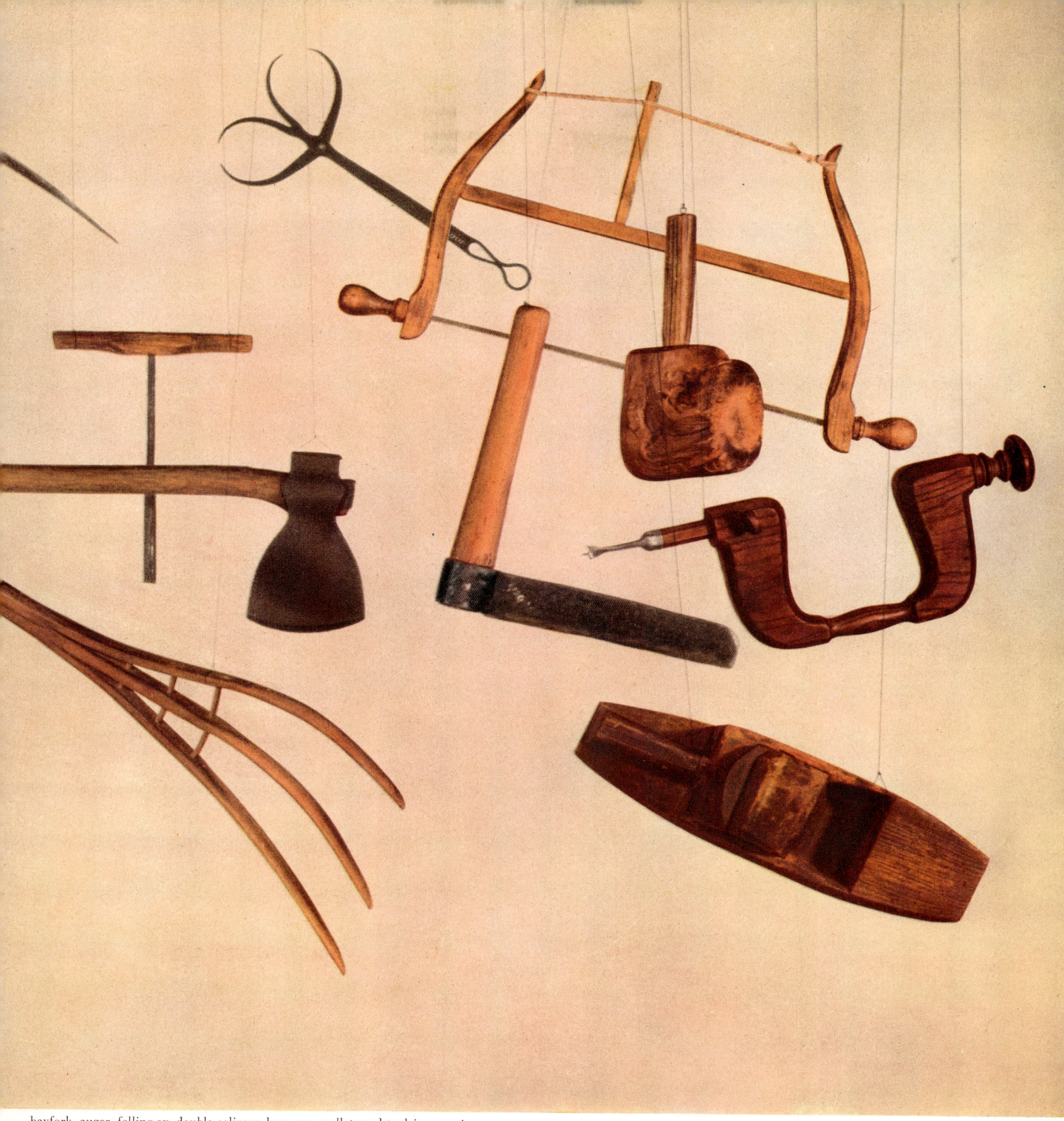

hayfork, auger, felling ax, double calipers, bow saw, mallet used to drive pegs in house frame, L-shaped frow used for splitting shingles, carpenter's brace, plane.

As the nation grew, the arts became more elaborate, the crafts more detailed. Spacious Georgian mansions were built in the South, great Gothic houses along the Hudson. Artisans fashioned the deadly Pennsylvania rifle, inventors perfected mass production. The clipper ships crossed the world's seas, stagecoach and Pullman car crossed the expanding nation. And finally American energy and ingenuity burst into a world of skyscrapers, a myriad of gleaming and running devices made of modern plastics and alloys and a million Cape Cod cottages built on lines laid out by Puritan carpenters. All this, seen in the chapters of this book, not only explains the designs of the American past but provides the values by which to judge the taste of America today.

STUDDED DOOR (*opposite page*) of Parson Capen house in Topsfield, Massachusetts was decorated with wrought-iron nails in diagonal pattern.

YOUNG PURITANS David, Joanna and Abigail Mason of Boston posed in their Sunday best for unknown artist who painted this picture about 1670.

The Practical World of the Colonists

PRODUCING FOR USE, THEY CREATED BEAUTY

With a few hand tools and such skills and memories as they brought from their homelands, the English colonists in Virginia, Maryland and New England, the Dutch on the Hudson and the Swedes on the Delaware attacked the wilderness. Out of these, and the rich raw material of the American land, grew cities, homes and much wealth. And out of the things the colonists made to use in their new world came a surprisingly beautiful heritage of decorative objects.

A successful colonist had to be able to do many things. Of the first arrivals in North Carolina a preacher wrote: "Men are generally of all trades, and women the like within their spheres. . . . Men are generally carpenters, joiners, wheelwrights, coopers, butchers, tanners, shoemakers, tallow-chandlers, watermen and whatnot; women soap-makers, starch-makers, dyers, etc. He or she who cannot do all these things . . . will have but a bad time of it." From this widespread versatility developed the tinkering Yankee who could make or fix anything, from a fine watch to a water wheel.

In the so-called fine arts there was no such rapid progress. Though the wealthy commissioned family portraits which were executed with neatness and grace, the colonists looked down on mere artists. "The Plow-Man that raiseth Grain, is more serviceable to Mankind, than the Painter who draws only to please the Eye," wrote an early New Englander. But human eyes have always yearned to be pleased. Even the Puritans liked color in their homes and dress; when beautiful form was combined with practical purpose they were willing to accept it. Many a colonial carpenter was an artist as well—as the nail-studded door and boldly carved bracket on the opposite page show. In their silverware, their furniture and even their everyday wooden drinking cups and bowls the colonists showed that they knew a good-looking thing when they saw it.

Because of the restrictions of materials, and limited time, the colonial artisan did not indulge in elaborate design. But the limits became a challenge and in American art colonial design became a style —simple, sturdy, never trying to hide the material used nor twist it to unnatural uses. It has had an obvious influence on American taste through the myriad colonial reproductions, which never seem to lose popularity. But it has had an equally strong, if subtler, impact on the work of generations of American designers who, following the colonials, found that usefulness and simplicity go hand in hand with beauty.

The changing architecture

OLD NEW YORK was a hustling center of worldwide trade when the panorama above and below was drawn in 1717 by William Burgis of Boston. The artist stood on what is now Brooklyn Heights and sketched the East River front from the fort at the Battery (marked by flag, *above left*) to the foot of modern Catherine Street (*far right, below*). The lower town which stretched up to Trinity Church (*far right, above*) was largely built by Dutch colonists who imported their

NEWER NEW YORK north of Wall Street (*far right in upper panel*) shows immediately the influence of the British who took over the city in 1664. Here the Dutch houses are mixed with mansions done in the Renaissance style which was popular in 17th Century England. They can be identified by their broad fronts, dormer windows, galleries across the roof and pediments. Here and there is also a house in the more recent Georgian manner, which was to sweep across

16

# of an early American city

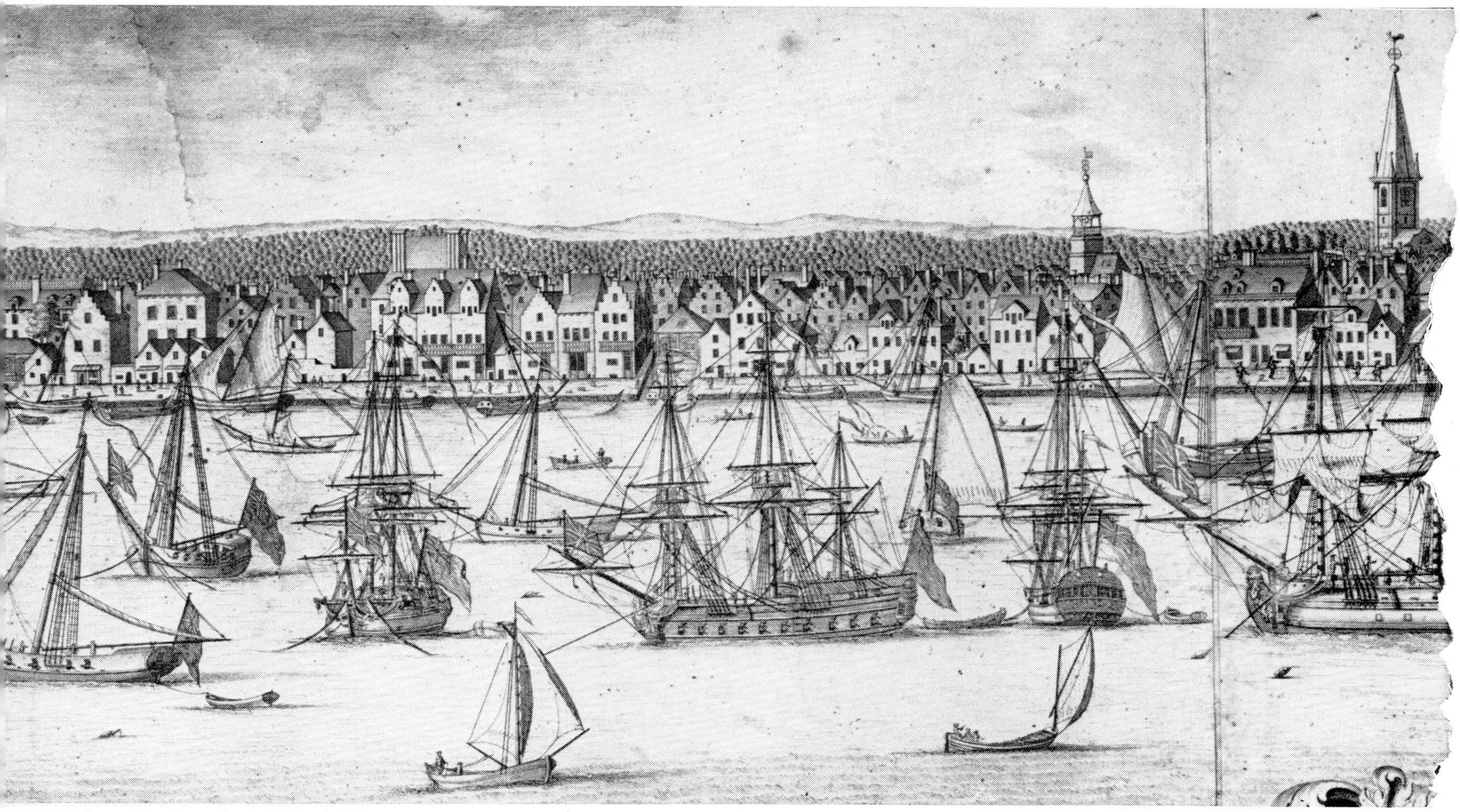

architecture direct from Holland. Their narrow, steep-roofed houses with crow-step gables were crowded together. In their brickwork they used many patterns and colors. Most of Dutch New York was burned during the Revolution and the original Dutch style is seen now only in a few survivals farther up the Hudson. The low, wide-roofed "Dutch Colonial," so familiar today, is really a Flemish cottage style—an example in white brick and blue shutters is seen on page 33.

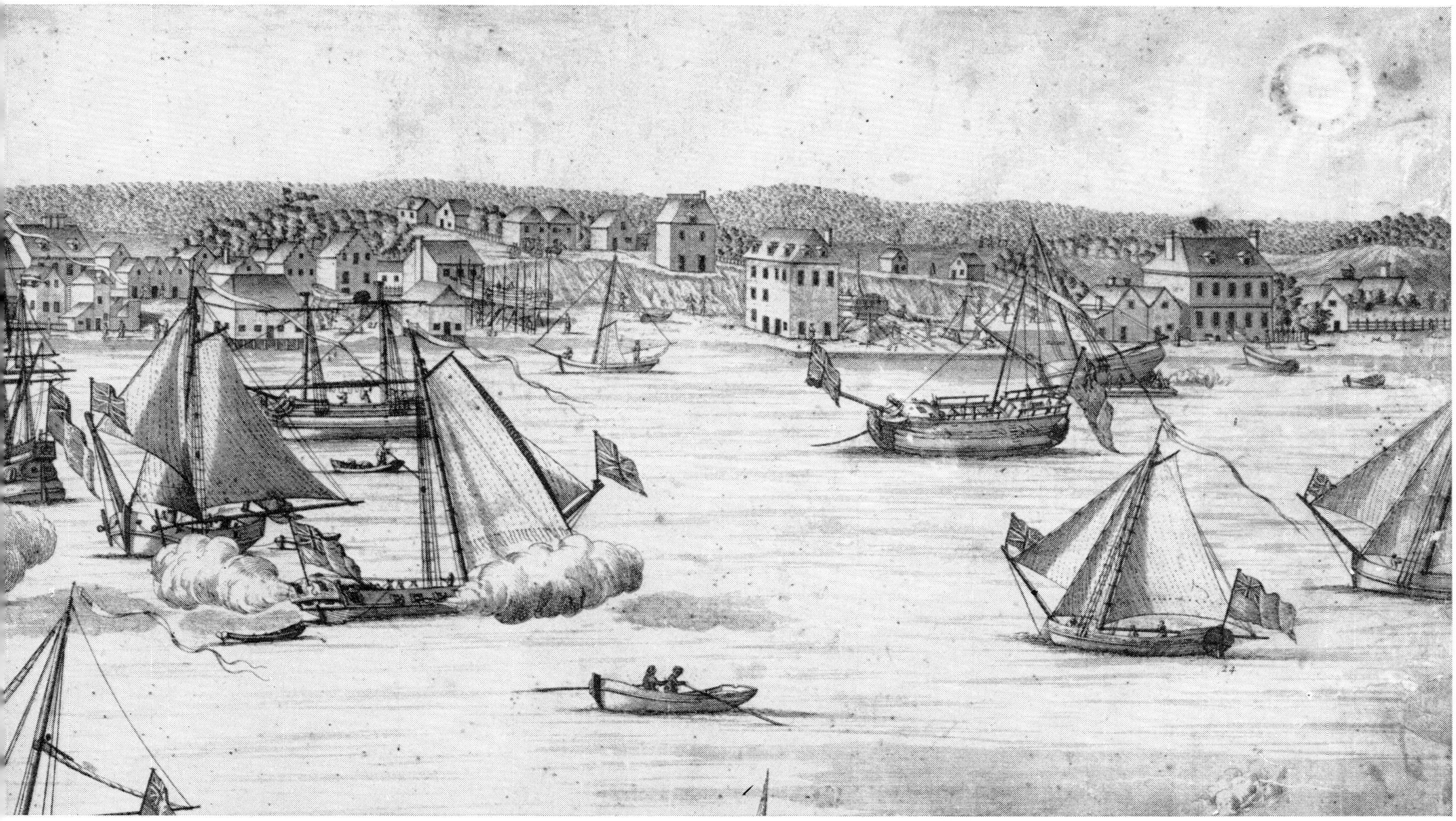

NEW YORK HISTORICAL SOCIETY

seaboard America in the 18th Century, and is still prevalent today. The two finest houses in the lower panel belonged to burghers who adopted Renaissance modes —Abraham de Peyster (*left*, just north of second spire) and Abraham Wendell (*extreme right*). The British ships crowding the river are apparently saluting the king's birthday, May 28, 1717. At lower right on river can be seen one of the first New York yachts, the noted *Fancy*, owned by Colonel Lewis Morris.

NEW YORK SHIPYARD, a detail enlarged from Burgis view on previous page, shows carpenters swarming over two partly finished hulls while another vessel (*far right*) waits repairs. Fancy coach on the bank above probably belongs to shipowner. In center stands a ship captain's house with widow's walk on top.

Wealth along the waterways

Good harbors and navigable rivers were the keys to wealth in the colonies. On them rose towns and plantation houses whose inhabitants could support a growing number of fine craftsmen. The silversmiths prospered in the seaboard cities and produced the pieces shown on pages 20 and 21. In Boston alone, by 1680, there were 24 silversmiths at work. Newport in Rhode Island and Williamsburg in Virginia produced America's first two competent architects, Peter Harrison and Richard Taliaferro. Colonial Charleston was noted for its beautifully landscaped gardens and goldsmiths' shops. Waterfront merchants of Philadelphia, which outstripped all other American ports in the 18th Century and became the second largest city in the British Empire, were famous for their showy houses and elegant taste in furniture.

In New York the rich Dutch families tended to move to country houses along the Hudson River, which they decorated with paintings both imported and local. There, in the early 18th Century, developed the first native American school of gifted—and largely self-taught—portrait painters. An example of their fresh, unsophisticated and wholly charming style is shown on the opposite page. Unlike the portrait of the Mason children on page 15, which still follows a provincial English style, this painting of an Albany girl is entirely American in its use of bold, contrasting colors and its background of formalized nature.

No one today knows the names of this artist or of any of his colleagues who are collectively called the "Patroon Painters." But the numerous pictures they left behind are proof that there was a sizable demand in at least one American colony for art of this kind.

FERRY LANDING in Brooklyn, detail from another section of Burgis drawing, shows scowlike sailing ferry at wharf. Though colonial boats were built abroad or copied from European models, these ferries were local designs, the precursors of the fast flat boats that were soon sailing the American rivers.

GIRL WITH RED SHOES is said to be Magdalena Douw, of Albany, later wife of Harmon Gansevoort, great-grandfather of Herman Melville. The portrait shows colonial love of color and decoration. Stiffly posed Magdalena is almost gaudy in bright shoes and bodice.

GOLD PAP spoon with bells was fashioned for a New York City child by Jacobus van der Spiegel. Buckle to fasten man's stock (cloth neckpiece) is a Philadelphia product.

Shapers of silver and gold

In colonial America the silversmith was a kind of investment banker for the wealthy who took a client's surplus coin and hammered it into objects of lasting value. Though designed for beauty, they were made for use. The oldest piece of colonial silverware known is the dram cup—a cocktail glass of the time—on the opposite page, made in 1651. The teapot was made in 1725, shortly after tea drinking came to the colonies. The porringer, however, was made just to commemorate a horse race at Hempstead. L.L, March 25, 1688.

This ware was for people who demanded distinction. They got it in pieces that are austere but elegant. Colonial silverware alternates plain surfaces with simple ornament, following timeless principles of design. That buyers should demand such artistry is not surprising. But it is surprising that in the new world they could find so many artisans who could supply it.

YALE UNIVERSITY GALLERY, MABEL BRADY GARVAN COLLECTION

EARLIEST AMERICAN SILVER is sampled in this array. In foreground are tobacco box by John Coney, salver by Thomas Savage, dram cup by John Hull and Robert Sanderson. At left are teapot by Pieter van Dyck, plain communion cup by Coney, engraved communion cup by Hull and Sanderson. At right are sugar caster (like salt shaker) by Bartholomew Le Roux, oval mustard pot by Van Dyck, porringer by Peter van Inburgh and two-handled cup by Edward Winslow.

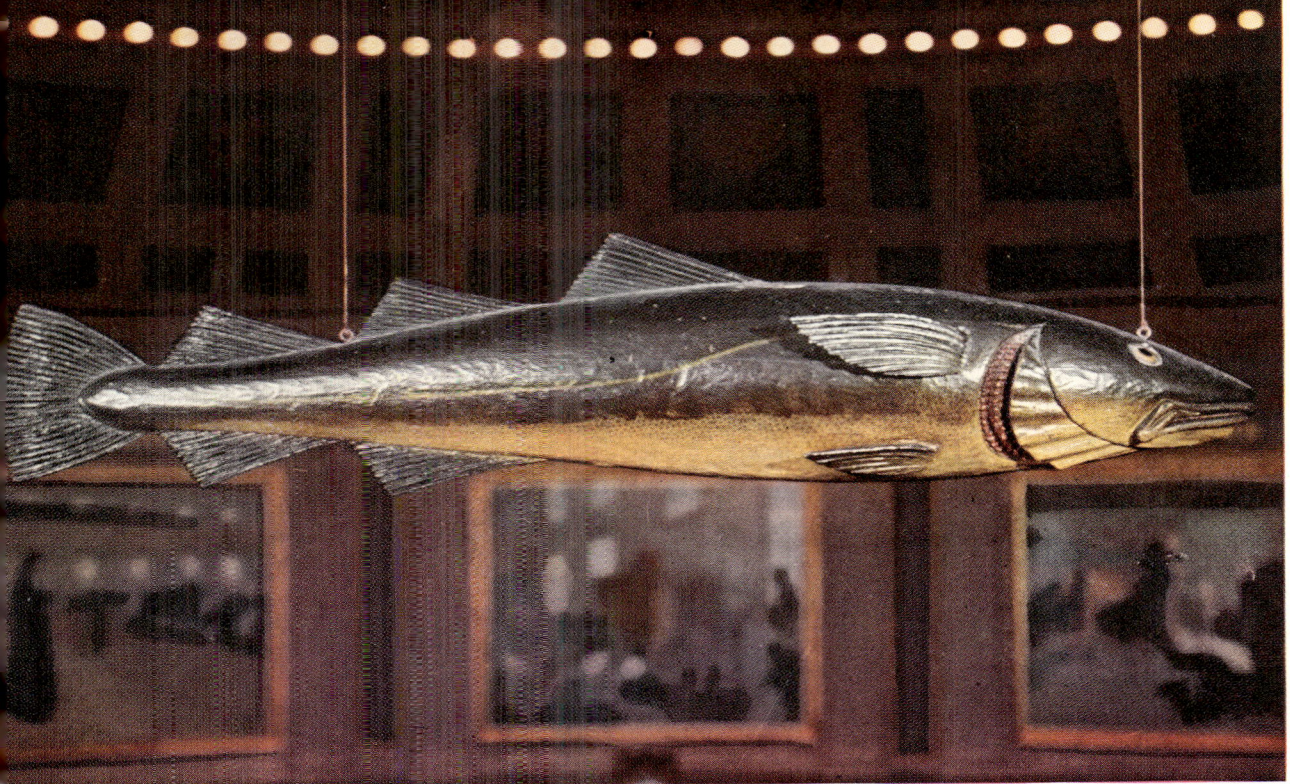

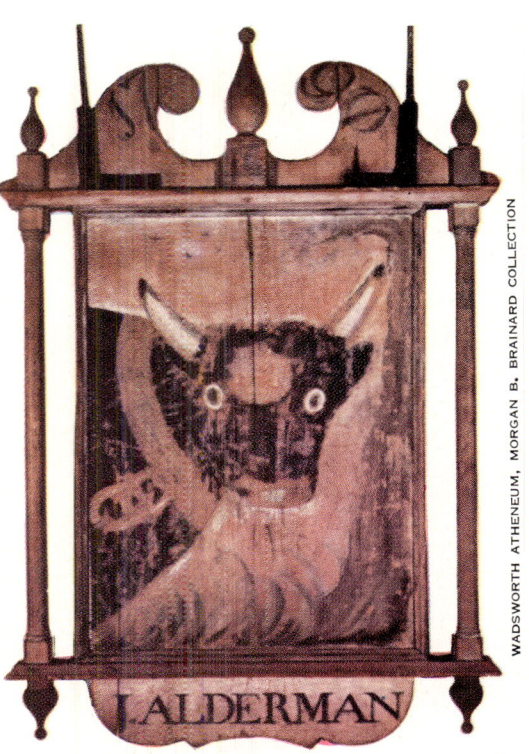

"SACRED COD," cut from wood in 1760s, hangs in the Massachusetts State house. Intricately and subtly carved, it is a masterwork of wood sculpture.

TIN CHANDELIER below, sturdy enough for 24 candles, was delicately wrought. Large chandeliers were a luxury item because candles were costly.

WADSWORTH ATHENEUM, MORGAN B. BRAINARD COLLECTION

BULL'S HEAD sign painted on wood hung in front of Bissell's tavern, East Windsor, Conn., about 1760. The starkly realistic animal portrait is in striking contrast to the exquisitely carved wood frame.

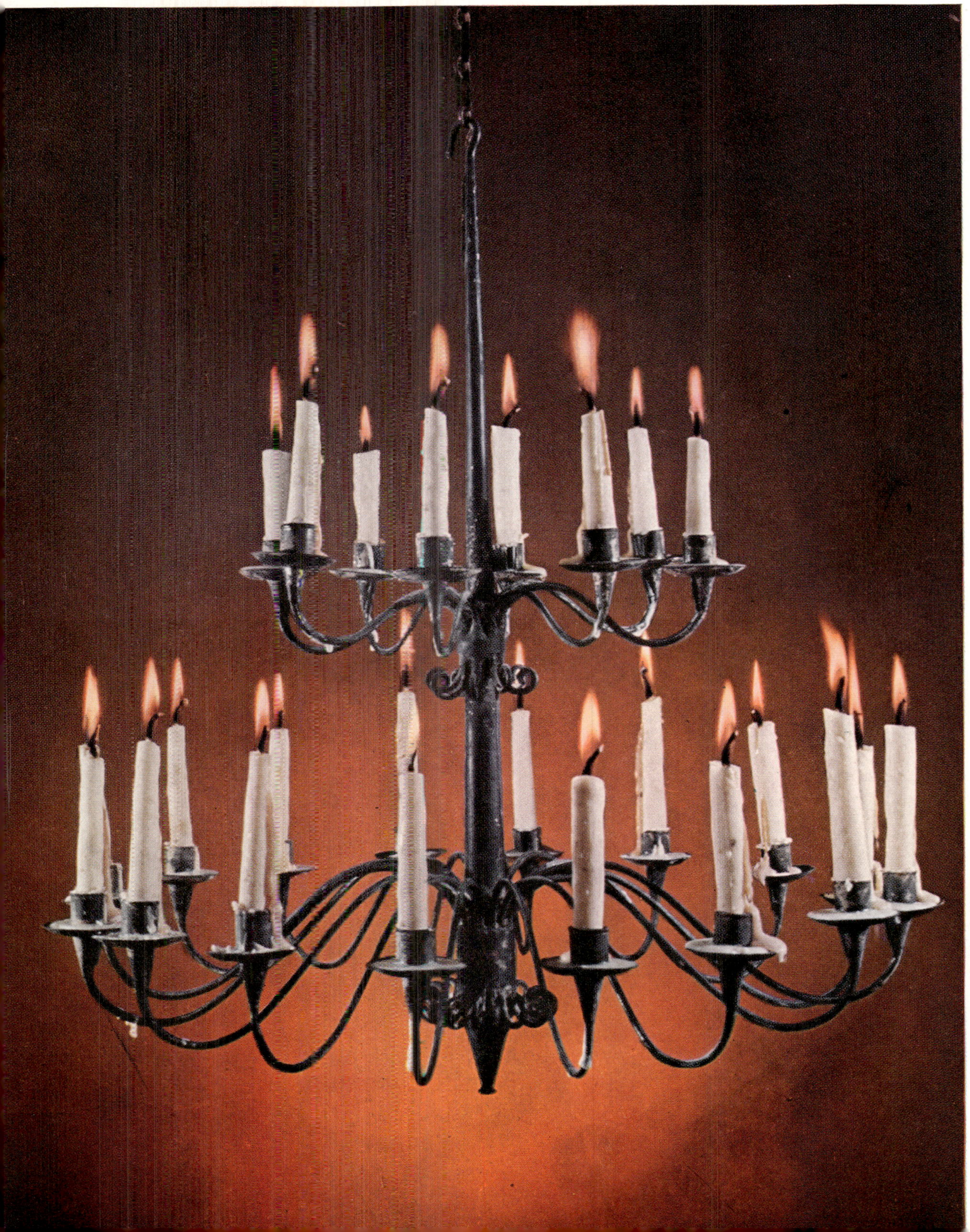

DU PONT MUSEUM, WINTERTHUR, DEL.

Craftsmen in common materials

The great forests which came down almost to the water's edge offered a seemingly endless supply of working material in early America—oak for house framing, cedar for shingles, walnut for gunstocks, hickory for ax handles, ash splints for baskets and barrel staves. The wood turners used white pine for cheeseboxes since it had no taste or smell. Chairmakers learned to make their rockers of black walnut which did not slide easily on the floor.

In all the colonies the most common utensils were made of wood, usually hard maple, which cut smoothly across the grain. Village craftsmen also used poplar and soft white basswood for "dish timber," turning out bowls, ladles, trenchers (plates) and noggins (drinking mugs) which were often small masterpieces of practical design. Because they were made for hard everyday use, these utensils were necessarily simple and hence their design graceful. Handles and lids had to balance or fit properly, which made for proper proportions. Most pieces were not painted, leaving grain of the natural wood to enhance their beauty. Decoration was indulged in only when it did not complicate the making or the using of the utensil. Only occasionally did the woodworkers soar into the realm of fine art, as an unknown carver did in the sacred cod at left, above.

For many people fine metalwork was out of the question, gold and silver being much too expensive. Tin also was "dear" but came into growing use by colonial craftsmen for such handsome decorations as the chandelier at left.

WOODEN UTENSILS above were made from a variety of native woods. The object at upper left is a bed wrench, used for tightening rope springs of an early bed; a whimsical artisan has given it a man's head. The pail with a hole in the handle is a piggin, used as dipper for water or for carrying food to the hens. At lower left is a trencher. The other utensils (*top to bottom*) are burl bowl made from a hard knot of chestnut, a funnel, mortar and pestle, butter paddle.

NEEDLEWORK, a skill colonial girls were supposed to acquire, was amateur art of the period. This fanciful portrait of Adam and Eve was embroidered in 1760 by Mary Sarah Titcomb, of crewels (twisted threads) on linen. It served in place of paintings as colorful wall decoration, also helped keep out drafts.

WEATHER VANES were usually a sideline for metalworkers. First specialist was Shem Drowne of Boston whose 4-foot-6-inch-tall copper Indian with a glass eye swiveled atop the governor's residence. Drowne also made the famous grasshopper which crouched above Faneuil Hall. Handsome vane below was made in Pennsylvania in 1670.

SCULPTURED GRAVESTONE in Dorchester, Mass. cemetery marks the plot of John Foster who did woodcut below.

Art of the amateur and the artisan

As the colonies grew in population and wealth, skilled artisans emerged as the third most important class, next after farmers and merchants. Many of them proved to be artists as well as successful businessmen. The men who made the two weather vanes at the left were producing objects of special utility to a people whose lives depended much on the weather. They were also expressing a picturesque sense of humor and a feeling for the kind of design which looks well against any skyline. John Foster, who carved the pioneer American woodcut below, was a printer who did the portrait as a frontispiece for a book which he published. A strong image of the Puritan priesthood in its heyday, it is also a human portrait of a man whose life was given to plain speaking and a powerful purpose. Foster also may have sketched the design for his own gravestone above, a grinning figure of Death snuffing out Life's candle, while Father Time tries to stay his skeleton arm. In works like these, and in Miss Titcomb's needlework on the opposite page, colonial craftsmen were able to satisfy their artistic impulses without displeasing their practical-minded friends and neighbors.

PURITAN PORTRAIT, the first American woodcut, depicts Richard Mather, ancestor of 80 New England preachers.

GARDEN OF EDEN, pictured in iron, decorated a Pennsylvania German stove. The inscription reads: "The snake betrayed Adam and Eve." Stovemakers cut pattern in wood, pressed wood into sand mold, then poured in molten iron.

CAIN KILLING ABEL was shown on another Colonial stove. Stove plates also taught the Commandments, the miracles of Christ and teachings of the Prophets. Religious pictures later gave way to floral and secular designs.

Scenes on stoves and Ben Franklin's big improvement

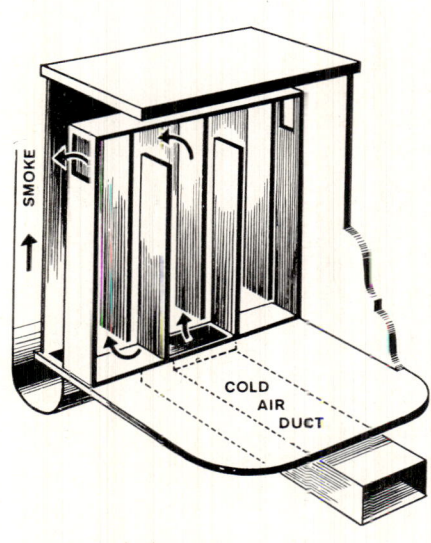

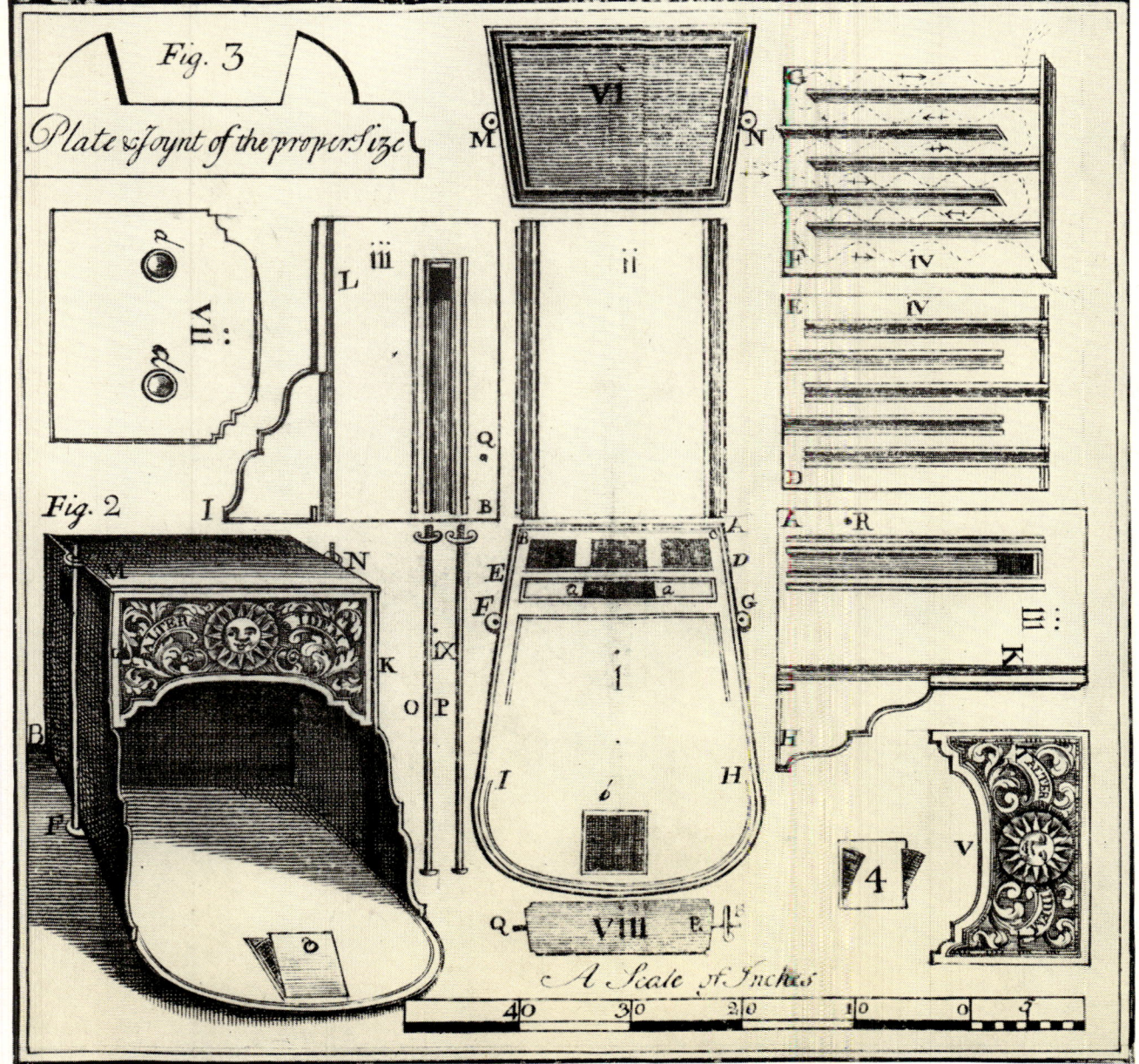

THE FRANKLIN STOVE, invented in 1742, saved much wood, produced better heat, and rid small rooms of smoke and other "filthy vapors." The ancestor of modern stoves, it also presaged the products of modern American industry: it was designed to be made of standardized parts which could be easily assembled in any fireplace. At right is Franklin's design. Above is a modern drawing showing how it worked. Fresh air was drawn through a floor duct into a separate chamber where it was heated by the surrounding fire and passed into the room through vents on either side. Smoke was drawn over the hot-air box and up the regular chimney. Franklin correctly boasted that his invention was more efficient than the German stoves which heated only by radiation and not air circulation, or the open fireplace, whereby, said Ben "a man is scorched before, while he is froze behind."

FIELDSTONE HEARTH—4½ feet high and 9 feet wide—is an ornament of Hyland house in Guilford, Conn., built in 1660. Massive, the fireplace still gains rude grace from its balanced proportions. Roughly made, it gains textural beauty from unfinished wood, hand-cut stone, plaster and brick. Andirons made by a local blacksmith have curved feet, with popular gooseneck upright. Trammel rods on which pots hung were notched so height of pots could be adjusted.

Designing the ways to keep warm

In the northern colonies heat was the basic problem in designing a home. English houses were heated by fireplaces which sent their smoke up through separate flues. The Americans, in a stroke of ingenious design, brought all the flues together into one huge chimney, or stack, which soaked up heat and radiated it through all the rooms. Such a chimney had two or more fireplace openings. Its central position determined the compact design of most American homes for 150 years.

In the main fireplace (*above*) the wife did her cooking, using a built-in oven and a variety of utensils. At first she hung pots in the fire from a green wood lug pole running crosswise above the hearth. Such poles often charred through and spilled the soup, so trammel rods and swinging iron cranes were substituted. In the 1740s Benjamin Franklin invented a new apparatus (*opposite page*) which was to end the need for fireplaces and led eventually to the American kitchen stove. This, in turn, changed American diet: biscuits, muffins, corn pone and flapjacks all came in when the stove's quick heat replaced slow-baking masonry.

RICHARD JACKSON HOUSE built around 1664 in Portsmouth, N.H. is believed to be the oldest in the state. The owner followed the common colonial trade of shipbuilding. Lean-tos are additions to the original structure. The windows shown here replaced early leaded pane types.

The first functional homes

The first settlers of New England brought with them in their minds two basic house designs which were typical of their homeland. One was the two-story medieval house of East Anglia, with its overhanging gable ends, leaded casement windows, center entrance and ornamental outside woodwork. The other was the simpler Flemish cottage, one story high with a loft on top and a steeply pitched roof to shed the North Sea rains. Such cottages were built in large numbers by Flemish weavers who flocked to England from the 14th Century on; the Puritans saw them everywhere in the counties they came from.

Both of these early New England types are illustrated here by photographs of surviving examples. The Jackson house (*above*) is basically a Flemish cottage with additions. The Parson Capen house, at the left, is purely English; it would look as natural in the hamlet of Toppesfield, in English Essex, as it does today in Topsfield, Essex County, Mass. It was built in 1683 for the parson of the Congregational Church and was the finest house in the village. The medieval overhangs along the front and at the gable ends, the dark clapboards and weathered shingles give it a look of quiet dignity and strength. Contrary to legend, the projecting overhangs, or jetties, were not intended as defenses against Indians. The same construction was common in ancient English towns where Indians were no menace but where overhangs served either as protection from rain or just as decoration.

For the builders of the Capen and Jackson houses it was natural to follow traditional patterns. Colonists are always homesick; they always try to rebuild the world they knew. But American conditions soon forced them to change their methods. Old England had a permanent shortage of wood; the walls of Tudor houses, between the timbers, were often enclosed with nothing but plaster or porous brick "nogging." The colonists tried this, but it did not keep out the weather. So they nailed strips of wood over the brick and plaster. Soon they found they could make a better house wall from rough wood sheathing, covered with overlapped clapboards. From all this emerged a house of clean lines and compact look, the decoration either omitted or simplified. Considering the materials available—much wood, little glass and hand labor—the New England home was for its time a magnificent example of functional architecture—in every sense of this word so often applied to modern building.

From the two houses shown here evolved two styles now most popularly associated with New England. The Parson Capen house with its small entrance hall—instead of the later large center hall—is a predecessor of the Cape Cod house. The Jackson house with its long roof slanted down over an added lean-to is the ancestor of the salt box. Oddly enough, none of the early English colonists built log cabins, which were introduced by the Swedes on the Delaware. Instead, in New England, they did a typically American thing: they mechanized their lumber industry. In 1634 a water-powered sawmill was erected on the Piscataqua, between Maine and New Hampshire. At that time there was no such mill in England.

PARSON CAPEN HOUSE was built in 1683 at Topsfield, Mass. Casement windows, each with 30 glass panes, were a relative luxury at time house was built. Pilastered chimney, borrowed from English manor house design, was also unusual.

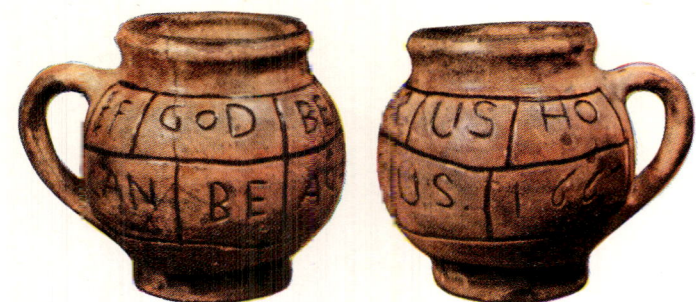

POTTERY JUG from Maine, was made in 1667, has pious inscription, "If God be for us-ho [who] can be against [against] us."

The Old World furniture

Colonial furniture, like colonial houses, followed fashions from abroad. Wealthier families, especially in the South, imported what they needed. But in the northern and middle colonies were American craftsmen who showed great skill in imitating English styles, often adding small touches of their own and working gradually toward lighter forms, easier and cheaper to produce. This was especially true when they used native woods and produced the humbler benches cupboards and beds for everyday use.

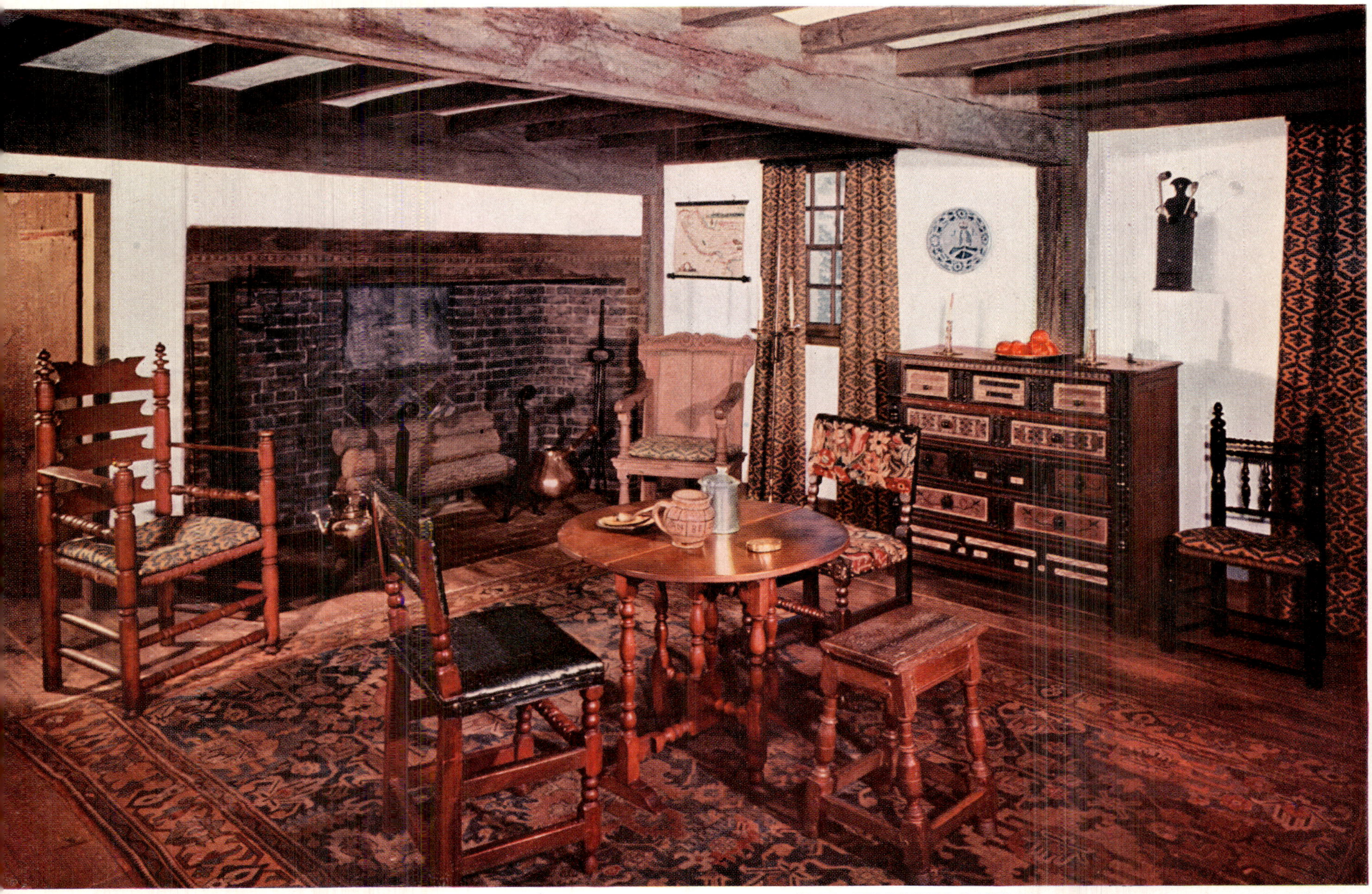

DU PONT MUSEUM, WINTERTHUR, DEL.

17TH CENTURY PARLOR from Oyster Bay, Long Island home is enlivened by red turkey work, a popular form of embroidery, on the chair behind the table, and also by the colorfully painted and carved Ipswich chest.

DU PONT MUSEUM, WINTERTHUR, D.L.

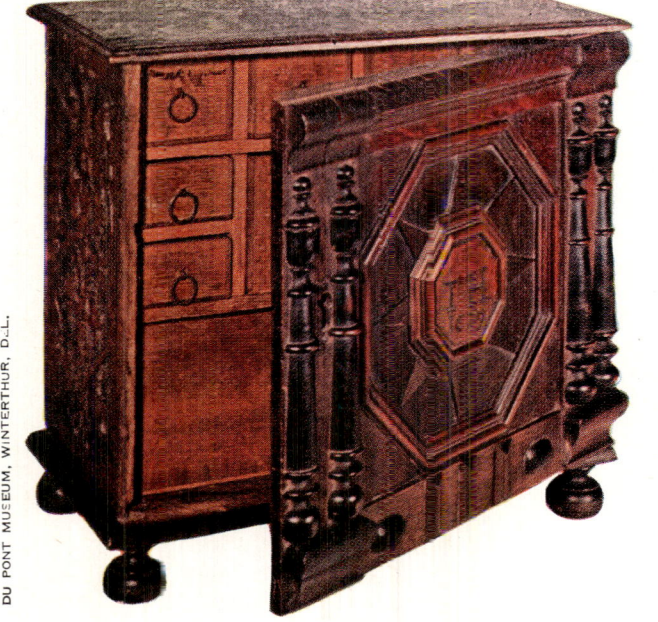

SPICE CABINET (*left*) made at Ipswich, Mass. in 1679 shows early use of ball feet. Paneled door bears the carved initials of owner, Thomas Hart Jr.

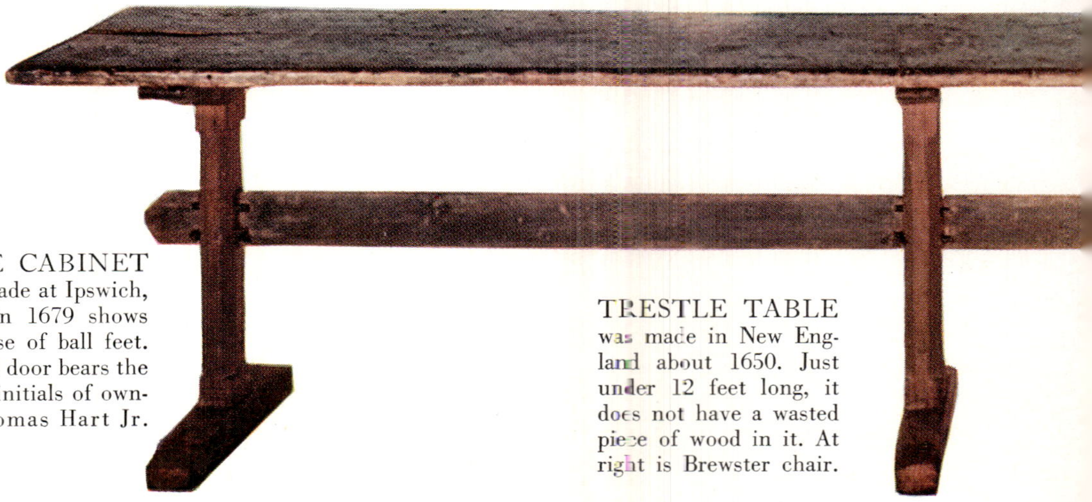

TRESTLE TABLE was made in New England about 1650. Just under 12 feet long, it does not have a wasted piece of wood in it. At right is Brewster chair.

with New World touches

What they accomplished in about 100 years is indicated in the two period rooms below. The elegant 17th Century parlor is almost purely English in appearance, though the colorful polychrome chest and the Carver chair beside it are characteristic of New England. In the kitchen at right the tall slat-back chairs, made in the Delaware Valley, are distinctly American in their slim lines and boldly curved backs. The scalloped open cupboard which holds the pottery is also an American design.

BOSTON MUSEUM

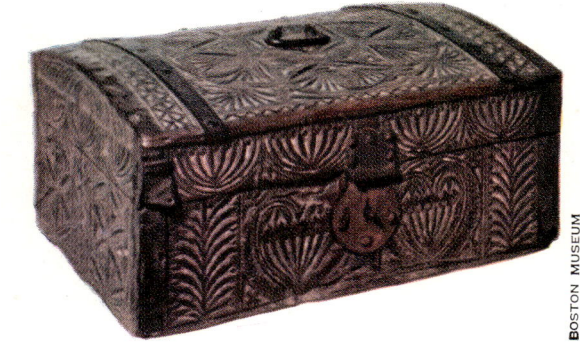

ORNATELY CARVED box made in Massachusetts, dated 1650, was used to store valuable papers, as well as to hold family Bible.

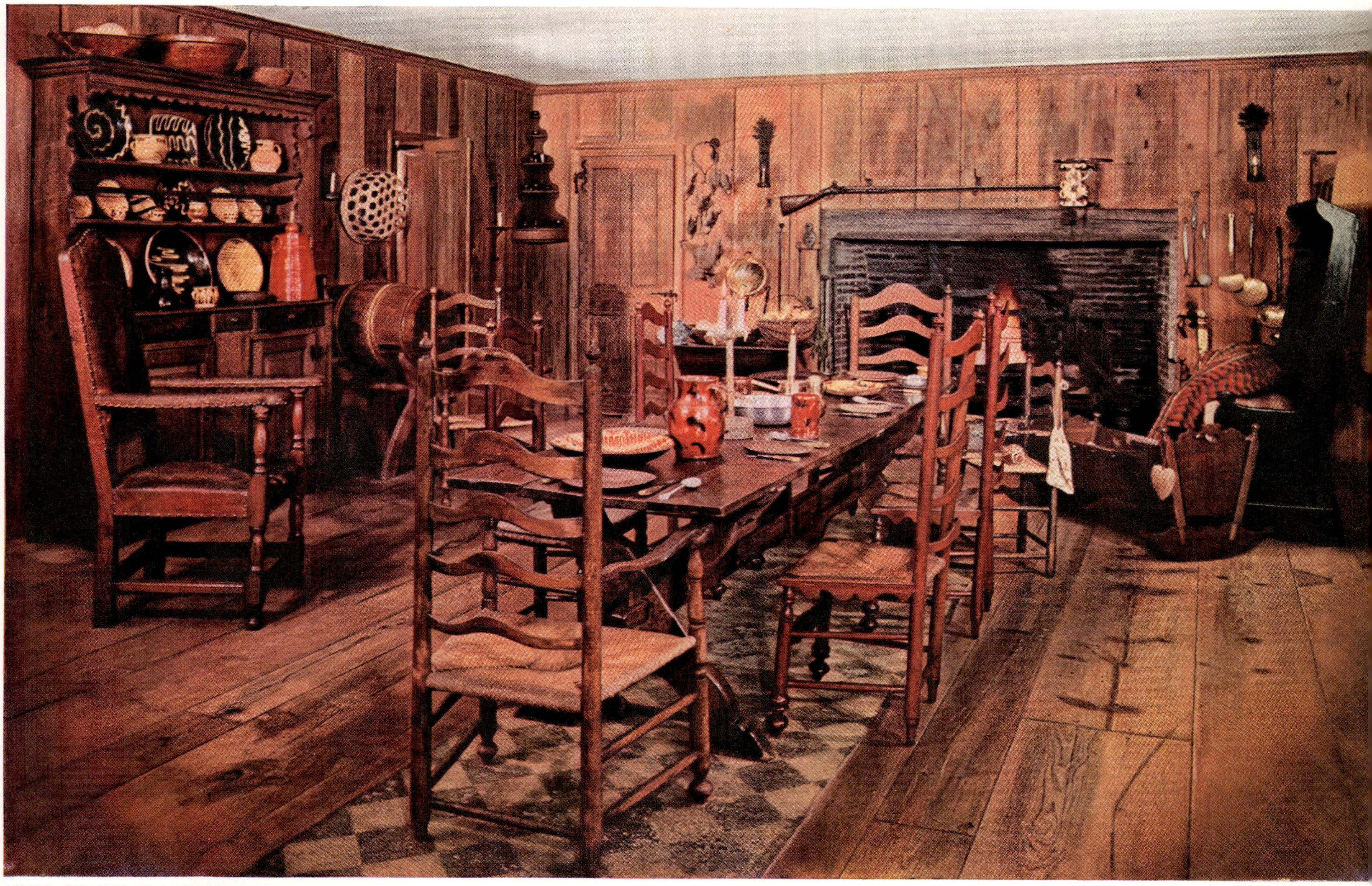

DU PONT MUSEUM, WINTERTHUR, DEL.

18TH CENTURY KITCHEN paneled in pine is furnished mostly with items from Pennsylvania. In cupboard at left is comb ware pottery. Beside fireplace is settle bed where guests slept, warmed by fire but uncomfortably upright.

THE METROPOLITAN MUSEUM OF ART

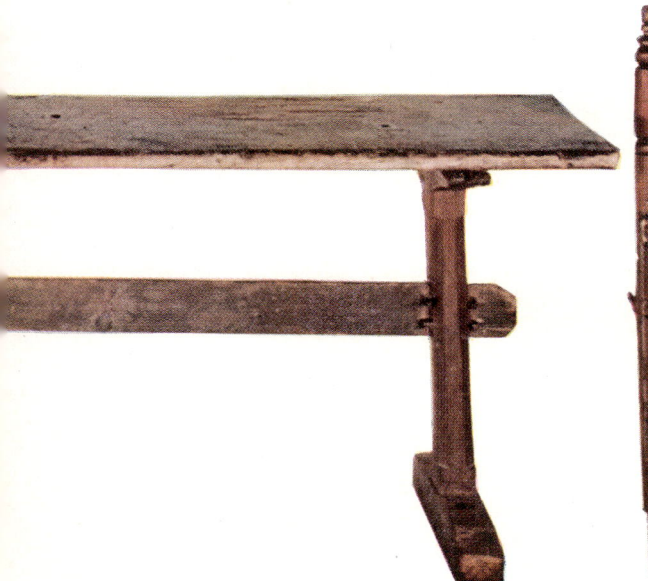

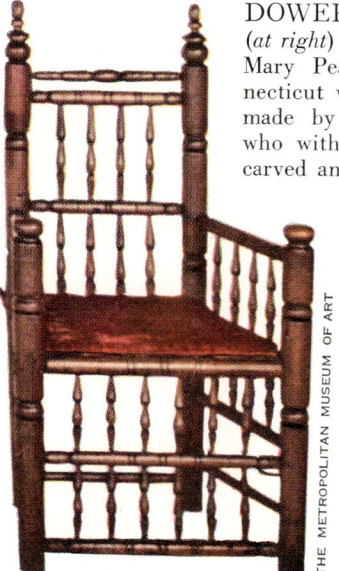

DOWER CHEST (*at right*) belonging to Mary Pease of Connecticut was probably made by her father, who with loving care carved and painted it.

MUSEUM OF FINE ARTS, BOSTON

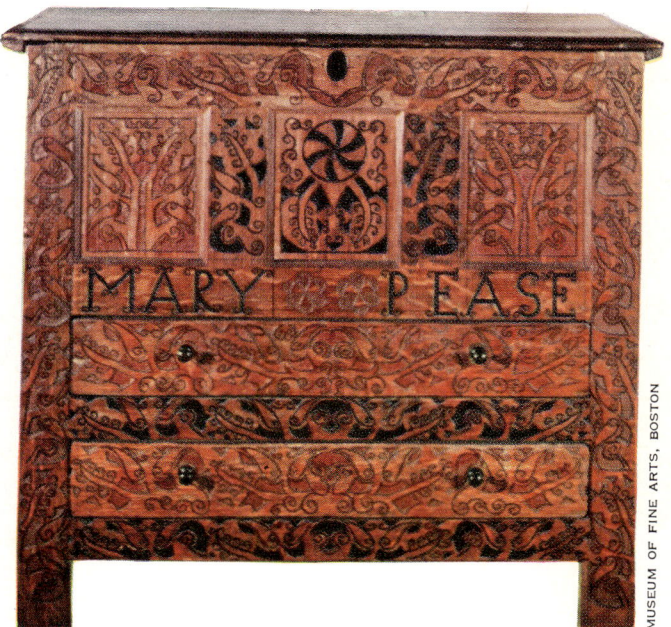

OLD SHIP MEETINGHOUSE at Hingham, Mass. has been continuously used for worship since it was built in 1681. Its interior is shown at right.

Proportion and patterns

The distinctive patterns and architectural details with which the colonists embellished their lives have mostly been rubbed out by time. But here and there they can still be seen, in the fading tracery of an old brick wall, or the thrust of massive timbers. The most remarkable survival is the Old Ship meetinghouse at Hingham (*above and right*), erected in 1681 when Massachusetts was still a Puritan commonwealth. Its builders designed an exterior both sturdy and graceful, its square mass lightened by the slender tower which points toward heaven. The cavernous interior is saved from gloom by its perfect proportions and the soaring sweep of the tremendous beams and rafters, some of which are 45 feet long, the equal of the widest Gothic cathedral nave in England. Inside, it resembles nothing more than the hull of a great ship overturned to make a house of worship (to get the effect, turn picture upside down).

The Old Ship meetinghouse is the only example left of the first purely American contribution to architecture—the four-square meetinghouse of 17th Century New England. The Puritans invented it because they hated the word "church" and would not build one in America. They permitted no cross or spire; instead there was a central tower which held the bell and supported a useful weathervane.

PENDILL OF WOOD, main New England building material, hangs from Parson Capen house. The ornament was designed and carved by the carpenter who built the house.

WALL OF STONE, a very popular material of the early middle colonies, gleams in lively contrast to painted door and shutters. This is the Van Deusen house in Hurley, N.Y.

DESIGN OF BRICK, material of South, though laid in 1663, still glows in wall of "Make Peace" in Somerset County, Md. Masons used glazed brick which sparkled in the sun.

The durable house of Cape Cod

RIVALS of Cape Cod style in early New England were the four house shapes shown above: one-room cottage, two-story English overhang, lean-to salt box and full two-story house with widened eaves.

A triumph of colonial technique was the snug Cape Cod house, whose familiar block shape and low symmetrical roof still dots the U.S. landscape. The ground-hugging Cape Cod style was developed along the coast to resist hard winters and Atlantic storms. It has endured because its simple design is not only pleasant to the eye but comparatively easy and cheap to build. Like a modern skyscraper, the Cape Cod's outward appearance was determined entirely by its wooden skeleton, or frame.

Colonial carpenters used 10 types of hand-hewn timbers, and the names they used then are still current today (*see diagram at right*). The *sills* lay on the foundations to support the whole structure. The *posts* were the main vertical members; they carried the crosswise *girts*, on which rested the second floor. The *summer beam* was an especially large timber which spanned the middle of a room and was dovetailed into the girts. All other joints were fastened with wooden pegs, or "trunnels" (tree nails). *Joists* were small beams which carried the floor boards. *Plates* were horizontal timbers on which rested the notched, slanting *rafters*. *Purlins* crossed the rafters to support roof boards and shingles. The *ridge* ran along the top. *Collars* were braces for the rafters.

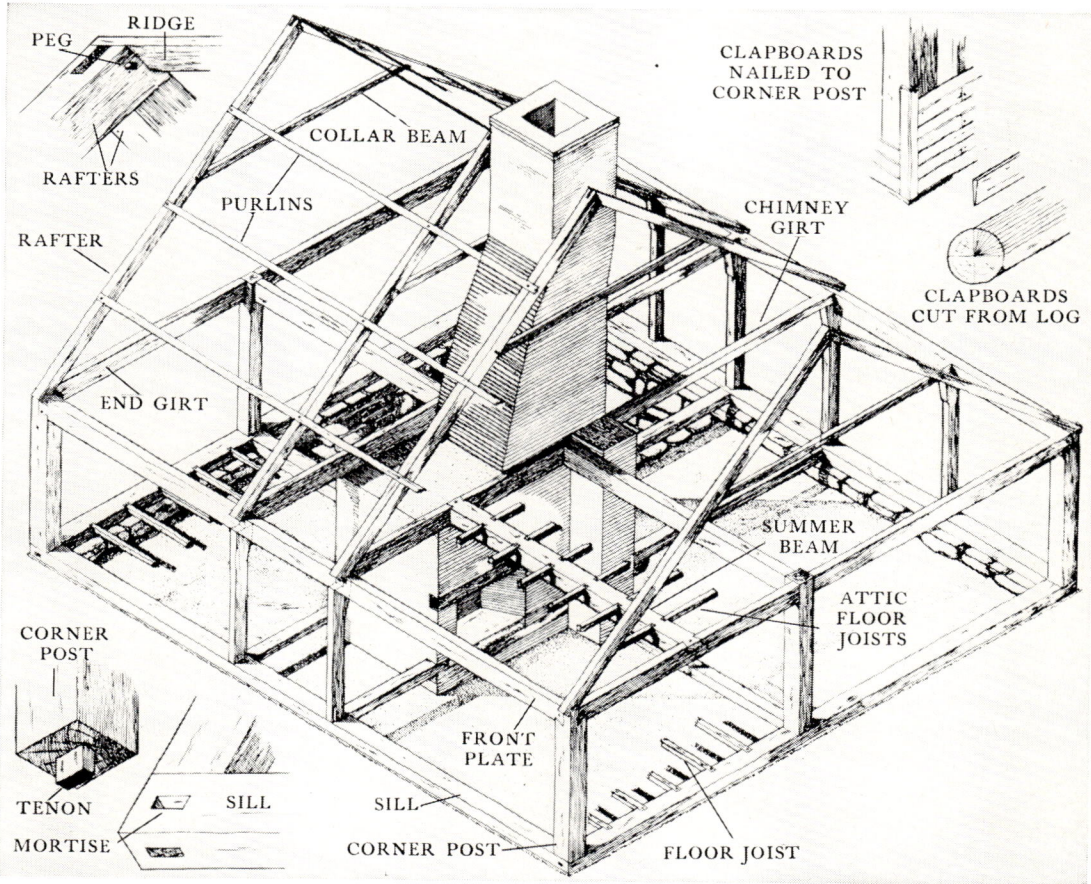

CONSTRUCTION of Cape Cod house is shown in diagram of basic frame. Corner drawings at left show mortises and tenons cut and fitted by hand. Clapboards (*right, above*) were split from long oak log.

← CHIMNEY (*opposite page*) of Cape Cod house pictured above rises through center of house and combines flues from three fireplaces into a central stack.

SHINGLED CAPE COD built in 1792 at South Orleans, Mass. was variation on clapboard style. Shingle idea may have come from New Amsterdam Dutch.

ANCIENT IRONWORKS at Saugus, Mass. was divided into separate buildings, now restored. Forging was done at left, rolling and slitting at right.

Necessary business of ironmaking

Iron was the industrial product the colonists needed most—for horseshoes, nails, wagon axles and weapons. They began very early to make their own. In 1619 an ironworks was established in Virginia but was soon destroyed by Indians. A more successful manufactory was begun in 1646, at Saugus, Mass., halfway between Boston and Salem.

The Saugus ironworks was powered by water wheels and produced a ton of cast iron every day from bog ores dug nearby and forest-fired charcoal. Some of the raw iron was cast directly into large pots and firebacks. The rest was reheated in the forge, converted to wrought iron and beaten into bars under a huge water-driven hammer. The bars were carried next door to the slitting mill and worked into strips and rods from which other craftsmen made farm tools and other finished products.

The first American inventor, Joseph Jenks, who received a Massachusetts patent for a scythe-grinding machine in 1646, was a Saugus workman. The plant fell into decay about 1670 but has been restored recently with the aid of a million and a half dollars contributed by the American Iron and Steel Institute.

The three-century-old home of the ironmaster at the Saugus Ironworks.

Part II

THE LOOK OF LIBERTY IN CRAFTSMANSHIP

PAUL REVERE, with silversmith's tools and a teapot he made, was painted around 1765 by John Singleton Copley, America's first major artist. Copley introduced a revolutionary realism into American portrait painting at a time when most English artists were still following the worn-out conventions of Van Dyck.

The Look of Liberty in Craftsmanship

PATRIOTISM BECOMES THE AMERICAN THEME

Long before 1776 the independence of America was being declared by its arts and manufactures. Colonial craftsmen of the 18th Century made silverware as handsome as any from England, and equally handsome guns which were much more deadly. Furniture-making reached its all-time peak of perfection and branched out in a number of particular American designs. Houses grew larger and ceilings higher; paint and window glass became necessities instead of luxuries; graceful paneled doorways with overhead pediments and fanlights replaced the thick nail-studded portals of pioneer days. A taste for the exotic, a love of ornament sheerly for ornament's sake began to appear. But in general, American design still showed a strong preference for the simpler, more functional forms.

The standard of living of the 13 American colonies by 1750 was already higher than that of any comparable area in the world. Their population was booming at a rate that has never been equaled. Wealth was piling up, not only in the strongboxes of the wealthy, but even more in the hands of a fast-growing and widely distributed middle class. The colonists did an amazing amount of traveling, to Europe, and up and down the Eastern seaboard. Even a Boston tallow-chandler's son like Benjamin Franklin managed to get part of his education abroad.

Colonial prosperity and colonial enterprise made the American Revolution almost an inevitable event. But it was a revolution which sought to conserve and enlarge the thriving American *status quo*, rather than overturn it. Paul Revere, pictured on the opposite page, is an excellent example of the American revolutionist: a craftsman who infused the look of liberty into his handiwork; a patriot who did much more for his country than risk his neck on a midnight ride.

Revere was the most gifted Boston silversmith of his time and his most famous creation is the punch bowl shown above, whose classical purity of shape tends to obscure the fact that it was fashioned in a fever of political excitement. Revere made it in 1768 after the Massachusetts legislature refused to withdraw an anti-British protest it had sent to the other colonies. On one side he etched a liberty cap and an inscription: "To the Memory of the glorious NINETY-TWO: Members of the Hon'bl House of Representatives of Massachusetts-Bay, who, undaunted by the insolent Menaces of Villains in Power . . . voted NOT TO RESCIND."

Revere also engraved patriotic cartoons (*below*) and propaganda pictures like his *Boston Massacre*. During the Revolution he printed currency, cast cannon and ran a gunpowder mill to supply Washington's army. After the war he went into the metal business in a big way. He made church bells, copper boilers for the first steamboats on the Hudson River and rolled copper for the Boston State House roof. The impetus of independence, which turned the artist-artisan Revere into an industrialist, also carried the country along—to an originality of architecture, an enterprise in technology and, in a way no period in American life has surpassed, a mature richness of decoration.

BOWL (ABOVE) MUSEUM OF FINE ARTS, BOSTON

REVERE'S RATTLESNAKE, symbol of the colonies, confronts British griffin in cartoon engraved for the *Massachusetts Spy* in 1774. Paul Revere took the nine-part snake idea from Ben Franklin. His drawing is crude but he was only interested in getting his idea across to as many readers as possible.

'The most fatal widow and orphan makers in the world'

In the Pennsylvania rifle the American patriot and the American craftsman joined forces. The early colonials brought over rifles like the one fourth from the top above—a short-barreled German gun with thick butt and awkward trigger guard. From this colonial gunsmiths developed a new weapon suited to the frontiersman's needs. The Pennsylvania rifle, a true American product, had a long barrel (45-50 inches) which gave steadiness and balance to the gun and greater accuracy to the shot. To engage the bullet snugly in the barrel, a hunter wrapped each piece of shot in a patch of greased cloth or buckskin, and to hold the patches the guns had a hinged patch box at the end of the butt.

From a long rifle, which was the most accurate in the world, the most important single shot of the Revolution was fired—by Tim Murphy of Northumberland County, Pa., who killed British General Simon Fraser at 300 yards at the Battle of Saratoga and began the demoralization of the British troops. The British honored the long rifles with a rueful epithet: ". . . the most fatal widow and orphan makers in the world."

Having produced a good weapon, the gunmakers took pains to make it good looking—keeping lines clean, the butt thin, the trigger guard graceful, the decorations refined. The rifle at top above, made for a pre-Revolutionary hunter, is decorated by carved scrolls and a brass patch box. The elaborately decorated one beneath, which was of later make, was probably the exhibition piece of an expert marksman. It has 40 silver inlays in addition to the scrolls and its cheek piece is an explosion of star, crescent and fish patterns. The third gun down, made about 1790, has a butt cut in a shoulder-fitting crescent, and among its rich ornamentation a formalized bird.

Some Revolutionary soldiers liked to decorate their equipment. At left is drum adorned with flags of France and North Carolina militia. Below are an officer's sword with lion's head handle, an enlisted man's sword. At right is a leather hunting pouch, powder horn, knife, bullet mold (like a pair of pliers), flintlock pistol. At bottom right is a halberd used by sergeants to measure distance between ranks. At upper right is fringed jacket, three-cornered hat and a buckskin bullet pouch lying on a manual of arms drawn up by Baron von Steuben for Revolutionary troops.

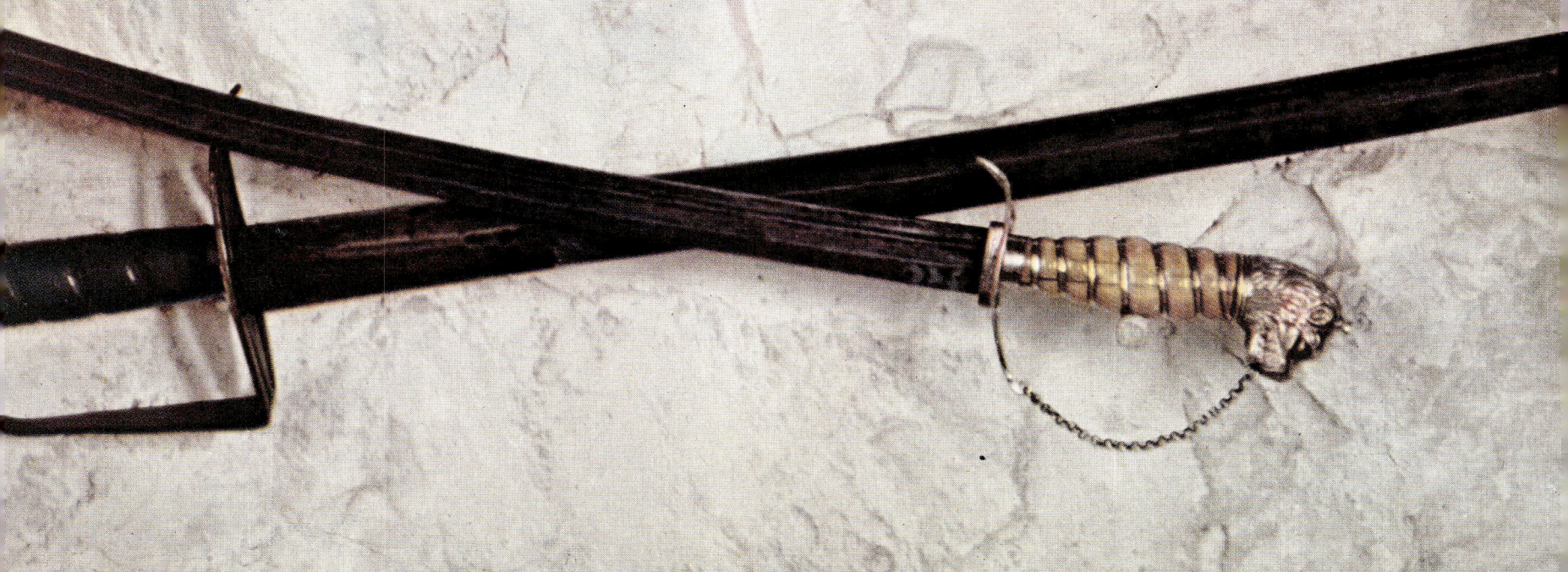

symmetry of form and the contrast of mellow bricks and white woodwork than to formal decorations.

express the young nation's dignity. This was the federal style which was highly developed in the work of a brilliant group of New Englanders, led by Boston's Charles Bulfinch. A magnificent federal house, built by Samuel McIntire of Salem for a wealthy merchant named Jerathmeel Peirce, is shown at far right. Here the favorite American material, wood, has been carved and planed to the smoothness of antique marble. The whole effect is closer in spirit to republican Rome than to royal Britain. In work like this, American architecture finally achieved a mature professional status.

CEILING at Kenmore, another Georgian mansion at Fredericksburg, Va., is richly decorated with leaf, fruit and flower designs in molded plaster. Such continental elegance was rare in colonial America.

STAIRCASE of Peirce House at Salem, Mass. (below) has rail of many small pieces of mahogany and Chippendale latticework. Codfish on upper wall once ornamented home of rich Salem fish merchant.

CARTER'S GROVE near Williamsburg, Va. was built originally with the central house separated from the matching office (*left*) and kitchen (*right*). It has a central hall with two rooms at each side on the first and second floors. Like other American Georgian houses, it pays more attention to

Houses independence built

Architecture in the colonies flowered most impressively in the South, and especially among the planter aristocrats of Virginia. When British officers rode through Virginia in 1781, on their way to Yorktown and surrender, they must have been struck by the great Georgian houses they saw. One of the finest, Carter's Grove, is pictured above. It was built about 1750 for Carter Burwell, and fully expresses the solid social standing and financial independence of its owner.

In design the house follows the Georgian style which developed in the American colonies from the brick buildings of England's Christopher Wren. The original arrangement of separating the house from kitchen and office was characteristic of the Southern colonies, where ventilation was a problem and a house was often the headquarters of a large-scale business. A plantation like Carter's Grove was surrounded in colonial times by stables, workshops and slaves' cabins, and shipped its main product—tobacco—direct to England from its own riverside docks.

After the Revolution a new American architecture arose to challenge the Georgian and

DU PONT MUSEUM

ESSEX INSTITUTE

DU PONT MUSEUM

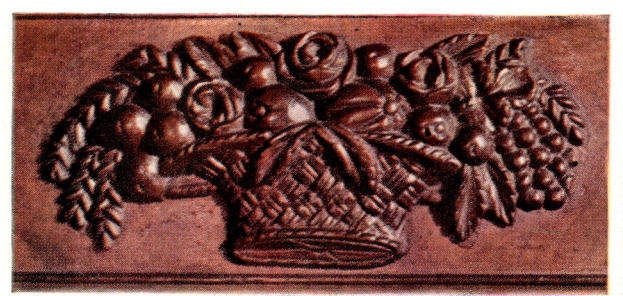

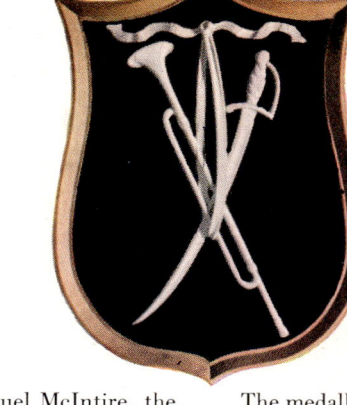

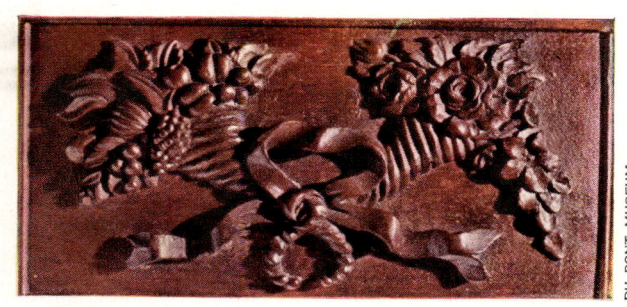

WOOD CARVING became a fine art as practiced by Samuel McIntire, the master carpenter of Salem. Fruit basket at left was a favorite McIntire design.

The medallion with crossed sword and bugle once decorated wood gate of Salem's Washington Common. Cornucopia at right was made for a McIntire card table.

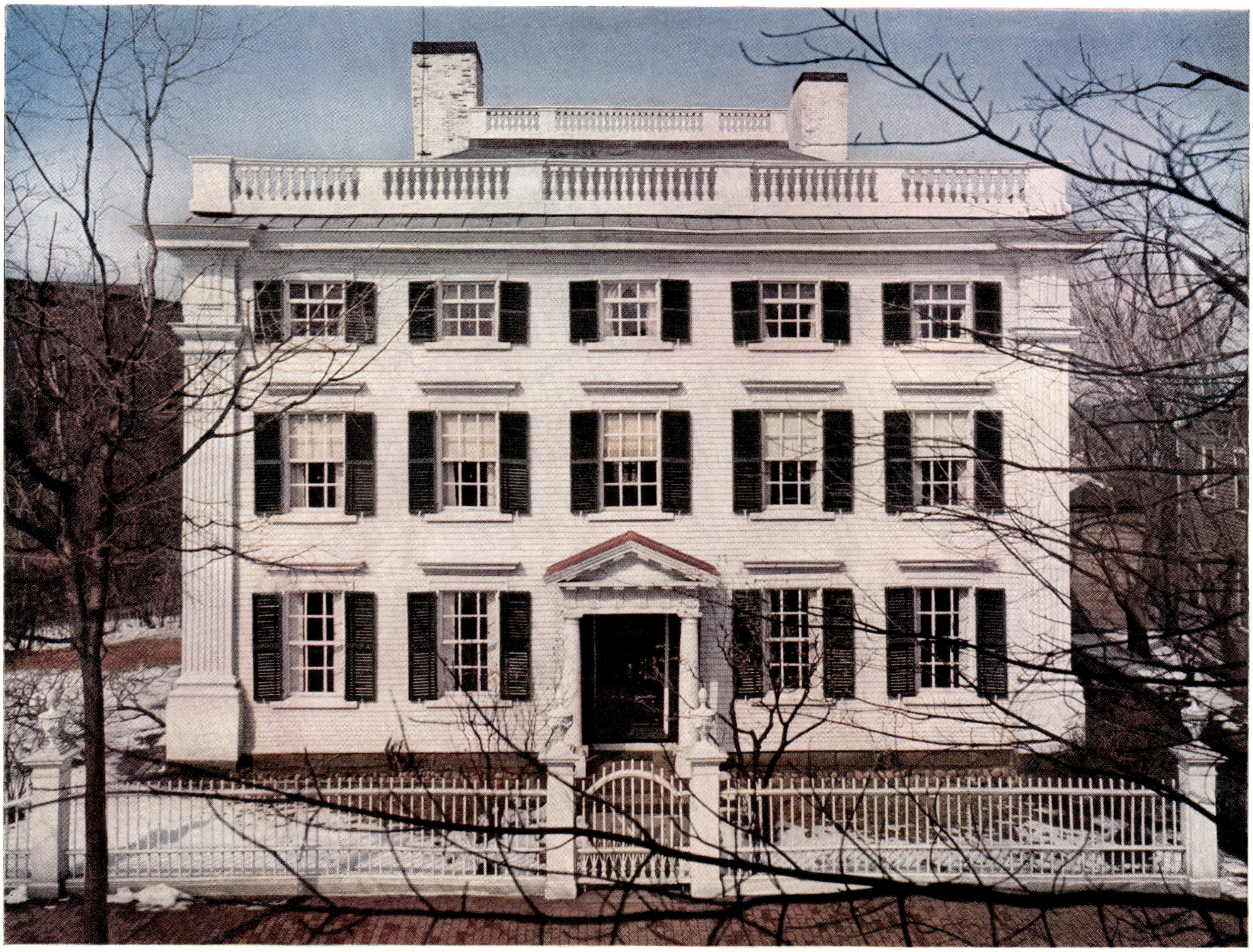

THE ESSEX INSTITUTE, SALEM, MASS.

PEIRCE HOUSE, now a Salem museum, was built by McIntire about 1782. Its chaste facade is perfectly framed by the roof railing and classic corner pillars.

DU PONT MUSEUM

ESSEX INSTITUTE

ESSEX INSTITUTE

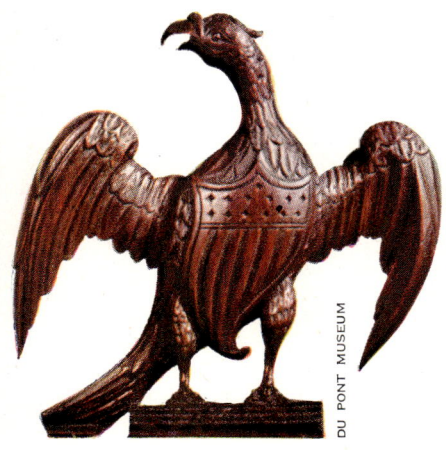

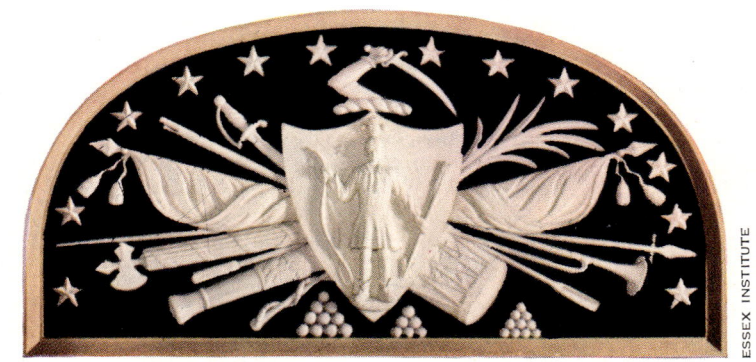

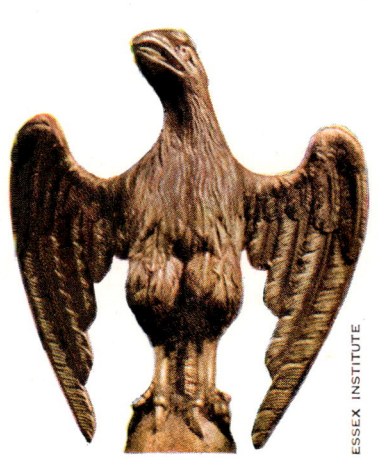

ARMS OF MASSACHUSETTS were carved by McIntire, who also did eagle at right. One at left was made in Baltimore by unknown carver to top a tall chest.

YALE UNIVERSITY ART GALLERY

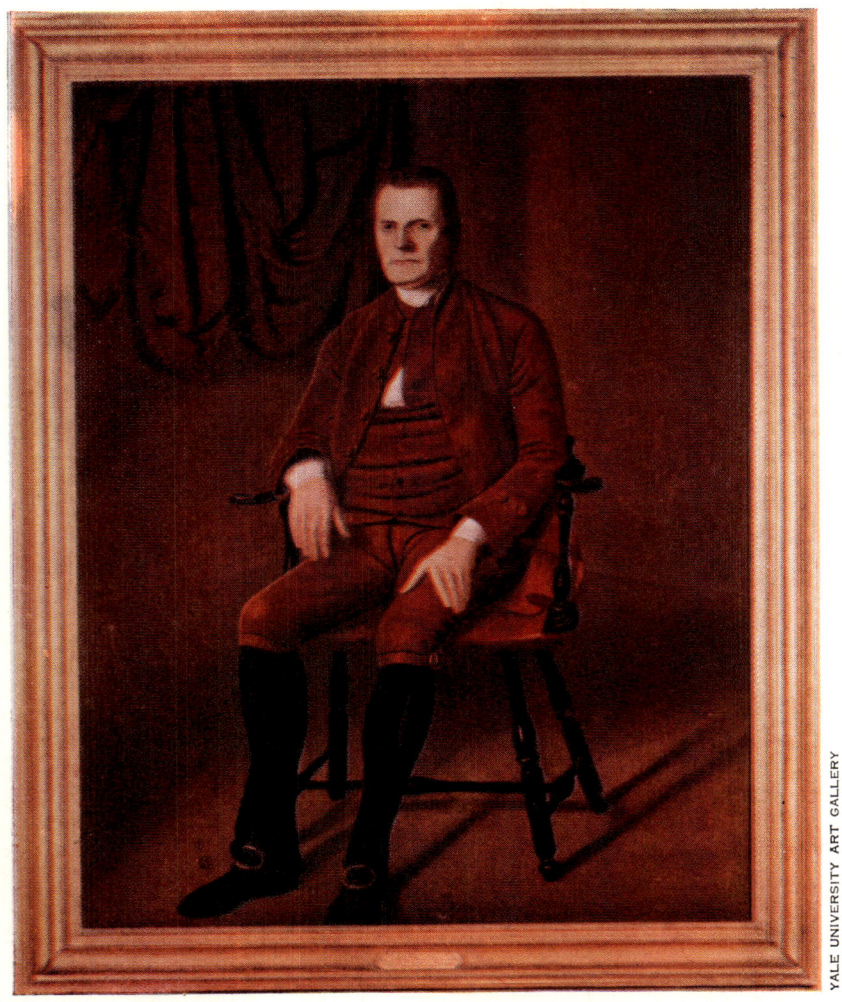

SEAT FOR PORTRAIT of Roger Sherman, who signed Declaration and U.S. Constitution, was a Connecticut Windsor chair. Painter was Ralph Earl.

The versatile hoop-and-stick chair

The Windsor chair, an English production which supposedly got its name from George III, was vastly more popular in pre-Revolutionary America than it ever became in the motherland. Craftsmen reveled in its varied shapes and uses and their customers liked its form-fitting, hoop-backed comfort. The seats were hollowed out of unseasoned wood; as they dried they formed tight sockets for the legs which were turned in shapes to give extra strength where needed. The backs, of resilient spindles fastened across the top by strips of hickory or ash, formed a light and strong, yet cheap, construction. American woodworkers showed the same freedom and versatility in making the more expensive chairs of the period (*below*).

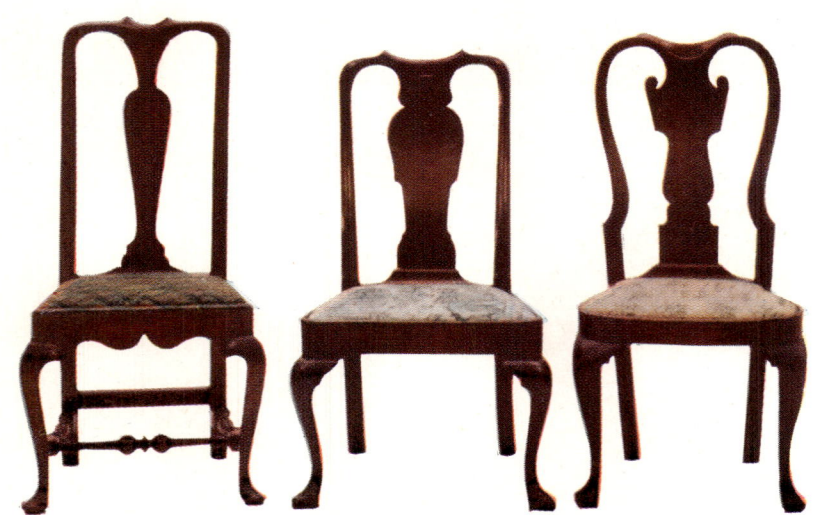

QUEEN ANNE STYLE varied with region. Chairs above (*from left*) are stiff, prim New England, solid, squat New York, gracefully curved Philadelphia.

ALL CHAIRS: DU PONT MUSEUM, WINTERTHUR, DEL.

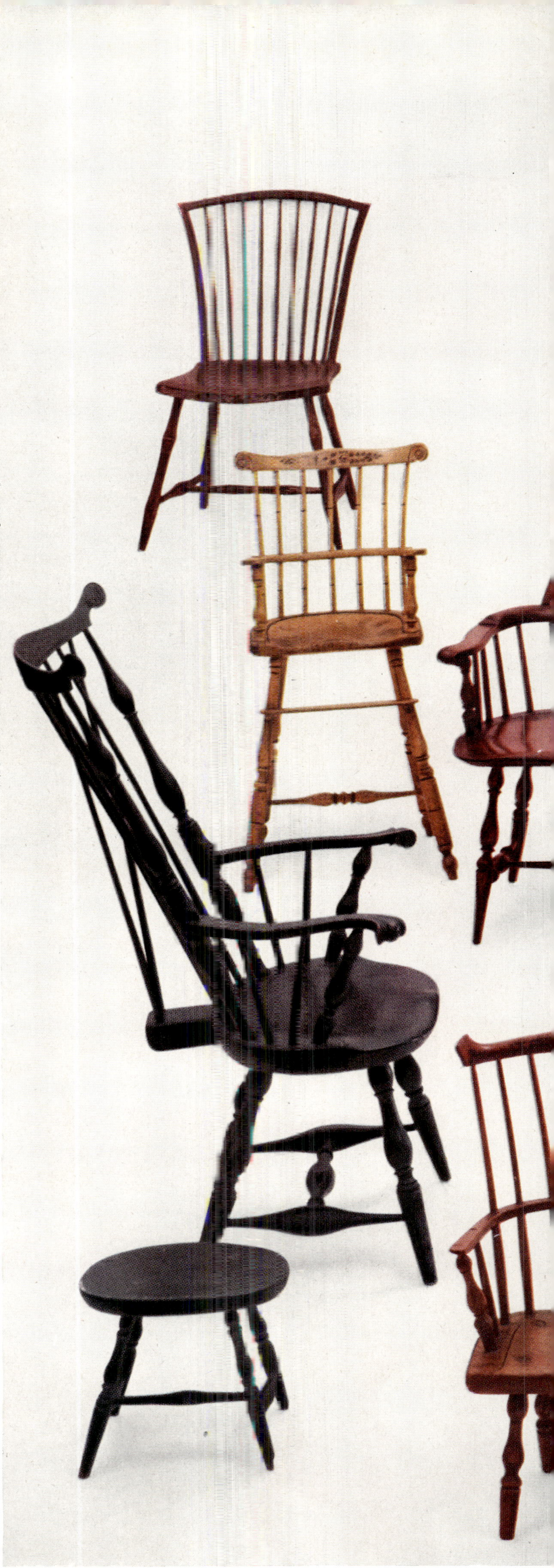

VARIED WINDSOR FORMS are arrayed here. At top, from left: fan-back chair, step-down settee with rockers cradle, stool. Next row: comb-back

high chair, triple hoop-back settee, comb-back writing chair. Next row: brace-back armchair, comb-back rocker. Bottom row: stool with vase-turned legs, child's settee, miniature bow-back, possibly carried as sample by chair salesmen, low-back armchair. The woods, painted in many colors, included maple, pine, tulip, ash.

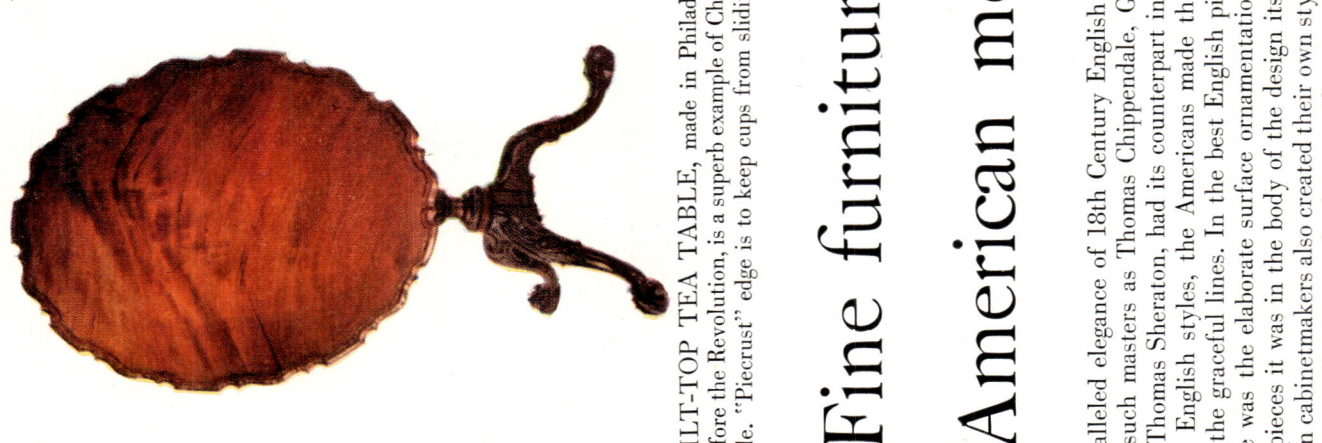

TILT-TOP TEA TABLE, made in Philadelphia before the Revolution, is a superb example of Chippendale. "Piecrust" edge is to keep cups from sliding off.

Fine furniture in American modes

The unparalleled elegance of 18th Century English furniture, designed by such masters as Thomas Chippendale, George Hepplewhite and Thomas Sheraton, had its counterpart in America. But in copying English styles, the Americans made them simpler to emphasize the graceful lines. In the best English pieces the striking feature was the elaborate surface ornamentation; in the best American pieces it was in the body of the design itself.

American cabinetmakers also created their own styles. John Goddard, a Newport Quaker, made the magnificent secretary at right and helped to originate its uniquely American block-front pattern.

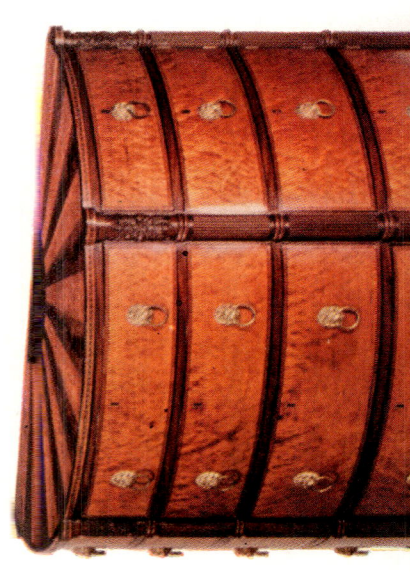

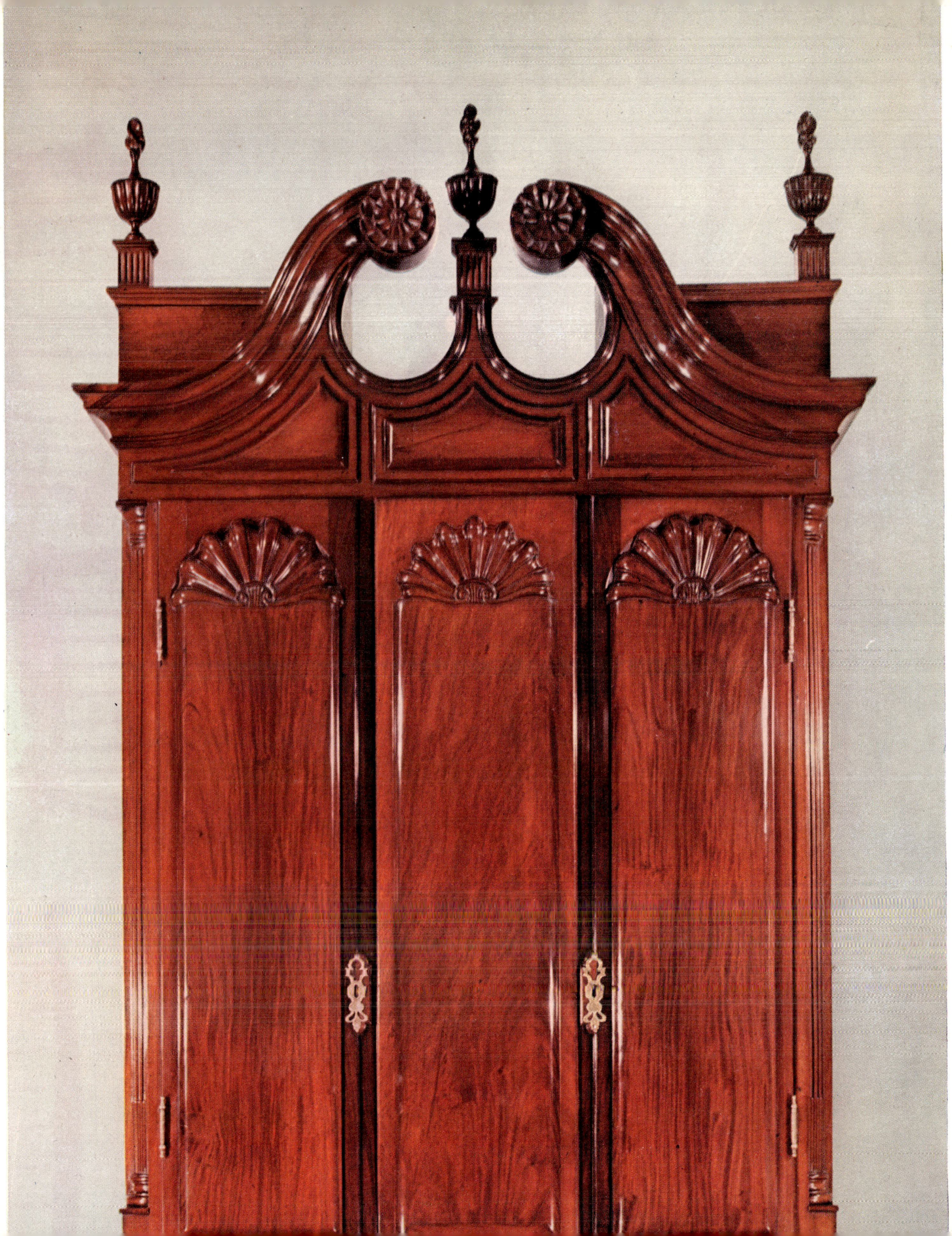

BLOCK-FRONT SECRETARY of warmly colored and perfectly matched mahogany was made about 1759 by John Goddard for Joseph Brown of Providence. The block-front pattern, with its alternating high and low panels, was an American design which had no counterpart in England. Here it is accentuated by the nine shell ornaments, carved in contrasting relief, and urns, rosettes and molded scrolls of the pediment.

ELLIPTICAL COMMODE made by Thomas Seymour of Boston about 1800 follows no one style. He was showing his skill in joinery and inlaying rare woods.

TAMBOUR SECRETARY made by Seymour or his father is Boston version of Hepplewhite style, with special American touch shown in economy of ornament.

"BOMBÉ" DESK, named for its flaring front and sides, was made in Massachusetts before 1760. Basic style is Italian baroque but indented fans are American.

49

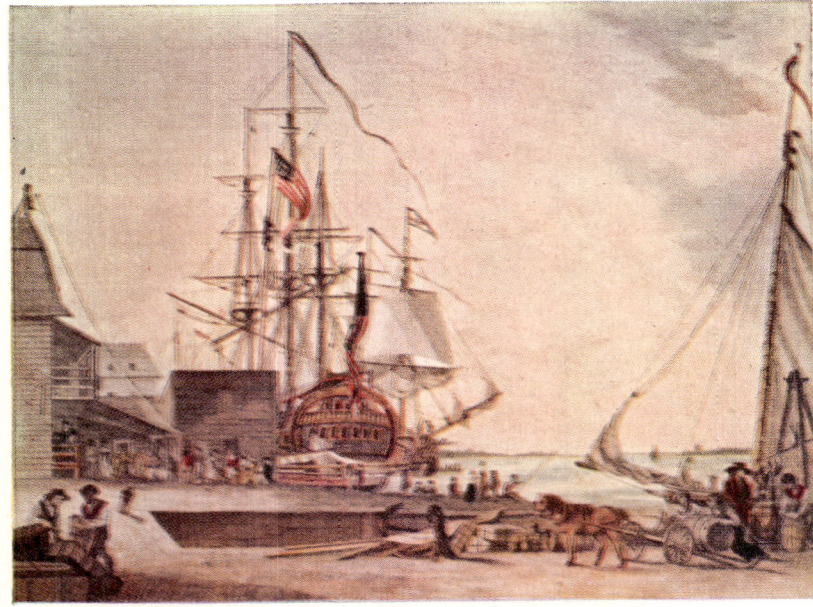

PHILADELPHIA EAST INDIAMAN, shown at Delaware wharf, was in China trade. Robert Morris, who signed Declaration, financed first trip in 1784.

Chippendale style and China trade

During and after the Revolution a sudden desire for things Chinese swept the wealthier homes of America, in part due to a wartime urge to get rid of British influence entirely. Soon after the fighting ended, scores of handsome, fast-sailing American ships were turned toward China, whose tea, silks and porcelains were in great demand and produced huge profits. The ships also brought back lacquered screens, Oriental carvings and carpets, and exotic wallpapers to brighten the merchants' drawing rooms. The furniture of Thomas Chippendale, who was strongly influenced by Chinese design, fitted perfectly with such decorations, and all these things together produced the style called Chinese Chippendale.

The parlor at the right illustrates the style at its peak, about 1790. The Chinese wallpaper sets the tone—an idealized landscape of peace and beauty, completely foreign to the troubled American scene, and more restful for that reason. The furniture in this room was made in Charleston and Philadelphia. Although based on Chippendale's designs, its American workmanship is strongly evident in the straight, sensible legs of the Chippendale side chairs and the magnificent sofa, which is upholstered in faded damask of the 18th Century. The mantel, with rococo carvings, is from the home of a former Philadelphia mayor.

PEABODY MUSEUM, SALEM, MASS.

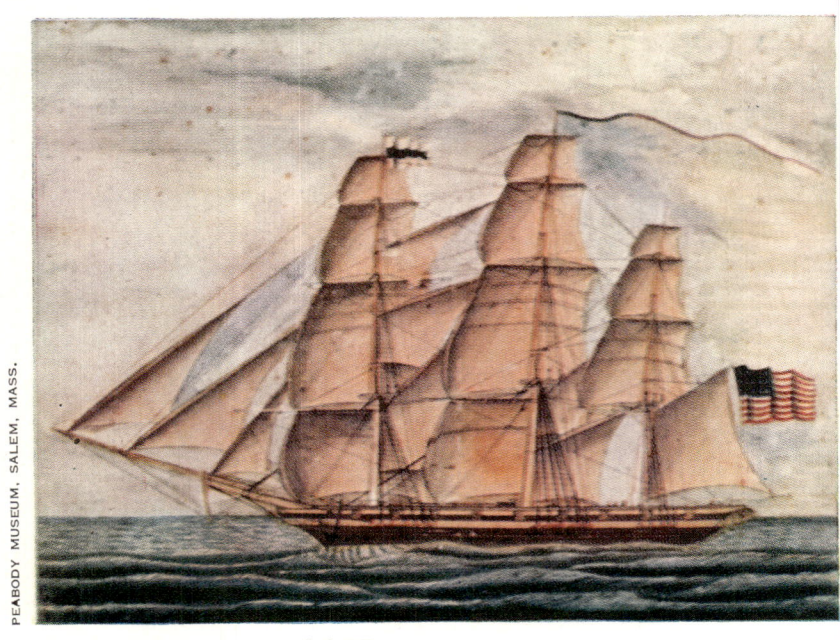

SALEM SQUARE-RIGGER, *The George*, was owned by Joseph Peabody. Salem's fleet brought fabulous wealth from China just after the Revolution.

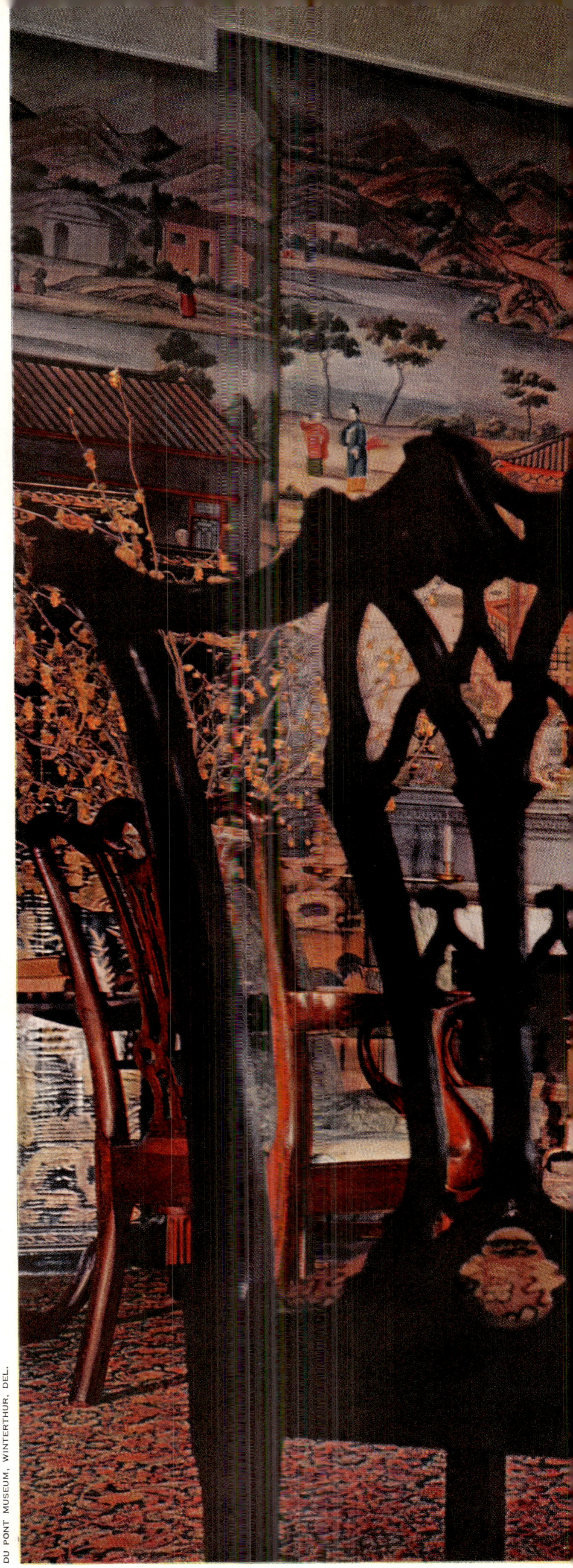

DU PONT MUSEUM, WINTERTHUR, DEL.

CHINESE PARLOR in the Du Pont Museum at Winterthur, Del. is a rich assemblage of American taste in the Revolutionary period. Oriental influence

extends to such details as the porcelain in the shell-shaped cupboard, japanned bellows and lacquered screens, and small pagodas which top the American-made andirons and are carved as "ears" on the Chippendale side chairs. The two-armed candlestands are purely American, designed to give better balance and light.

RARE, HISTORIC PLAYING CARDS

CARD TABLE TOP of needlepoint, made about 1740, features cards of conventional design, chips and fish-shaped counters.

Cards for Americans

After the Americans got rid of a king as a ruler they decided to eliminate royalty from their playing cards. General Washington himself became the king of hearts in the rare historical deck illustrated on the opposite page. Thomas Jefferson is the king of clubs, John Quincy Adams the king of diamonds. In this deck, the queens are classic divinities—Minerva the queen of spades, Venus the queen of hearts, Ceres of clubs, Justitia of diamonds. Jacks (or knaves) are Indian chiefs—Gy-ant-wachia the jack of diamonds, an unidentified chief the jack of spades, the Iroquois Joseph Brant the jack of clubs, Red Jacket the jack of hearts. All these cards were made by J. Y. Humphreys of Philadelphia. The ace of spades in the bottom row is by Jazaniah Ford of Milton, Mass., who about 1815 printed a deck featuring the battles of Stephen Decatur.

The wealthier colonists played "Pope Joan," quadrille and whist. Few of them kept as full a gambling record as George Washington, whose diaries show that he lost six pounds, three shillings and threepence between 1772 and 1775. After he took command of the Continental army he banned card games among his men, as it was impossible to discriminate between "innocent play" and "criminal gaming."

CARD TABLE of walnut was owned by Governor William Dummer of Massachusetts. His wife made table top. When not in use it folded against wall.

BOSTON MUSEUM OF FINE ARTS

The official eagle

The American bald eagle, grumbled Benjamin Franklin, is "a bird of bad moral character . . . he is generally poor, and often very lousy. Besides, he is a rank coward; the little *kingbird*, not bigger than a sparrow, attacks him boldly and drives him out of the district." Franklin thought the wild turkey would make a "much more respectable" national emblem. But Congress thought otherwise and in 1782 it directed that an American bald eagle grasping in its talons the arrows of war and an olive branch of peace should be the main feature of the Great Seal of the United States. The first official seal was based on a drawing (*bottom, in group at left*) made by Charles Thomson, longtime secretary of the Continental Congress, from suggestions supplied by an amateur student of European heraldry named William Barton. The seal itself is at right above. This eagle wore a crest that no American eagle has.

For the artists and designers of the young nation the eagle was a godsend. Promptly they broke out in a rash of carved, painted, engraved, embroidered and stenciled eagles, which were used to decorate mirrors, butter molds, documents and bedsteads. Two such productions in wood are shown on page 45. Meanwhile the Great Seal itself underwent various transformations. In 1834 it was redesigned in its present form by Messrs. Tiffany & Co. of New York. They gave the eagle a proper haircut, as anyone can see who has a $1 bill in his pocket.

PROPOSED DESIGNS (*left*) for Great Seal of U.S. included a rifleman, montage of small State seals, the Goddess of Liberty. Sketch of eagle at left evolved into the official design (*top right*) which was adopted in 1782.

Part III

THE STURDY AGE OF HOMESPUN

◄ FARMHOUSE KITCHEN of about 1820 is reconstructed in Lippitt house at Farmers' Museum in Cooperstown, N.Y.

FARMHOUSE PORTRAIT shows homestead of Marten Van Bergen of Leeds, N.Y., who had scene painted over mantel.

The Sturdy Age of Homespun

SELF-RELIANCE SHAPED ITS RURAL ARTS

As the nation grew and expanded westward the mass of Americans were forced to lead self-sufficient lives. Factories were few, roads bad and imported luxuries rarely got beyond the seacoast. So the majority who lived in the interior depended on what they and their neighbors could make.

Unlike the cities, where styles changed fast and elegance was in demand, rural America carried on and improved the colonial tradition of simple, practical design. The table, chair and bed in the Lippitt kitchen (*left*), along with the open fireplace and beamed ceiling, follow the styles of a people who demanded sturdiness, had no time to make things fancy and, all unself-consciously, achieved a lasting beauty. The farm wife herself created the colors and patterns which decorated her home. On the table are some of her dyestuffs. The butternut hulls on the wooden plate at left gave a strong brown color when simmered for hours in an open pot. On the pewter plate is powdered indigo, which was blue by itself, green when used with goldenrod. The small bowl has ground madder root, which made reds and browns, and the large bowl at the right holds onion skins which made yellow. The clusters of staghorn sumac at left produced a warm beige. At the far right are dried heads of teasel, a plant used to raise the wool nap. Dyed yarn is heaped on the table and hangs from a rack above. Wool ready for spinning is in a splint basket on the floor.

American homespun fabrics had fresh colors and generally simple designs. The barn-frame looms on which they were woven limited them to geometric and abstract patterns. But in their embroidery work American women created many unique designs, like the "rose wheel" coverlet folded at the foot of the bed at left.

The painting above was another kind of house decoration, reflecting the pride and prosperity of its rural owner. It was painted on a panel above his mantelpiece, probably by an itinerant craftsman whose saddlebags were packed with cat's hair brushes for painting, a sponge and cork for mottling chests, a leather comb for graining woodwork. The resourcefulness shown by such artist-peddlers was displayed in other folk crafts, as shown in the following pages. Invention itself became a recognized profession in this period, in the careers of country-born mechanics whose innovations changed the world's way of life.

Tin, clay and

The vivid colors and freehand decorations on the objects around these pages reveal their rural origin. Toleware (painted tin) was popular in New England and Pennsylvania. Pottery was usually made in tiny shops with one small kiln and a single potter's wheel. Pennsylvania Germans liked to add an extra coat or "slip" of creamy clay to plates, squeezing it into patterns or scratching designs into it. Pewter, an

TOLEWARE BOX for documents is painted in classical designs which were typical of New England.

TIN PITCHER, gaily painted and cheaply made, was an expendable substitute for pewter or silver.

EARTHENWARE PLATE relates a religious parable: a pelican feeding her young with her blood.

STONEWARE JUG with eagle design was fired at a higher temperature than red clay plate above.

ARRAY OF PEWTER, set out in 18th Century walnut pewter dresser, includes: (top shelf) sugar bowl with distinctive pear shape, largest (19-inch) American charger known, prized William Will coffee

pewter ware

alloy of tin with copper or lead poured in iron molds and beaten to a soft luster with hammers, was the Sunday best of farm families.

The people who bought these hardy wares demanded pitchers and jugs which would not tip over and were easy to use. Slender shapes and delicate decoration were not for them. But still the practical shapes produced were attractive and the decorative patterns striking.

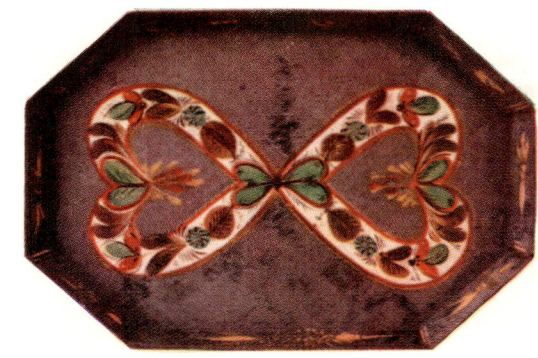

TOLE "COFFIN TRAY" from Pennsylvania, named for its shape, has gaudy hearts and flowers.

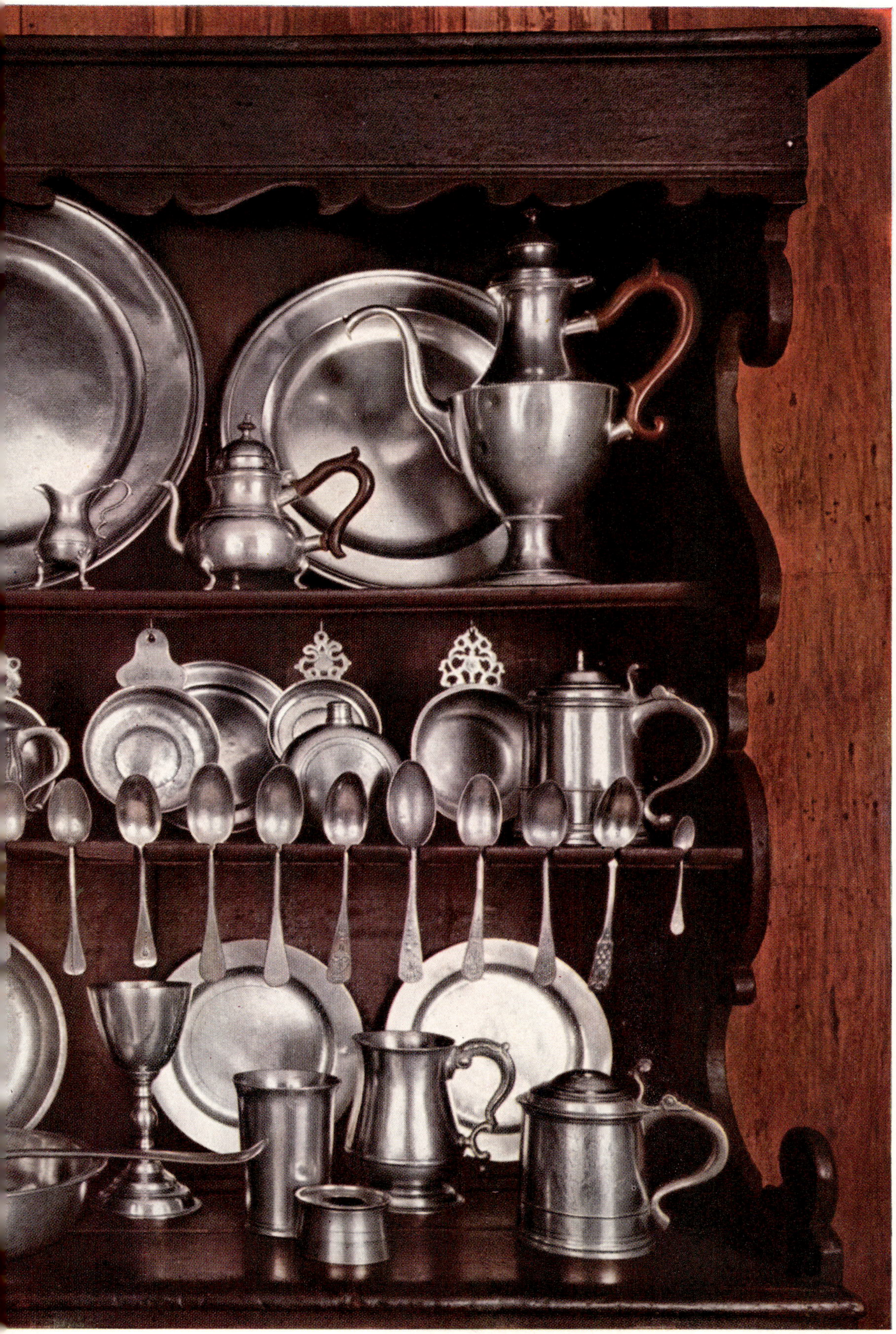

DU PONT MUSEUM, WINTERTHUR, DEL.

pot (*right*); (middle shelf) porringers with variously designed handles, nursing bottle (*left*); (bottom shelf) covered tankards, inkwell (*right*), a chalice (*right center*), one of handsomest American pieces.

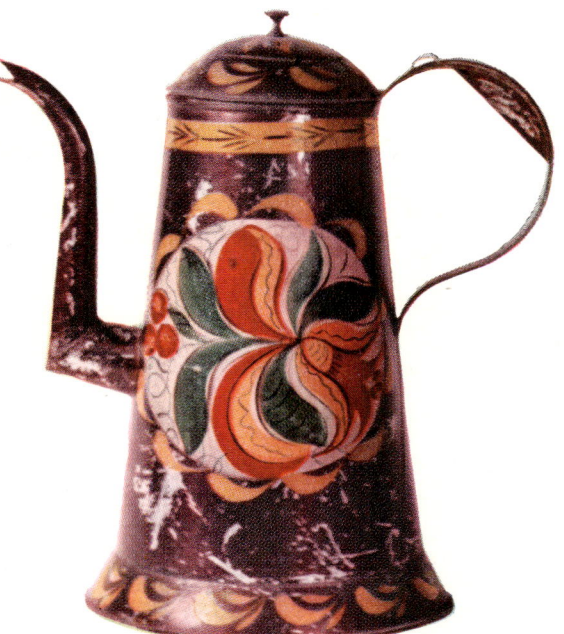

TIN TEAPOT with graceful gooseneck spout was cleverly copied from an expensive silverware design.

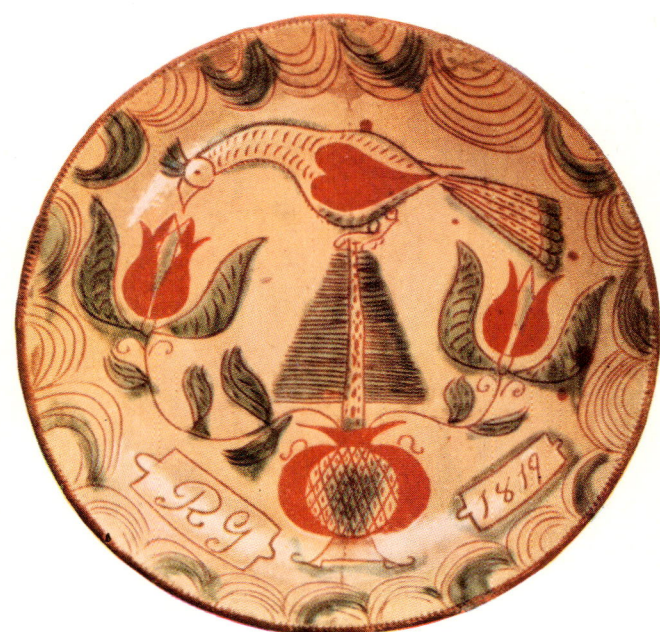

SLIPWARE PLATE symbolizes remorse (folded peacock tail), love (open heart), Christ (tulips).

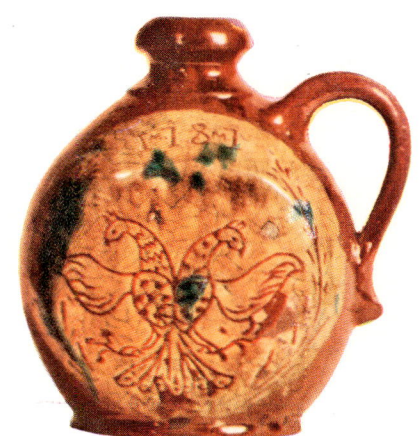

SGRAFFITO JUG, made in 1781, is "scratched ware" with design cut in top coat to clay underneath.

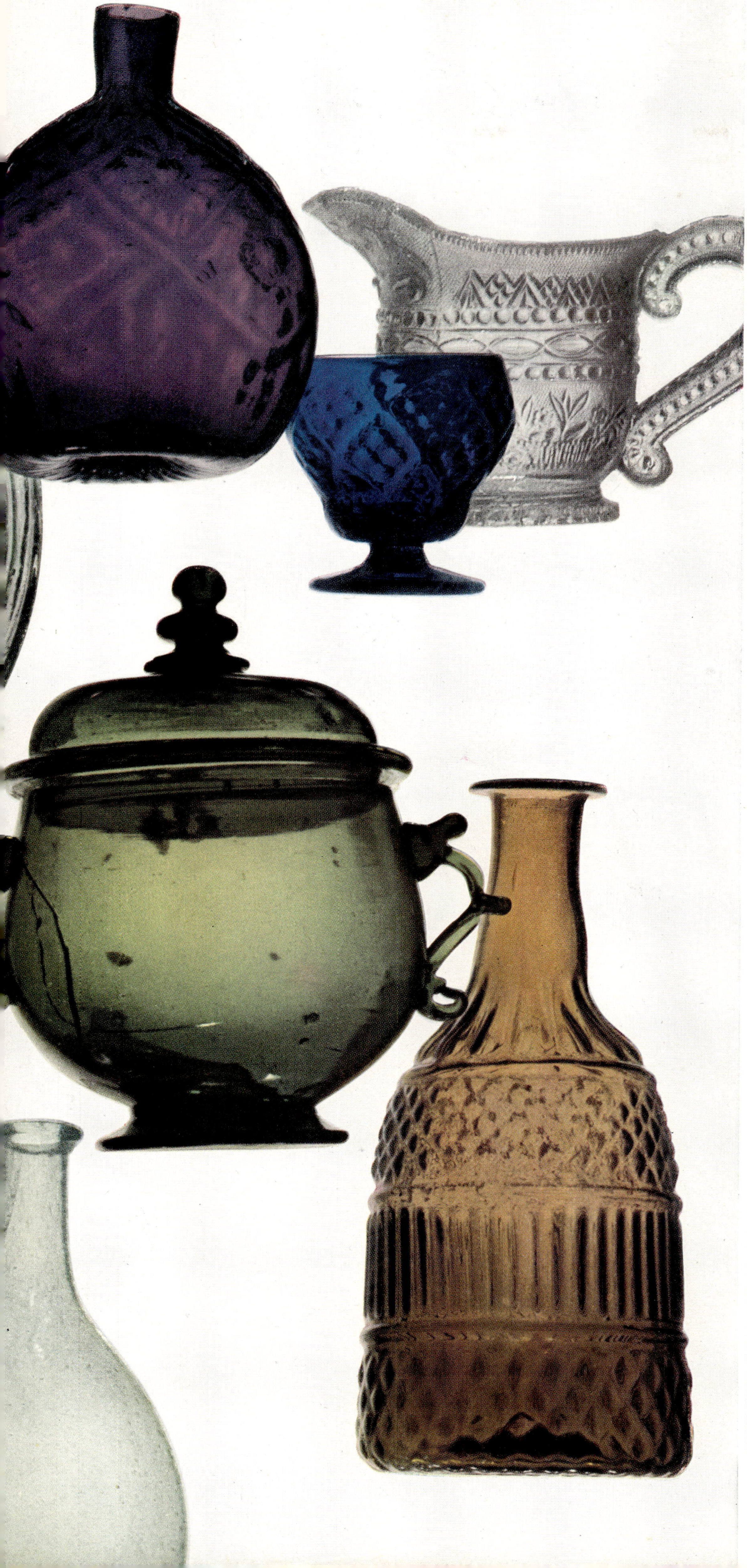

NEW YORK PUBLIC LIBRARY

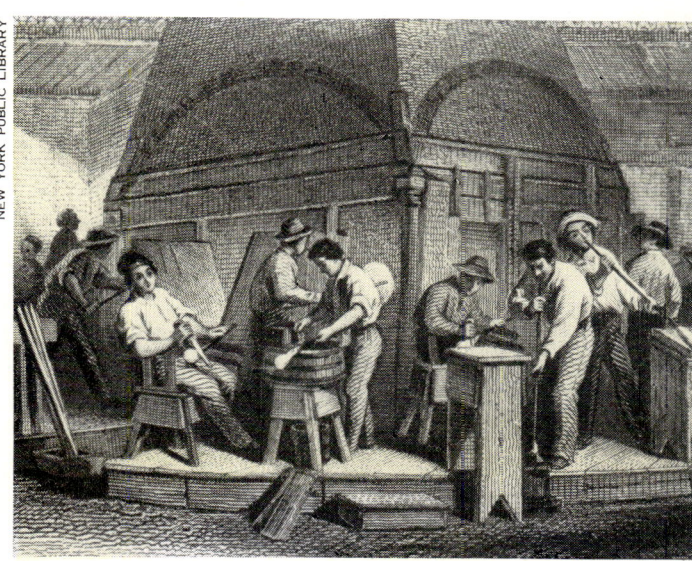

GLASS BLOWERS in New Jersey are shown in engraving from a $5 Millville, N.J. banknote.

Glass in myriad shapes and colors

The first successful American glassworks was started in 1739 in rural Salem County, N.J. near some fine deposits of silica. Caspar Wistar, its owner, made rum flasks, windowpanes and a line of tableware. His "Wistarberg" glass was free-blown by ancient techniques but shaped in designs which were distinctively American. Two of these are shown in the large aquamarine pitcher at far left: the "lily pads" which form the base and the delicate spirals around the neck.

William Henry Stiegel of Manheim, Pa., a flamboyant man who called himself "Baron," and John Frederick Amelung of Fredericktown, Md. also made 18th Century glassware in handsome styles of their own. But the big boom for U.S. glass began after 1815, when American inventors perfected molds which made flasks in exact quart and pint sizes. These were decorated with an exuberant variety of national symbols—Columbia, eagles, flags. A log-cabin flask used by a Philadelphia distiller named Booz helped add a new word to the language.

Meanwhile New Englanders patented the world's first practical glass press, using it at first to manufacture glass doorknobs. From this American invention came the great lines of Sandwich and the other pressed glassware which are so highly prized by collectors today.

CORNING MUSEUM OF GLASS, CORNING GLASS CENTER

EARLY AMERICAN GLASS valued at more than $5,000 is arrayed at left. Top group from left: Ohio flat bowl, Stiegel sugar bowl, Stiegel enameled tumbler, Columbia molded flask, Stiegel "daisy-diamond" blown flask, Amelung salt holder, Pittsburgh creamer. Middle group: bullseye windowpane, South Jersey-type "lily pad" pitcher, South Jersey sugar bowl. Lower group: Amelung wine glass, Sandwich pressed bowl, Ohio "grandfather" flask, Wistar candlestick, Ludlow bottle, Ohio three-mold decanter.

HOTEL KITCHEN in York in 1800 was drawn from memory by Miller, who boasted "no better cooks can be found nowhere." Here the cook bakes bread on old open hearth. On mantel is coffee mill.

"AN ACCIDENT," wrote Miller describing this drawing of Peter Witt house. "Frederick fell from

A carpenter's lively views of

A SELF PORTRAIT of Lewis Miller shows him as a bachelor dandy of the 1830s.

This was an age of busy, productive people, and its spirit was caught in a series of crude contemporary sketches by a carpenter named Lewis Miller, who was born in 1796 at York, Pa. and worked there at his trade for 40 years. Somehow Miller found time to make nearly 2,000 drawings of his neighbors and compile a unique autobiography in pictures.

The U.S. that Miller lived in was just beginning its great transition from a nation of farmers and craftsmen to a nation of factories and mechanized power. Miller's drawings show what the country was like at the start of that change.

A craftsman himself, he was interested in the jobs of other craftsmen. He portrayed cooks, masons, an aproned bootmaker, brewers and a carpenter—Miller himself. The tools and techniques they are using are not much different from colonial times. But here and there is a sign of change, like the coffee-mill gadget at left above, and the sheet-iron stove at right below. The Pennsylvania Germans, to whom Miller belonged, were especially conservative in their architecture. The 1740 Lutheran church below, with its canopied pulpit, arched doorways and painted balcony railing, is straight out of

YORK BREWHOUSE in 1801 has women and boys waiting to buy some yeast from John and George Barnitz. "They made good beer," the artist added in his sketchbook. Codorus Creek ran beside brewery.

CARPENTER MILLER smooths a long board with a plane. Although he had his own shop, the

the scaffold . . . in topping out the chimney . . . broke two ribs." Picture shows collapsing scaffold.

TAVERN KEEPER of York, Mrs. Lottman was drawn by Miller "frying sweet potatoes . . . some of the first I ever tasted." The artist, aged 3, stands in center. A dish of sausages stands before the hearth.

crafts and creature comforts

Medieval Europe. The church has long since been torn down. But there are still houses in rural Pennsylvania which resemble the one at center above, with fieldstone walls terminating in a square chimney at the gable ends, its small windows and overhanging eaves.

Very few of Miller's sketches have been published and these appear for the first time in their original watercolors. A self-taught "folk" artist, Miller's drawing was faulty and his use of perspective childlike. But his pictures vibrate with life and rough humor. Under some portraits he jotted descriptions, such as "fond of liquor," "stinks of ink," or "his mind not right." Functioning as reporter and artist combined, he recorded the accidents, hangings, political parades, preaching which provided excitement for rural America in the early 19th Century. He made hundreds of individual portraits of the citizens of York. Among them were some remarkable examples of American enterprise: an entomologist who collected local insects and sent them to Europe, a flute-playing silversmith and a master mechanic, Phineas Davis, who made watches, an iron steamboat, the first coal-burning locomotive in America.

BOOTMAKER Henry Wagner works while boys stuff pipe of new-style sheet-iron stove.

routine tools shown here indicate that Miller was satisfied to be a day worker rather than contractor.

OLD LUTHERAN CHURCH in 1800 shows the balcony railing painted with portraits of Biblical figures and Apostles. While Pastor Jacob Goering preaches, the sexton (*left*) goes after an intruder.

STREET LAMP powered by candles lights way to the tavern at right. The four-sided globe was suggested by Franklin to give more draft, prevent smoking.

Designs for travelers in a mobile nation

In the 1820s an American who had just climbed out of a stagecoach wrote home: "We were rattled from Providence to Boston in four hours and 50 minutes. If any one wants to go faster he may send to Kentucky and charter a streak of lightning." Speed was what U.S. stage lines provided first. Comfort came behind. The coaches they used were designed in an oval which foreshadowed modern streamlining (*below*). They were suspended on thoroughbraces, or heavy leather springs, which lifted the body off the axles and cushioned the worst jolts. But foreign travelers complained of their limited space for legs and baggage.

Along the roads were hundreds of small taverns which offered hearty meals and modest comfort for a one-night stay only. Reservations were not necessary; the landlords felt obliged to take all comers. The bar was usually on the first floor and served as a registration desk. Near it (sometimes above) was a "common room" where guests sat and ate together. Bed chambers were on the upper floors, and few taverns had more than half a dozen. When these were full the overflow slept on the barroom floor.

ELLIPTICAL SHAPE of American stagecoach was designed to give more speed. But it cramped the nine passengers. Baggage went in rear "boot."

COMMON ROOM of the Red Lion Inn (Delaware) was on the second floor, above taproom and kitchen. Patrons entered from a cobbled court and

climbed rear stairs to spend the evening in cozy games and talk. The walls were finished in white plaster and decorated with useful pipe rack, sconces and clock. Fold-back window shutters could be closed and bolted quickly in case of storm outside or disturbance inside. This 1820 room is now in the Du Pont Museum.

TALL CLOCK by David Rittenhouse of Philadelphia is enclosed in superb Chinese Chippendale case.

SHELF CLOCK by Aaron Willard has half as many parts as tall clock, is both shorter and cheaper.

BANJO CLOCK by Simon Willard is a masterpiece of graceful design and practical purpose.

Handsome clocks in quantity

In the growing nation the exact time of day became a significant fact. Stagecoaches ran on schedule, more people worked in factories, businessmen set their appointments for a specific hour. American clockmakers met this need by producing new kinds of clocks which, while within the average family's means, were gracefully made and handsome to look at. Here came a history-making step in the development of American arts and skills, the first large-scale production of objects of everyday use.

In colonial times clocks were costly works of art. Their long pendulums were enclosed in tall "grandfather" cases of expensive wood. The magnificent example at the left was made by David Rittenhouse, who was an astronomer as well as a clockmaker. This clock has five extra dials which show the positions of the sun, moon and stars, and it sold for $690, the equivalent of $6,000 today.

Soon after the Revolution, American clockmakers perfected new and simple clock mechanisms which could be put in a case less than half as tall as a grandfather's clock, thus saving much expense. In 1792 Eli Terry opened a shop at Plymouth, Conn. where he later produced a beautiful pillar and scroll clock with wooden works that sold for $15. He made his wooden clock movements by the techniques of mass production; a division of labor under which workmen made standardized parts, the assembly of these parts by men who specialized in this one process. The parts were interchangeable, could be replaced at minimum cost.

Wood was used because it was locally available, cheaper and easier to work than metal on the machines of the time. It was also durable; many wooden-works clocks 100 to 150 years old are still running today.

Connecticut became the center of the clock trade. Seth Thomas bought the patent to Terry's wooden movement and started a factory of his own. Another Terry-trained workman, Chauncey Jerome, pushed the price of a good shelf clock down to $1.

The wooden-works clock marks a great dividing point. From now on, the U.S. consumer would be buying less and less of the artisan's wares, more and more of the factory's products. The American manufacturer learned that his mass-produced goods would not only satisfy existing markets but also create new ones. He also learned he had to develop new ways of selling so people would demand his goods, of distributing so people could get them, and of designing so customers would be pleased by them.

WOODEN 30-HOUR CLOCK MOVEMENT, patented by Terry and made by Seth Thomas, has a brass escapement wheel (*top center*). Other wheels are of cherry, the pinions of ivy or laurel, the mounting plate of oak. Because the wood used was so hard and so well machined, the clocks kept excellent time.

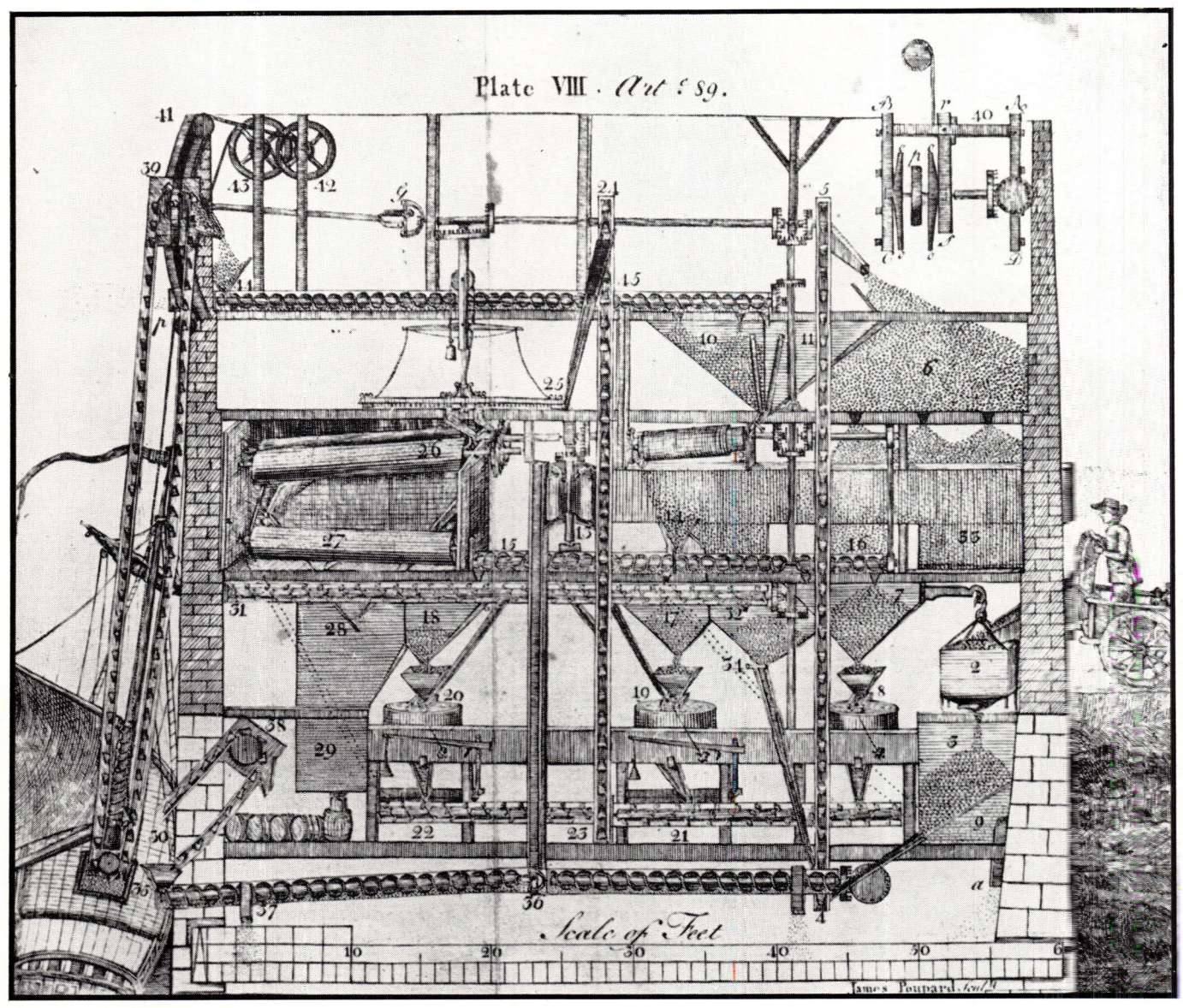

HOW MILL WORKED is shown in diagram published by Oliver Evans in 1795. Principles of this design spread westward, ran mills up to Civil War.

Before 1800, signs of automation

Automation, which today takes on increasing importance in U.S. industry, first came to the U.S. in the 1790s. The thoroughly practical one-man flour mill shown here was designed by a self-taught inventor named Oliver Evans for a friend who operated it on the Occoquam River in Virginia. The wheat was delivered by boat (*lower left in diagram*) or by wagon (*at right in diagram*). It was measured and poured into conical iron hoppers and conveyed by long, narrow screw-type elevators to the top floor of the mill. Here (*marked 6 in diagram*) it was evenly distributed in piles and fed by gravity through funnels (*marked 7, 17, 18*) to several sets of revolving millstones. The ground meal fell into conveyors (*marked 21, 22*), was raised by another set of elevators to the bolting hopper (*marked 25*) which sifted the flour. A conveyor (*15*) dropped it down chutes to waiting barrels (*at 29*). Other machinery weighed and headed the barrels and kept them moving toward the delivery door at left (*marked 30*). All of this was run by the power from three water wheels and directed by one man.

Evans was a farmer's son in New Castle County, Del. who read about Newcomen's steam engine when he was 17. Thereafter he could not rest until he made one himself. He was the first American to specialize in making high-pressure steam engines and became a large-scale manufacturer. In 1804 he rumbled through the streets of Philadelphia in his celebrated "Oruktor Amphibolos," a self-propelled steam dredge which could run on land or water and was really a crude forerunner of both the automobile and the steamboat. He also invented an important machine for making the teeth used to card wool and cotton.

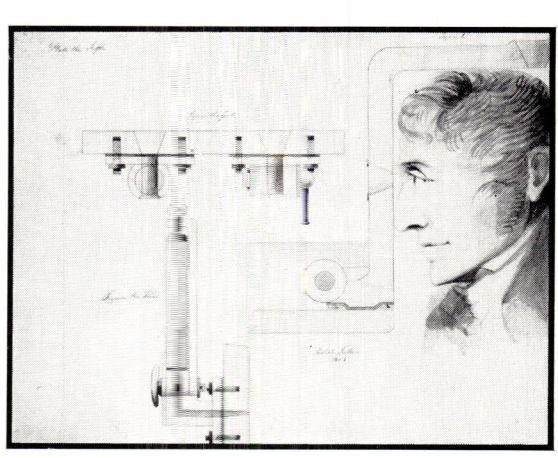

The fertile mind of Robert Fulton

ROBERT FULTON, whose self-portrait (*above, right*) shows how he could direct the placing of bombs from 1800 submarine, summed up in his career all the self-sufficient aspects of the homespun age. Detail at upper left shows submarine window reinforced against water pressure. Bathometer below registered depth. Fulton, a Pennsylvania farm boy who learned the gunsmith's craft, earned his living painting miniatures at 17, and then, with little education and no technical training, became a sensational success as an engineer and inventor.

Part IV

THE MAGNIFICENT GREEK REVIVAL

STATELY FACADE of Andalusia, added to older house in 1830–35 and facing Delaware River, is one of finest examples of pure Greek in U.S. architecture. The Doric design reproduces a famous temple to Poseidon, with rows of columns around three sides and original decorations translated from stone to wood.

BANKER-ROMANTIC Nicholas Biddle lived in Andalusia (*left*). The portrait is by Thomas Sully.

The Magnificent Greek Revival

IT GAVE THE U.S. A DURABLE STYLE

In the first half of the 19th Century, American architecture broke sharply with its English and colonial past and adopted the ancient Greek temple, almost as a national symbol. The great revolution in U.S. taste which we call the Greek Revival affected the design of furniture, clothing and even fire engines. It was inspired in part by a belief that old Athens and young America were akin in their political ideals. But mostly the Greek Revival occurred because the burgeoning U.S. needed new public buildings of monumental size and ageless beauty, and statelier homes to express the pride and cultural ambitions of its citizens.

The perfectly proportioned Greek Revival mansion shown here is Andalusia, in Bucks County, Pa. It was the home of Nicholas Biddle (*above*), a diplomat and poet who was the nation's leading banker in the 1830s. Biddle went to Athens while a very young man and was probably the first U.S. citizen to set foot on the Acropolis. On his return he declared, "There are but two great truths in the world—the Bible and Greek architecture!" Biddle's enthusiasm helped to convert Philadelphia into a center of the Greek Revival. His own bank in Chestnut Street was a flawless marble temple with porticoes like the Parthenon's. This was not bad for business because the vaulted interior was invitingly cool in summer.

The classic temple design was introduced to the U.S. in 1785 by Thomas Jefferson in his model for the Virginia State capitol. Jefferson also influenced the dome and wing design of the U.S. Capitol, and this influenced other large buildings. Americans now had leisure and money to indulge in beauty for beauty's sake; in Greek Revival buildings appearance counted most.

But the movement had practical results. It produced a sizeable body of trained U.S. architects and gave them an opportunity to experiment with ancient principles of form. In the best of their work the old Greek style became new and even "modern"—a style which boldly handled massive structures and spacious interiors and used them in a surprising variety of ways.

CLASSIC VASE of porcelain (*right*) now in the Philadelphia Museum of Art, was made in 1830s by a local firm which put a picture of its factory on the front.

PHYFE HEADQUARTERS on Fulton Street, New York included workshop at left, warehouse (*right*) and salesroom with customers seen through door.

Elegant furniture for a Grecian parlor

Duncan Phyfe was the most famous furniture maker the U.S. ever produced. In his handsome New York City workshop (*above*) he made pieces which graced many Greek Revival homes and are eagerly sought by collectors. Below, spread across two pages, are five of Phyfe's finest products. Classic features shown here are the delicate carvings of acanthus leaves and lyre, the animal paws used as table feet and the pronounced Grecian curves of the chairs and sofa, derived from ancient furniture.

Phyfe was not a creator of styles but rather a master of exquisite workmanship who used only choice woods and skillfully catered to contemporary tastes. He worked in the ornate Regency style (*see drawing, right*), and late in his career he made bulky overly decorated pieces in the French Empire manner. But he much preferred his light and graceful early work, as shown below. Experts today agree with him.

IDEAL INTERIOR of a pretentious Greek Revival home is shown in this 1845 watercolor by A. J. Davis, a New York contemporary of Duncan Phyfe. Ionic columns, along with pilasters set into the walls, separate the two parlors. Architectural

PHYFE FURNITURE includes these examples of his finest work. At left is a chair with spread-eagle splat and Grecian in-curved legs. Next is a folding table of mahogany, Phyfe's favorite wood; a large eagle forms the pedestal and the legs are adorned with carvings of acanthus leaves in Phyfe's personal

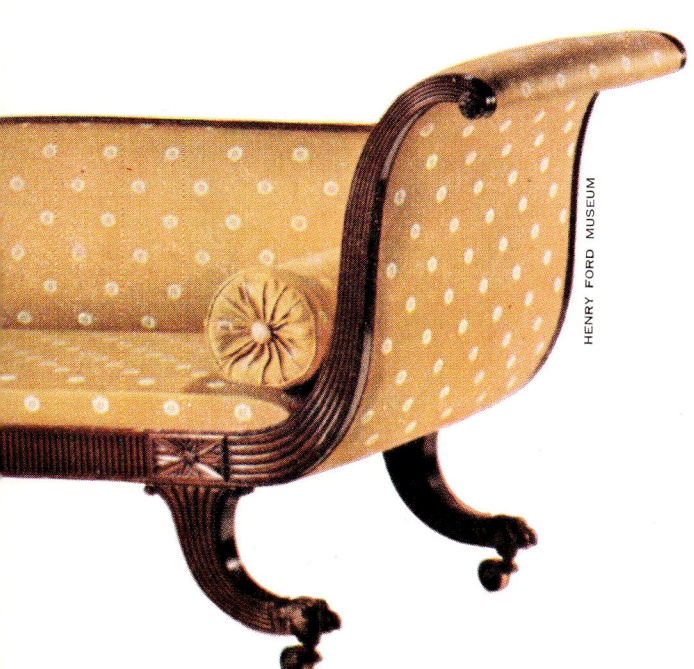

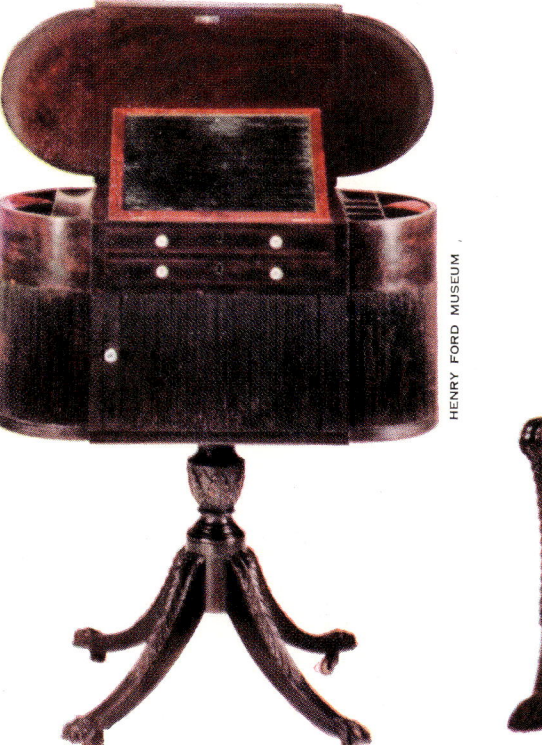

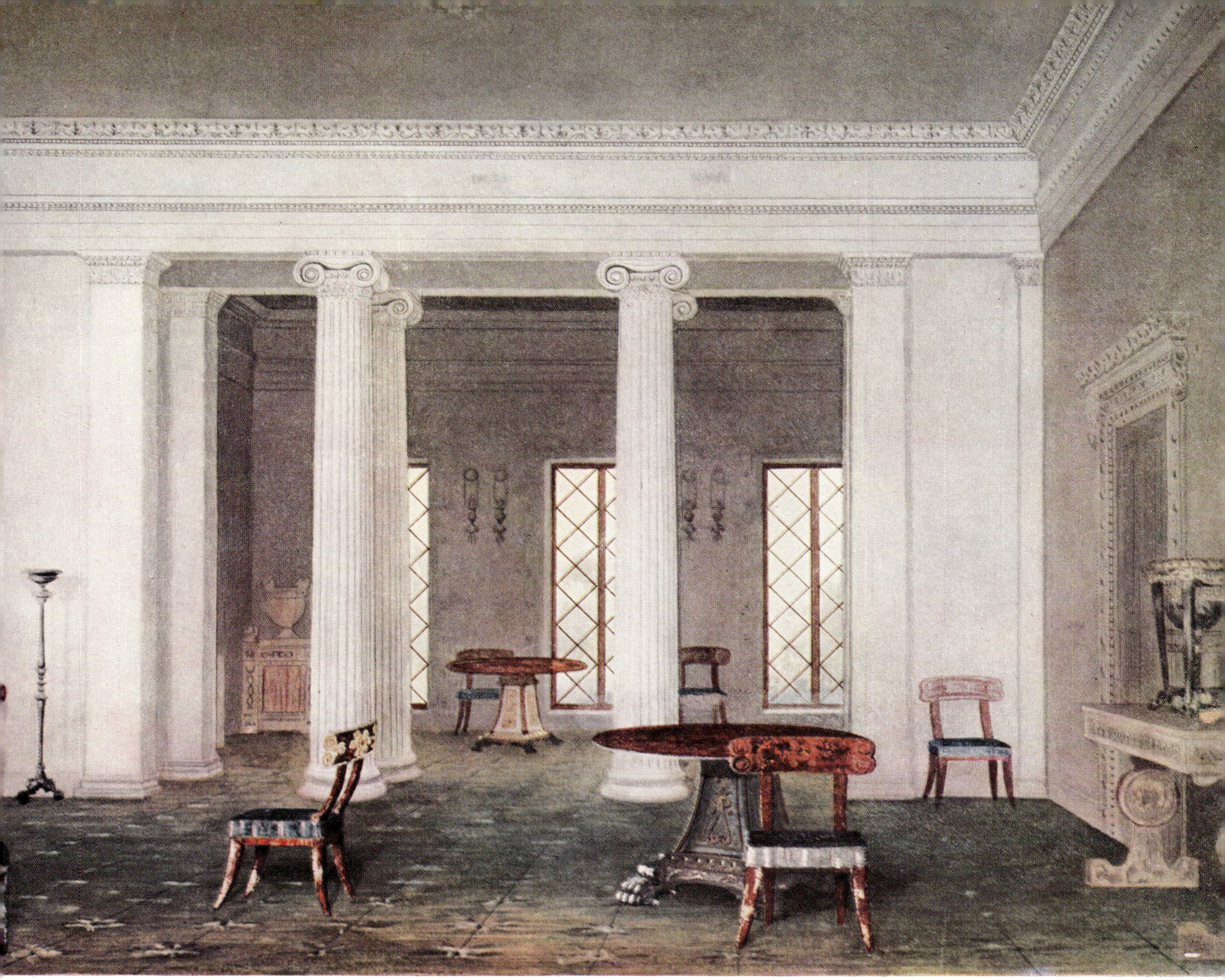

THE NEW-YORK HISTORICAL SOCIETY

trim is used around the ceiling and doorways, and windows are nearly full-length. The massive furniture is in the English Regency style, which was inspired directly by ancient models and was often heavily embellished with bronze or gilded inlays.

HENRY FORD MUSEUM

HENRY FORD MUSEUM

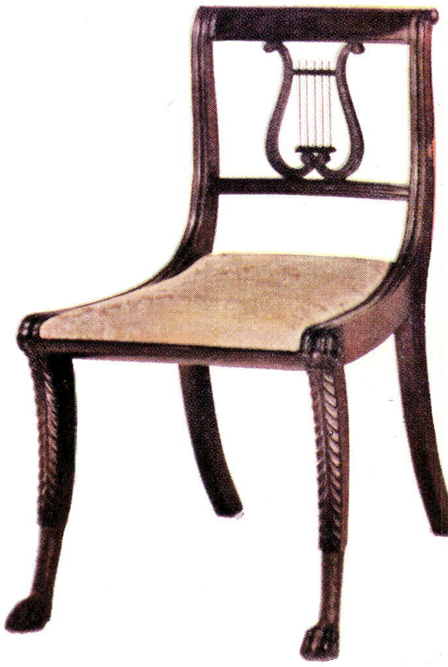

DU PONT MUSEUM

style. The richly upholstered sofa in center combines classic lines of the French Directoire with finely chiseled carving and reeding typical of the best Phyfe pieces. Next is a tambour sewing table with a vase-shaped pedestal and brass lion paws for feet. Lyre-back chair at right was one of Phyfe's most popular designs.

ACORN CLOCK of 1850 from Bristol, Conn., has Greek Revival house of its maker painted on case.

HAND-PUMPED FIRE ENGINE, made in 1843 for a Pittsburgh volunteer fire company, used a hollow classic column as decorative cover for central air compression chamber. On one panel firemen

"FOURTH OF JULY" in Centre Square, Philadelphia was painted about 1812 by John Lewis Krimmel. Women's dresses, domed pump house and William Rush's nymph (center) show taste of times.

Patterns that

In the world of fashion this was a time when women donned the clinging drapery of the ancient Greeks, with high bodices and revealing necklines. They also tied up their hair in Grecian knots or wore it across their foreheads in classic ringlets. These styles, transmitted to the U.S. from the Paris of Napoleon, are illustrated in the painting at left which shows a well-dressed Philadelphia crowd. In the background is the municipal pump house, which has a Greek portico and a Roman dome. The fountain statue of a nymph and water bird was carved from wood by William Rush, America's first professional sculptor. Following the precedent of antiquity, but scandalizing his neighbors, Rush persuaded a pretty Philadelphia belle to pose for this work in the nude.

It was also a time when American designers cut loose with creations which, freely mingling Greek Revival motifs with ideas of their own, further emphasized the sharp break with a utilitarian past. Household objects acquired new shapes which tickled the fancy and started

pasted a Currier & Ives print. In operation poles were run through holes in ends of the long metal rockers and pumped by rows of 30 men to a side. This created pressure to throw streams of water.

DUNCE-CAP STOVE was patented by Poughkeepsie man in 1816. Conical cap helped spread heat.

caught the eye

fads. The U.S. flourished during the Greek Revival, and people with money to spend were intrigued by such gadgets as the acorn clock and dunce-cap stove shown above. Both were unique American designs. The clock, which was invented and manufactured by Jonathan Brown, had a coiled spring works enclosed in a vase-shaped case which harmonized well with furniture of the period. The inverted acorn around the face and the rest of the frame were made of laminated rosewood.

The stove is a direct descendant of Benjamin Franklin's stove which is pictured on page 26. The inventor, James Wilson, found that the dunce-cap top added a great deal of heat.

The gaudily painted fire engine in the center was delivered by its manufacturer bearing no decorations whatsoever. The volunteer firemen in this period liked to beautify their own engines and when the work was completed they held a public celebration. In this instance a remarkable job was performed which succeeded in dazzling all beholders—and still does.

RICHARDSON MEMORIAL embroidered by Harriet Moore, 15, of Massachusetts, expresses grief over death of two friends. Mourning pictures with classic urns hung in Greek Revival bedrooms.

75

Lasting monuments to the

TOBACCO FLOWERS and leaves are used instead of acanthus leaf on U.S. Capitol column.

As the Greek Revival style was adapted to public buildings it took on a distinctively American look and made symbolic use of such native products as corn and tobacco. In Washington the U.S. Capitol was supported by graceful columns carved as bundles of cornstalks and topped with open ears of corn, or adorned with sprouting leaves and star-shaped flowers of tobacco. These much-admired designs were created by Benjamin Latrobe, a British-born architect and engineer who spent most of his career in the U.S., married an American wife and fathered a distinguished American family. For 14 years he was chief architect of the Capitol, which was designed first by William Thornton and completed by Thomas U. Walter.

ENDURING BEAUTY of the Greek Revival is illustrated by the scene below, on the Schuylkill River in modern Philadelphia. The charming temples in the foreground were built before 1850 to

imagination of Americans

Latrobe also designed one of the first complete bathrooms in the U.S., with bathtub, basin and water closet, for a Philadelphia family in 1810. He built the municipal Roman-domed pump house and influenced the chastely Greek design of the Philadelphia waterworks (*below*). Latrobe's pupils, Robert Mills and William Strickland, and Strickland's pupils, Thomas U. Walter and Gideon Shryock, were among the first professional architects who were trained inside the U.S. The state capitols and courthouses which they designed established a style —classic in its details, monumental in its size, versatile in its many uses—which dominated public architecture for almost 100 years and is still a familiar feature of the U.S. skyline.

house machinery for the city's expanding water system. On the hill behind them towers the enormous Philadelphia Museum of Art, built in the 1920s and now the largest Greek-style building in the world.

CORN COLUMNS with ears and husks for decorations were installed in Senate vestibule in 1809.

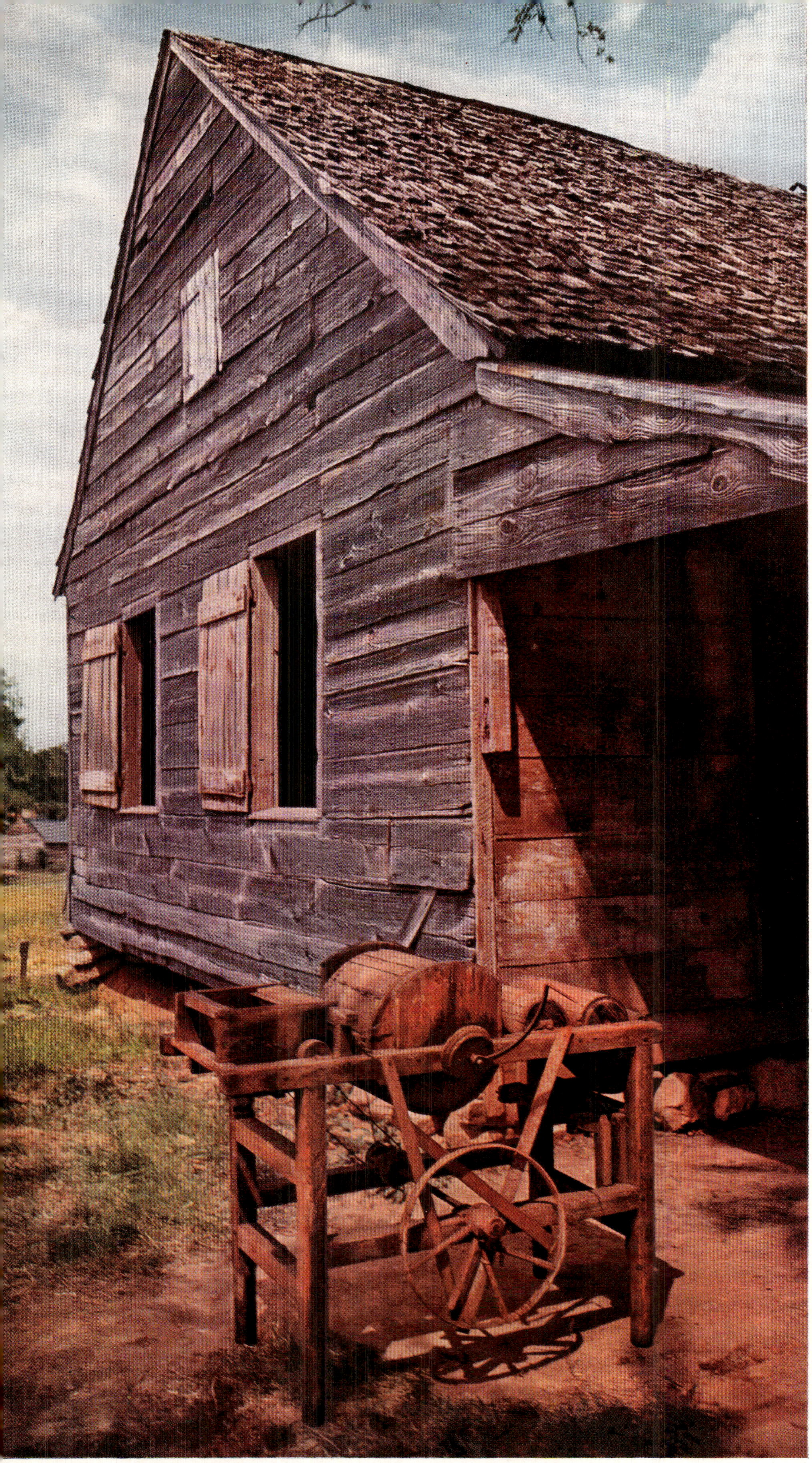

GIN FROM THE ATLANTA MUSEUM, GEORGIA

WHITNEY WORKSHOP now stands near Washington, Ga. In foreground is a combination gin and carder, developed from his invention. It prepared cotton for home spinning on the plantation.

YALE UNIVERSITY ART GALLERY

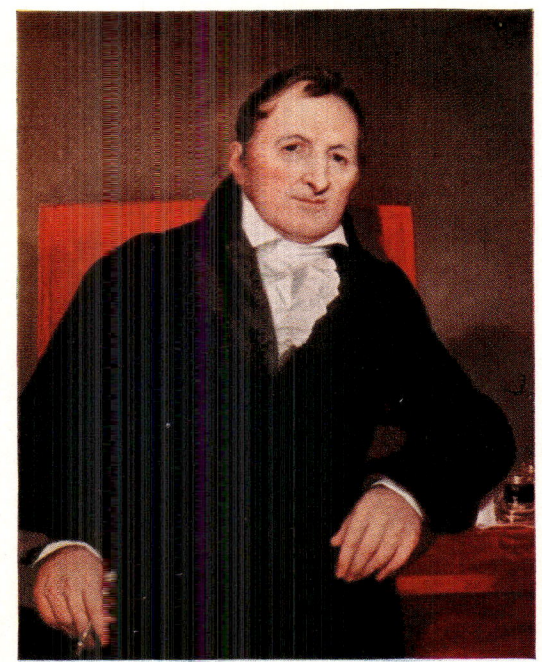

WHITNEY'S PORTRAIT was painted in 1822 by Samuel F. B. Morse, who later invented telegraph.

Eli Whitney and the cotton kingdom

In the South the Greek Revival reached a high level of opulence in the great homes of rich cotton planters whose fortunes were based on an invention by a Yankee named Eli Whitney (*above*). Following his graduation from Yale, Whitney went south as a tutor. At Mulberry Grove near Savannah, Ga. he saw slaves picking seeds from short-staple cotton at the rate of one pound of cotton per man per day. Whitney built a cylinder with wire teeth which pulled the cotton through a screen, separated fiber from seeds and, when used with horse or water power, made cleaning go 50 times faster.

In 1792, the year Whitney invented the cotton gin, the South sold 138,000 pounds of cotton to English mills. In 1811, after Whitney's patent expired, this figure soared to 62 million pounds at about 9¢ a pound. The tremendous boom in cotton dotted the South with extensive mansions like Rattle and Snap (*opposite*) in Maury County, Tenn., which got its name when the land was originally won in a dice game. The spacious house was built in 1845 by a cousin of President Polk. Here the sumptuous Corinthian style is followed instead of the simple Doric of Andalusia.

Eli Whitney, who made all this possible, did not wait to see it materialize. He returned to New Haven, invented the first important U.S. machine tool (a metal-milling machine) and manufactured guns for the government by new techniques which firmly established the principles of mass production. Thus in one lifetime he revolutionized both the agriculture of the South and the industry of the North.

SOUTHERN PROSPERITY and classic taste built Rattle and Snap (*opposite page*) in Tennessee.

PAPERED BANDBOXES were used both for carrying and storing clothes.
The designs were printed from wooden blocks hand-carved by an unknown artist.

PHOTOS COURTESY COOPER UNION MUSEUM

Bathrooms and a bandbox boom

GREEK REVIVAL BATHROOM of about 1845 was depicted in New York plumber's advertisement. It includes two washstands, toilet, tub with hot and cold water.

The lucky lady, soaking herself in a marble tub surrounded by classic columns and an elegant curtain arrangement, is enjoying one of the rarest luxuries of the Greek Revival period. Bathrooms were scarce in early 19th Century America because: 1) running water was not available except in a few large cities; 2) fixtures were expensive; and 3) most Americans thought baths were unhealthy.

The great surge of U.S. prosperity which brought bathrooms to a fortunate few also nourished more plebeian innovations. Bandboxes made of thin wood or cardboard and covered with hand-blocked wallpaper were a feminine fad of the period. Ladies liked them because they were light, used them to carry dresses and hats. American manufacturers liked them because they offered a wider market for their wallpapers. The bandbox boom gave U.S. designers a chance to try out all kinds of topical patterns—one example, above, shows a scene along the Erie Canal, whose opening in 1825 was a great national event.

80

Part

V

THE
ROMANTIC DECADES

SWISS GOTHIC HOUSE, Loch Aerie, was built in 1865 near West Chester, Pa. by William E. Lockwood, who made a fortune in the manufacture of paper collars. Gables and dormers are topped by Gothic finials, windows are rounded in Romanesque style. Mr. Lockwood's daughters still own and live in the house.

TUSCAN VILLA with tower and balcony is a setting for happy outdoor family life in this 1855 print. The heavy carved brackets under the eaves later gave rise to "Hudson River Bracketed" style.

The Romantic Decades

AN ENERGETIC AGE PRODUCED A LIVELY DIVERSITY OF TASTE

In the decades before the Civil War the U.S. was bursting with energy and new ideas. Before 1860 Americans had invented the telegraph, ether anesthesia, rubber-soled shoes, the sewing machine, bloomers and graham bread. They read the romantic novels of Cooper and Scott, paid more attention to the beauties of nature than ever before and rebelled against any limitations on their taste. Many of them thought that the Greek Revival style was much too formal for everyday living so, in their search for something different, they crowded the landscape with Tuscan villas (*above*), Swiss chalets, Tudor cottages and Norman mansions.

In the north and especially along the Hudson River the Gothic villa became a favorite. Inside, Gothic homes were cozy and personal, with furniture-filled rooms, bay windows and vine-draped verandas. The Gothic style was marked by sharply pointed arches and peaks, towers with skyward-pointing finials and narrow windows. These medieval details were freely adapted and mixed with other styles by U.S. builders who developed their own "carpenter Gothic" with a great deal of ornamentation cut out with scroll saws. Though the Gothic was a byway in American design, the variations (*next page*) and innovations of local craftsmen gave it a distinctive charm and character.

Other romantically minded and rebellious Americans wanted the U.S. to ignore all foreign styles and create its own architecture. But it was too early for that. Instead, the principles which they advocated were expressed in the two fastest objects on sea or land—the American clipper ship and the American trotting wagon. By stripping these down to the barest essentials of locomotion, their makers produced perfect examples of the functional design which was to be the ideal of the future.

Local variations on the Gothic theme

SNUG CLUBHOUSE was formerly used for its turtle dinners by the New York Yacht Club, at Hoboken. Sloping eaves, typical of Gothic design, drip with carved wooden pendants, are supported by heavy brackets. In windows are diamond-shaped Gothic panes.

SCROLLSAW GOTHIC ornaments porch of house in Mystic, Conn. (*opposite page*) now owned by Marine Historical Association. Cut-out patterns, which were popular through the 19th Century, are repeated in the arm of the 1845 cane-seated rocker.

TRIM CHURCH, St. Alban's Episcopal on Staten Island, N.Y., based its style largely on English Medieval churches. Here the Gothic appears in simple details: board-and-batten construction, a small rose wheel window and quatrefoil carving in the peaked gable.

QUAINT HOMESTEAD of Washington Irving at Tarrytown, N.Y. has a semi-Gothic tower (*right*) which Irving used for servants' rooms. Irving himself redesigned this house in a mingling of Dutch, Oriental and Tudor styles and called it Sunnyside.

COURTESY MUSEUM OF THE CITY OF NEW YORK

John Belter's Victorian parlor

Furniture in this period touched new extremes in ornamental lushness and functional simplicity. One is pictured above in a re-creation of an elegant parlor. The central ottoman with its tufted damask upholstery, chairs, and marble-top table are the work of John Belter, last of the great New York cabinetmakers. Belter worked with laminated rosewood, using a secret process to bind thin sheets of wood together and press them into shell-like forms which he carved in luxuriant patterns. Ornate as it was, Belter's work was done with a delicacy that saved it from seeming vulgar. His material was almost unbreakable. He used to throw sample chairs out of second-story windows to impress his customers.

The other furnishings in the room above—wax flowers, John Rogers statuette, Swiss landscape on the wall by Thomas Cole of the Hudson River School, heavy damask drape, imported chandelier and wallpaper—were the last word in stylish taste for Americans of the mid-Victorian era.

COURTESY MR. AND MRS. EDWARD D. ANDREWS

The Shakers' gathering room

To American Shakers who shunned the world of fashion John Belter's rich furniture was literally sinful. The Shakers lived in small religious communities and designed furniture that expressed perfectly the simplicity and serenity of their lives. They followed and refined colonial patterns. Since they were celibate and had no children, they could use more delicate legs and arms without fear of too-hard use and breakage.

Above is a Shaker common, or gathering, room of about 1850. The pegboard across the wall was used for bonnets, clocks or anything that had to hang out of the way. Like the window frame, it is painted "heavenly blue," a favorite Shaker shade. Other Shaker items above are: dual purpose cupboard chest of pine; two-slat maple chair, which hung on pegs while floor was cleaned; three-slat rocker with seat of woven tape; "spitbox" of molded maple; iron stove with bar attached for hanging tongs and shovel; trestle table; candle sconce (on peg) of unpainted wood.

87

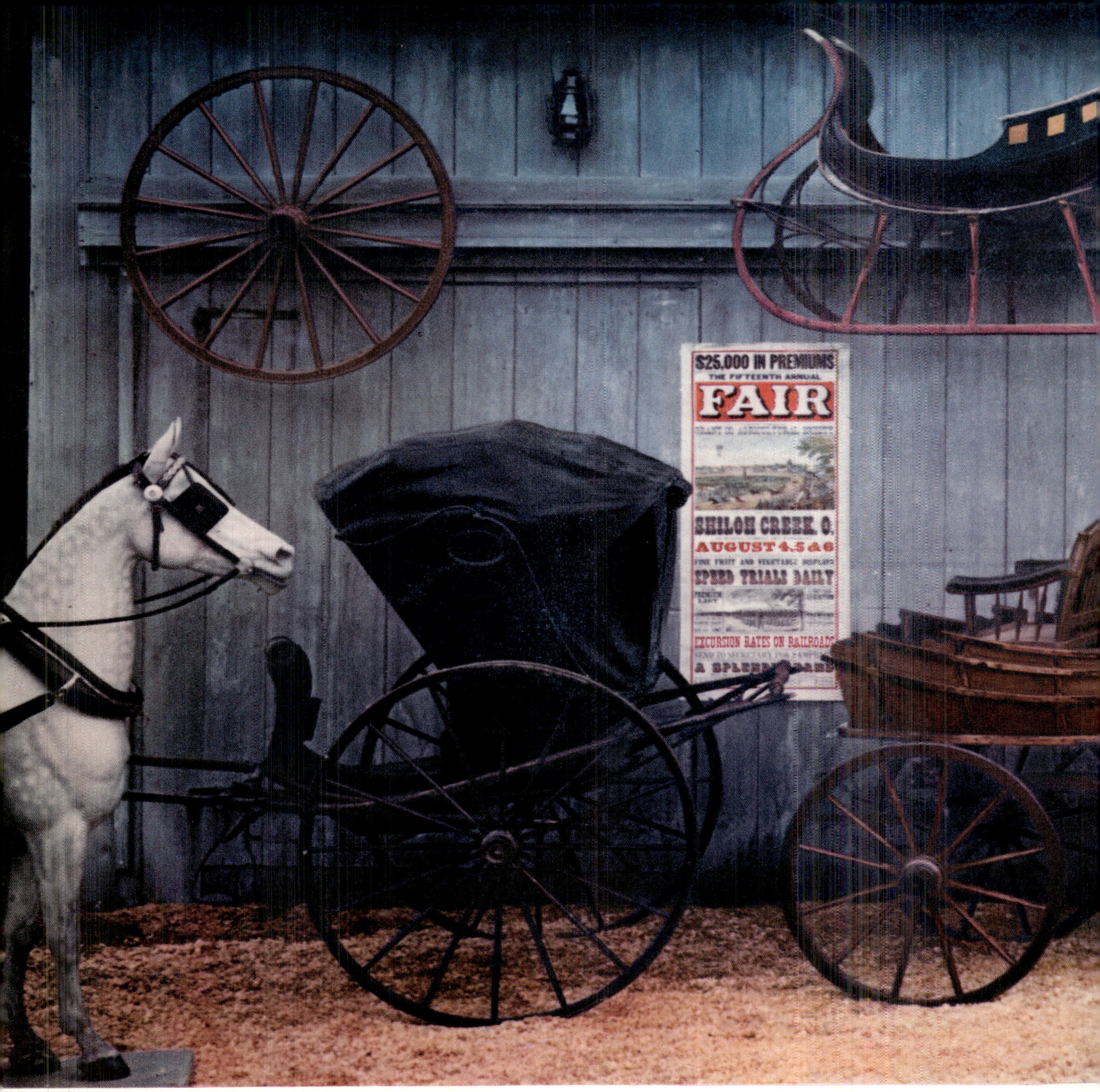

COURTESY MR. AND MRS. EDWIN GRABHORN

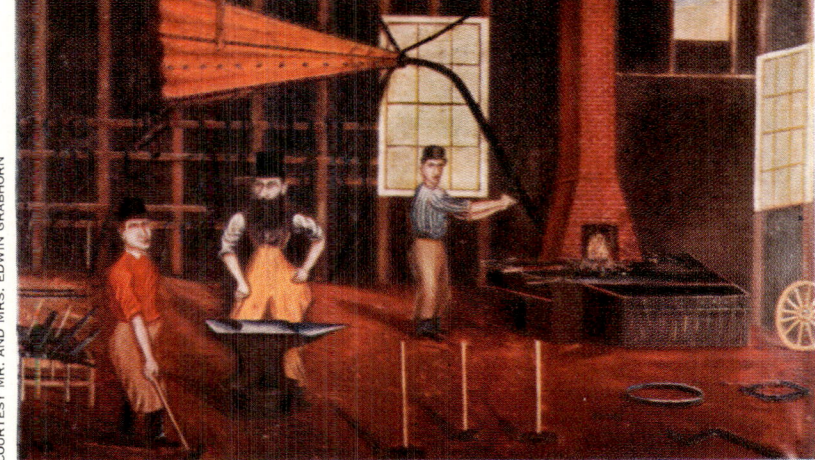

1850 WAGON SHOP at Hangtown, Cal. was run by J. M. Studebaker (*left*) who later made autos.

By 1860 the designing of fast, efficient vehicles was already an American specialty and four of the distinctive American types are pictured above. At the left is a Boston chaise used by doctors, parsons and businessmen for quick trips around town. The famous poem by Oliver Wendell Holmes celebrated the durability of the "wonderful one-hoss shay"—which fell apart just 100 years ago on "the first of November, fifty-five." The poem also lists details of its construction: spokes, floors and sills of "the strongest oak," thills of lancewood, crossbars of ash, and "the panels of white-wood, that cuts like cheese, But lasts like iron for things like

Smart equipment for the horse-drawn age

these...." The chaise above has a leather top which folded back in warm weather, as on today's convertibles.

Next is an American pleasure wagon used for family outings or for light hauling since the seats with upholstered arm rests could be removed. Next is a skeleton trotting wagon designed for American race drivers who, at this time, preferred a stripped-down four-wheeler (which kept the driver's weight off the horse's back) to the English two-wheeled sulky. At right is a three-seated Rockaway, resplendent with polished panels and top. The Rockaway, named for Rockaway, Long Island, was a symbol of U.S. democracy. It served families who could afford a carriage but not a coachman. The driver's seat was set down in the body and the head of the family drove. Rockaways had comfortable spring cushions. One day in 1853 a Watertown, N.Y. man took a nap on one of them while his wife was shopping and woke up so refreshed that he persuaded a local carriage maker to manufacture the first set of bedsprings.

Other accessories of the horse-drawn age are arrayed on the barn wall. James D. Sarven's patented "never-let-down" wheel (*left*), with iron braces pressed into each of its 16 spokes, was standard for heavy wagons,

CLIPPER'S HULL, shown above in scale model of the *Thomas Fitch*, was a masterpiece of streamlined design. The knifelike bow cut cleanly through the waves and the gently swelling curves of the "dead rise" (rounded part of the hull) offered minimum resistance to wind and water. Flat bottom added to its speed.

CLIPPER BUILDER Donald McKay, shown in 1854 daguerreotype, designed the *Flying Cloud*.

Thoroughbred racers of the seven seas

Yankee clippers were the fastest sailing ships in the world because of the cunning curves of their hulls, the tremendous load of canvas that crowded their tall spars, and the competitive daring of masters and crews who looked on each trip as a challenge. A clipper like the *Galatea* at right was a thing of beauty as it scudded along at 16 to 18 knots per hour. It was also the climax of 200 years of American seafaring know-how.

Because England ruled the waves by force of numbers the Americans had to depend on speed in war and peaceful commerce. In the 1790s, English merchantmen still lumbered along at two to six knots per hour. But the young U.S. was sending out traders designed for 10-knot cruising. The Baltimore clipper, a snub-nosed type with wedge-shaped bottom which sailed from that port from 1800 on, was even faster. The full-fledged clipper, long, clean and "smooth as a smelt"—with sharp, convex bow, rounded sides and flat bottom—appeared in the 1840s and gave spectacular service during the gold rush. The advertising slogans read "Eighty Days to the Golden Gate!" But the 15,000-mile route lay around Cape Horn where gales wrecked many ships and waves froze sailors in their bunks. A passage of 110 days was fast; two clippers, *Flying Cloud* and *Andrew Jackson*, made it in just under 90. On easier routes the clippers set many records: *i.e.*, 12 days from Boston to Liverpool (3,100 miles).

Next to the clippers the most famous U.S. ships were the far-ranging whalers whose crews created their own kind of folk art and used a remarkable American invention in their hunting (*far right*). The great era of American whalers and clippers faded fast after 1855 when wooden sailing vessels gave way before the onrush of iron ships propelled by steam.

← SPEEDY PASSAGE to the gold fields of California was offered in this poster advertising the *Galatea*. *Galatea* was built in 1854 at Charlestown, Mass.

HEADING SOUTHWARD in a favoring breeze, the *Galatea* is depicted here → without the skysails shown on poster, but flaunting a horse on its fore-topsail.

CARRIAGES AND OTHER OBJECTS ABOVE, COURTESY OF SUFFOLK MUSEUM, STONY BROOK, L.I.

stagecoaches and fire engines. The sleek "swell-body" Albany cutter at left and the one-horse open sleigh at right provided fast travel and sport in winter. Between them hang chains of sleigh bells and plumed collars of sleigh chimes which made music during the ride and gave warning at intersections. Below the bells is a pair of hames, which fit around the horse's collar to receive the pull of the carriage, and two straight whips with colored snaps. At upper right are two sets of pony harness and handsome silver carriage lamps which burned candles. Wooden horse (*left*) is a harnessmaker's dummy and the iron figure (*right*) a hitching post.

1858 TROTTING MATCH on Union Course, L.I. is won by Ethan Allen (*right*) in 2.28 per mile.

ALL PICTURES EXCEPT TOP LEFT COURTESY MARINE HISTORICAL ASSOC., MYSTIC, CONN.

WHALERS' HARPOON was invented in 1848 by Lewis Temple, a Negro blacksmith of New Bedford, Mass. The iron toggle, or barb, lay flat (*upper photo*) when the harpoon was thrown. When it lodged in blubber and whale tried to escape, the barb pulled out at right angles and took a firm death grip (*lower photo*).

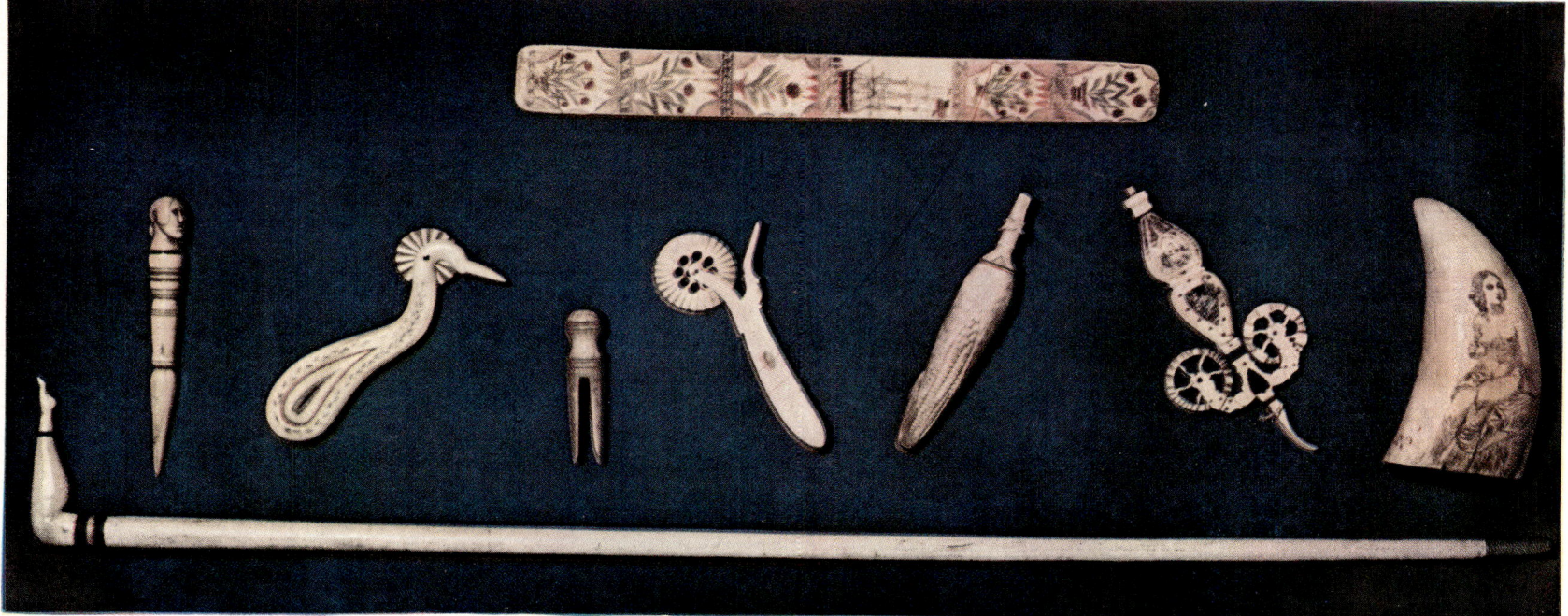

WHALERS' ART, or "scrimshaw," was whittled and carved from whalebone during tedious voyages. Examples above: an ornamented corset stay (*top*), cane (*bottom*) and in center, a dressmaker's bodkin with man's head, clothespin, ear of corn, and pin-up girl on whale's tooth. Three wheeled objects are pie crimpers.

GRATER crushed raw vegetable roots against a perforated tin cylinder, collecting the finished product inside. This was probably a craftsman's product.

SEWING MACHINE of 1859 was one of first home models. In a few years sewing machines were exported more widely than any other U.S. invention.

Mechanization of gadgets and guns

This was a period when inventors multiplied U.S. manpower—and womanpower—many times with devices which mechanized routine tasks. The Gatling gun (*opposite page*) was a crank-turned cluster of barrels which fired 350 shots per minute. The other objects around this page were contrived to lighten the labors of U.S. women, and they illustrate three phases of the industrial revolution which was moving ahead fast at the time. The milk warmer below was handmade in the old-fashioned way by a local craftsman. The apple parer beside it was also of craft origin but became a factory product and eventually found large-scale use in canneries.

Most characteristic development was the sewing machine, which was a combination of at least a dozen American inventions. The decisive feature was Isaac M. Singer's foot-powered treadle, which left both hands free for manipulating the cloth. Any of these household gadgets could have been made in 1500, insofar as their mechanical principles were concerned. But they did not come into being until the American housewife demanded them and convinced her husband she could afford them.

MECHANICAL AIDS were made for a wide range of household needs. The mousetrap at left crushed the mouse to death. Apple parer (*center*) applied the mechanism of the wood-turning lathe to paring fruit. The milk warmer at the right was probably made by a local tinsmith and heated with whale oil.

GATLING GUN, ancestor of the machine gun, was invented in 1862 by Dr. Richard Gatling of Indianapolis. The War Department was not interested but General Ben Butler bought 12 guns and used them successfully at the siege of Petersburg. The gun was officially adopted in 1866, after the Civil War was over.

EIGHT-SIDED HOUSE of modified Oriental mosque design was built in 1860 at Irvington-on-Hudson, N. Y. Author Carl Carmer now lives in it.

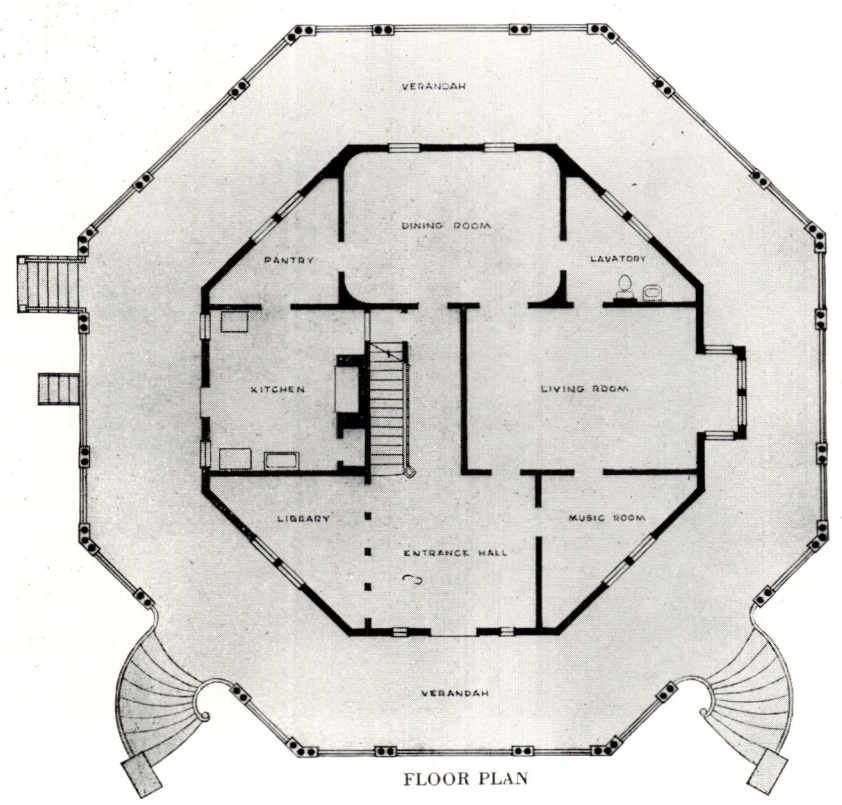

FLOOR PLAN

Octagonal houses and gymnastic rooms

A romantic U.S. innovation of this period was the eight-sided house, which was widely promoted by Orson S. Fowler, a New York phrenologist and lecturer on happy marriages. Fowler preached big families and big houses. Every well-planned home, he said, should include a playroom for small children, a dancing room for teenagers and a special "gymnastic room" where females of all ages could keep themselves in trim. By lopping off all the corners of a square house plan Fowler claimed he could enclose the same amount of room space at a 25% saving in basic building cost. His eight-sided design was striking and symmetrical in appearance, and offered views in all directions. By eliminating "waste" corners and extra hallways it saved housewives many steps and distributed light from the windows and heat from the cellar evenly through the interior. The octagonal style was also used efficiently in barns, schools and churches.

Many octagonal examples are still in everyday use. The imposing one shown above has 18 rooms grouped around a central stairway and a fifth-floor cupola looking out over the Hudson River. The wood veranda runs entirely around the house and is ornamented with a railing which repeats a cast-iron portrait of a former owner's dog Prince.

Part

VI

THE FABULOUS FRONTIER

"SHIPS OF THE PLAINS," a painting by Samuel Colman, shows covered wagons hauling Western freight. The oxen provided meat supply in emergencies.

The Fabulous Frontier

GENERATION AFTER U.S. GENERATION USED

Across the central plains of North America, over broad rivers and chains of mountains, poured the streams of human migration which gave the U.S. its national shape and a boundary on the Pacific Ocean. The move to the West began with the first colonists and swelled to a conquering flood in the mid-19th Century. Along its edge—the frontier—life was a continuous adventure in self-reliance, an endless retraining in the skills and crafts of the pioneer and homesteader.

Because the frontier was always in motion, its arts were transient and often crude. The main types of frontier architecture were the log cabin, sod house and wooden false fronts of the mining and cowboy towns. Frontier furniture was a mixture of homemade benches, cornhusk beds and such treasured heirlooms as each family brought with it from the east. The frontier's basic tools were the gun and the plow, and both of them had to be drastically changed and improved by American inventors to meet special conditions along the American frontier.

In the covered wagon, the frontier's great carrier, a graceful and practical design was combined with the utmost in rugged strength. The covered wagon was evolved by local craftsmen along the colonial frontier of Pennsylvania where it was called the Conestoga wagon after a stream in Lancaster County. Unlike the low-wheeled English wagons of the period, the fully developed Conestoga (*above*) was designed for the rough American terrain with high, finely ironed wheels that maneuvered well among stumps and stones and could ford a stream two feet deep. The Conestoga's carefully shaped bed sloped downward from both ends, so the load would shift toward the middle

CONESTOGA WAGON, built about 1770, is painted in colors used by Pennsylvania wagonmakers. Frame and flooring are oak, spokes hickory, axles of gumwood which does not split. Toolbox at center is decorated with wrought-iron designs. Brakeman sat on "lazy board" extending at side.

THE ARTS OF THE PIONEERS

and not spill out on hills. The whole body was tilted slightly forward, with smaller wheels in front, providing almost parallel drawbar pull for a powerful six-horse team.

The Pennsylvania Conestogas were used for hauling farm products and freight; some enormous ones could carry 10 tons. Their boatlike shape and their white cloth dust covers which resembled billowing sails gave them the name of turnpike schooners in the east. They were driven by a rider on the left rear horse and passed other wagons on the left. This frontier habit may have helped to make the U.S. a nation of left-seated auto drivers.

As the covered wagons rolled westward, their size and shape were altered to meet new conditions. The prairie schooner which was used on level plains and gradual mountain passes had a flatter bed than the eastern type. It was smaller and lighter and was often fitted up for family living on the 2,000-mile trek to Oregon or California. In emergencies it could serve as a fort or a boat. But its first and most necessary job was moving supplies across vast distances and maintaining the far-flung outposts of the fabulous American frontier.

FUR TRADE OUTPOST, Fort Laramie in Wyoming, was painted in 1837 by Alfred Jacob Miller. The log palisades enclosed a trading area 150 feet square, guarded by blockhouse and corner bastions.

FRONTIER FIREARMS are (from the top) a Hawken-type "plains rifle" prized by early buffalo hunters for felling power and accuracy. Next three pistols: a .44 Colt dragoon six-shooter (left) invented in 1847 and used in Mexican War; a single-shot Philadelphia derringer, sometimes called the gambler's pistol; and Colt 1861 Navy revolver. Next a single-shot Sharps' carbine of the type used in the fighting between pro- and anti-slave factions in Kansas and later in the Civil War; a seven-shot Spencer carbine; a Winchester 66 carbine and a Winchester 73 rifle, both repeaters, which replaced older types for hunting on the plains; Springfield carbine used by the Indian-fighting army of the 1870s. At bottom is the Colt .44 Frontier model, long the standard weapon of Western cowboys, sheriffs and outlaws.

FUR TRADE GOODS above include (upper left) a bear trap and beaver trap made at Oneida, N.Y.

The hardy

Fur traders were the first residents on every American frontier from Virginia to the Pacific Northwest. They made their living by exchanging craft and factory products for the skins of beaver, deer and buffalo, collected and brought to them by Indians. Fur traders supplied the Indians with cheap guns, scalping knives, iron

for Western trappers; snowshoes and fringed jacket which belonged to the Chouteau trading family of St. Louis; tomahawks, blanket, silver armbands and beads which were traded for furs. The bowie knife (*lower left*) was a favorite frontier accessory used for cutting meat or throwing or close-in fighting.

fur traders, first on the Indian border

tomahawks and alcohol, along with more innocent beads and bracelets. The traders adopted the Indians' tepee-style dwellings, copied their clothing and sometimes borrowed their wives. The snowshoes above were an Indian invention much used by white trappers. So is the handsome deerskin jacket whose decorations are porcupine quills dyed by an ancient Indian process and whose long fringes served the useful purpose of letting rain drain off quickly. For their weapons the traders used finely made firearms like those which are shown in the photo at left.

Fur traders crossed the whole continent by the 1820s; along their trails and over passes they discovered came the later pioneers and official explorers. Trading posts established by fur companies became Army forts and future cities. In a few decades the traders' frontier was swallowed up and lost forever in the frontier of the cattleman, farmer and gold-seeker.

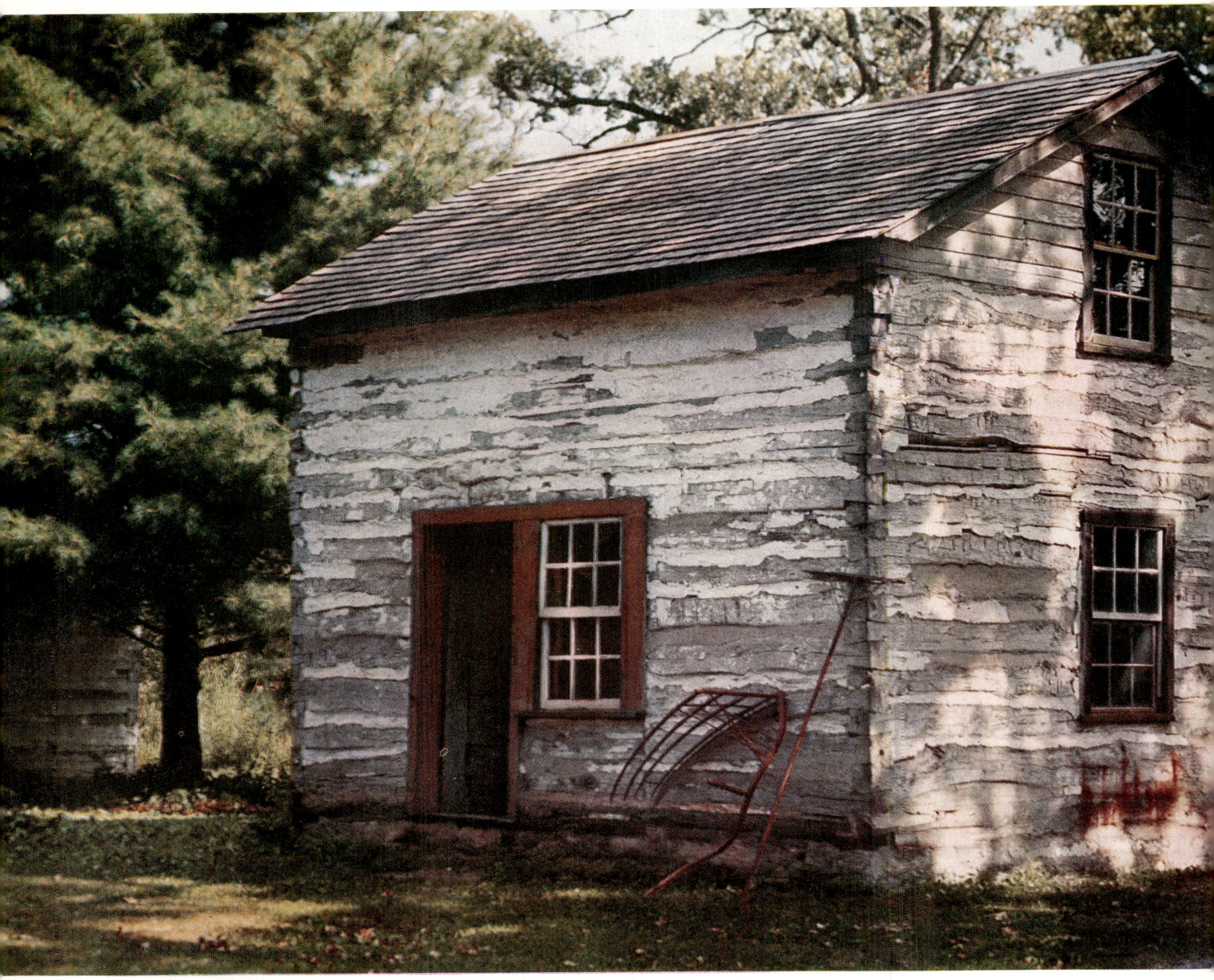

WELL-BUILT CABIN of squared oak logs was put up in 1852 near Decorah, Iowa, by Erick Egge, a carpenter-farmer from Norway. Rake and cradle scythe against wall were early frontier farm tools.

COZY INTERIOR of another Decorah cabin (*below*) is furnished in simple style of the Midwest frontier: turned bed with rope springs, sturdy gate-leg table, plain chairs, storage boxes and churn.

CABIN FROM NORWEGIAN-AMERICAN HISTORICAL MUSEUM, DECORAH, IOWA

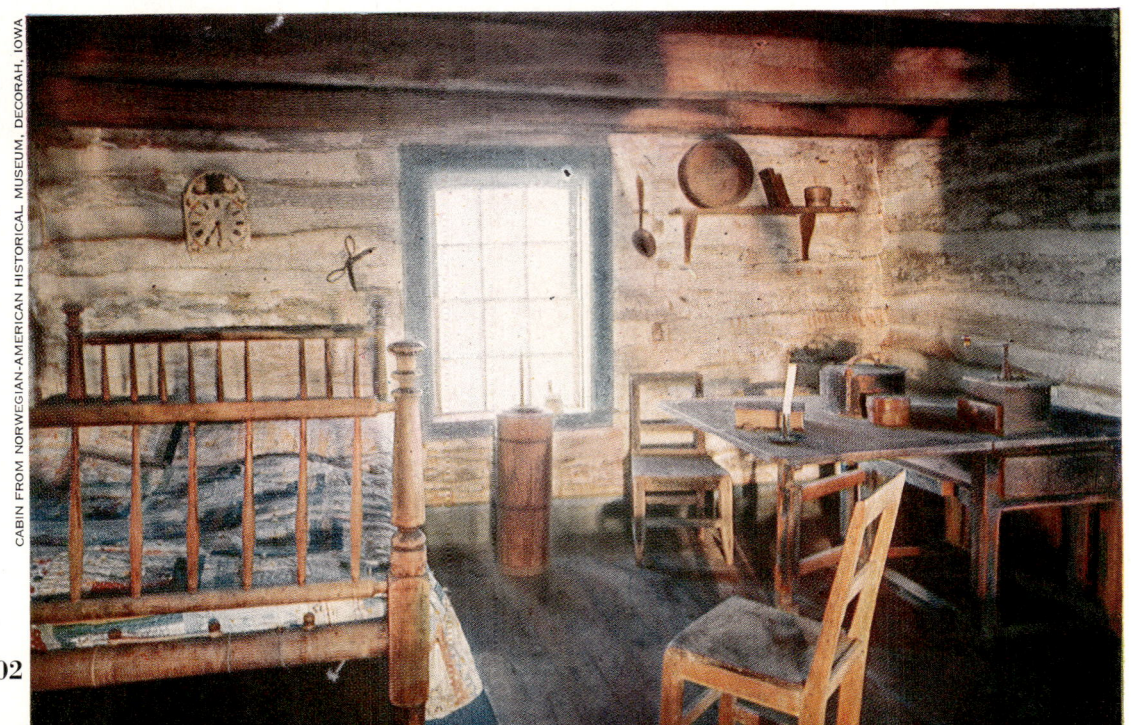

Homes, tools

The log cabin appeared fairly late on the frontier because the early English colonists never saw log houses in their homeland and did not build them here. The first American log cabins were built by Swedish settlers on the Delaware and the style was carried inland by German and Scotch-Irish farmers. The log cabin technique was perfectly suited to frontier conditions; from 1750 on, it flourished wherever there were trees.

An ax was the only tool needed to build a log cabin and a couple of men could finish the job in a week. In the rougher cabins the logs were left round, with shallow notches at both ends which interlocked and held the structure steady. Chinks in the walls were filled up with moss and mud. Windows were made of sliding boards, oiled paper or greased deerskin.

VITAL INVENTION of the frontier was the all-steel "singing plow," first made by John Deere of Illinois in 1837. The rich prairie soil quickly fouled cast-iron plows but slid smoothly off polished steel.

MECHANIZED RAKES were needed for frontier's bumper hay crops. Above, left is a horse-drawn rake with wood teeth lifted by a man on foot to release the hay. At right: a sulky rake with iron teeth.

McCORMICK'S REAPER, shown below in 1831 model, became a sensational success on level Midwest prairies. Revolving paddles pushed wheat toward cutting blade at forward edge of wooden bed.

for the farmer

Such dwellings were considered temporary, built by families who expected to move on or build a better home in a few years. But alongside them, as the frontier settled down, appeared other log houses like the one shown above, built with more care, and still snug and livable after more than 100 years. Here the logs have been squared and dovetailed at the corners. Windows are sliding sash and there is a second floor reached by a ladder.

The building of homes like this marked the end of one phase of the frontier and the start of another—the era of pioneer farming. From the 1830s on, the greatest agricultural revolution in history took place on the fertile and endlessly inventive farm frontier, with the perfection of mechanized planters, reapers, and balers, and the all-steel prairie-breaking plow.

OLD RIVER STEAMBOAT, built in 1882, has triple decks and a pilothouse in the center like the fast steam packets that Mark Twain knew. Stern paddle wheels like this were used on some boats; others had wheels at the sides. The lower deck was always open, for easy loading of freight; the second

BEFORE THE STEAMBOAT, the graceful keelboat (*center*) and the clumsier flatboat (*far left*) provided transport on frontier rivers. The keelboat could be rowed or poled or sailed going upstream.

Travel on the

Along the rivers that pierced the wilderness swarmed an array of native American craft designed for every frontier need. The fur traders used Indian pirogues (canoes of hollowed logs) to ascend the Missouri and bring back bales of skins. On the Ohio, the early gateway to the West, appeared the flatboat—an enormous cabin built on a raft, in which whole families floated hundreds of miles with their horses, cows, carts and plows. The more manageable keelboat had a heavy timber running along its bottom to give better balance and take the shock of snags.

Finally came the great Western steamboats which through competition and the pride of

deck held staterooms and the lushly decorated dining room and saloon where gamblers consorted. The third or "Texas" deck had quarters for officers and crew. The boat above, fitted with modern antennae and towing bumpers in the bow, is used today by Army engineers to haul equipment for levee-building.

inland waters

their owners soon became the epitome of luxury along the frontier. Mark Twain, a onetime pilot, never forgot how handsome and exciting these floating palaces were, with their smokestacks resembling "a spraying crown of plumes . . . gilt deer horns over the big bell; gaudy symbolical picture on the paddle box . . . porcelain knob and oil picture on every stateroom door . . . big chandeliers every little way, each an April shower of glittering glass drops . . . in the ladies' cabin a pink and white Wilton carpet, as soft as mush." The golden age of Mississippi steamboating was ended by the Civil War and the railroad. But a few survivors designed in the classic manner still ply the river.

ROUNDING A BEND, a Mississippi steamboat passes Indian mounds near Natchez. This scene is part of a 348-foot panorama of the river painted in 1850 and exhibited to audiences at 25¢ a head.

FRONTIER'S LOCOMOTIVE, the Genoa, is the standard American eight-wheeled type used everywhere in the early West. This engine was built in 1872 by the Baldwin Locomotive Works of Philadelphia and ran until 1912 on the mountainous Virginia & Truckee line which linked silver-rich Virginia City, Nev.

CONCORD COACHES provided the fastest travel in the West before the railroad. This light and handsome coach was operated by Wells Fargo between Hangtown, Calif. and Carson City, Nev.

Iron horses

"There is more poetry in the rush of a single railroad train across the continent than in all the gory story of burning Troy," wrote Joaquin Miller, the California poet. After the covered wagon and the speedy Concord stagecoach (*left*) the locomotive took over as the chief opener of the West.

Although England built the first railroads, the tremendous possibilities of steam transportation were realized first in the young and wide-open U.S. American inventors and engineers quickly transformed the clumsy four-wheeled English "platform" locomotive into a versatile eight-wheeled giant. Since sharp curves were the rule on American roads, the first problem was to keep the engine on the track. This was solved by John B. Jervis of the Mohawk & Hudson line in 1831. He mounted the front of the engine on four small wheels set close together and fastened to the engine by a center pin, so the front truck could turn by itself and follow the curves. The driving wheels in the back were later divided into four to distribute

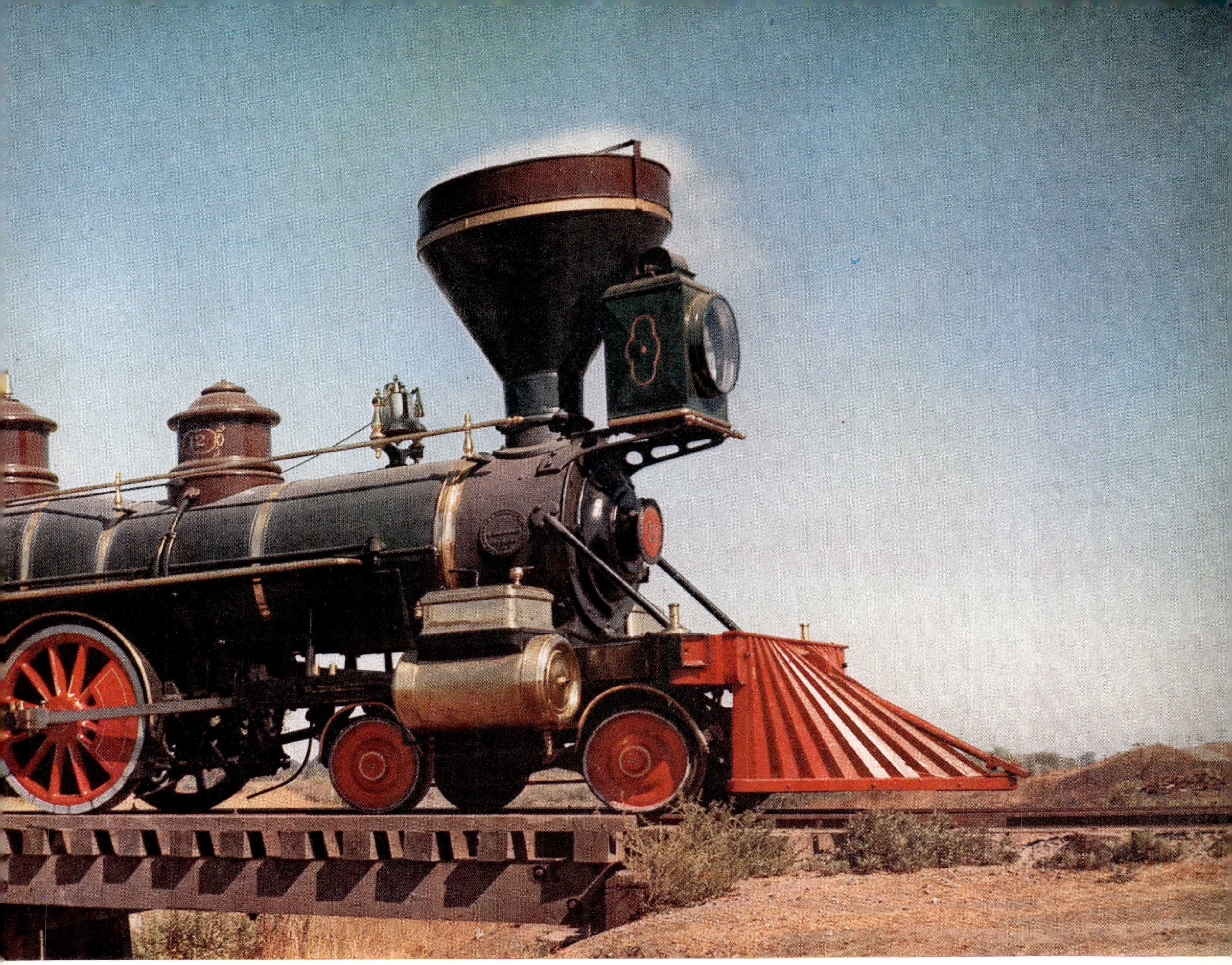

with Carson City and Reno. The towering funnel in front is a spark arrester, designed to reduce the danger of fires along the right-of-way. Other distinctive American features are the wooden cowcatcher, kerosene-burning headlight and bronze bell, all needed on American roads to clear and inspect the right-of-way.

for the West

the weight of the engine and supply added traction on long steep grades. Mathias Baldwin, whose Philadelphia plant built the engine above, perfected a steamtight metal joint that carried twice as much pressure as English locomotives. The enclosed cab at the back of the engine was an innovation of New England trainmen who got tired of standing out in the open on long winter hauls.

By the 1860s the railroads had crisscrossed all of the east and reached the Missouri River. In 1866, as soon as the Civil War was over, work began in earnest on a transcontinental line. Hordes of workmen, laying track simultaneously from Omaha in the east and Sacramento in the west, completed this prodigious feat in a little over three years to the amazement of the rest of the world. Thereafter the iron horse, with its gaudy colors and clanging bell, its cars filled with sightseers and emigrants and freight, and its widespread promotions and sales of farmland, pushed rapidly to every part of the receding frontier as civilization's advance agent.

M. H. DE YOUNG MEMORIAL MUSEUM, SAN FRANCISCO

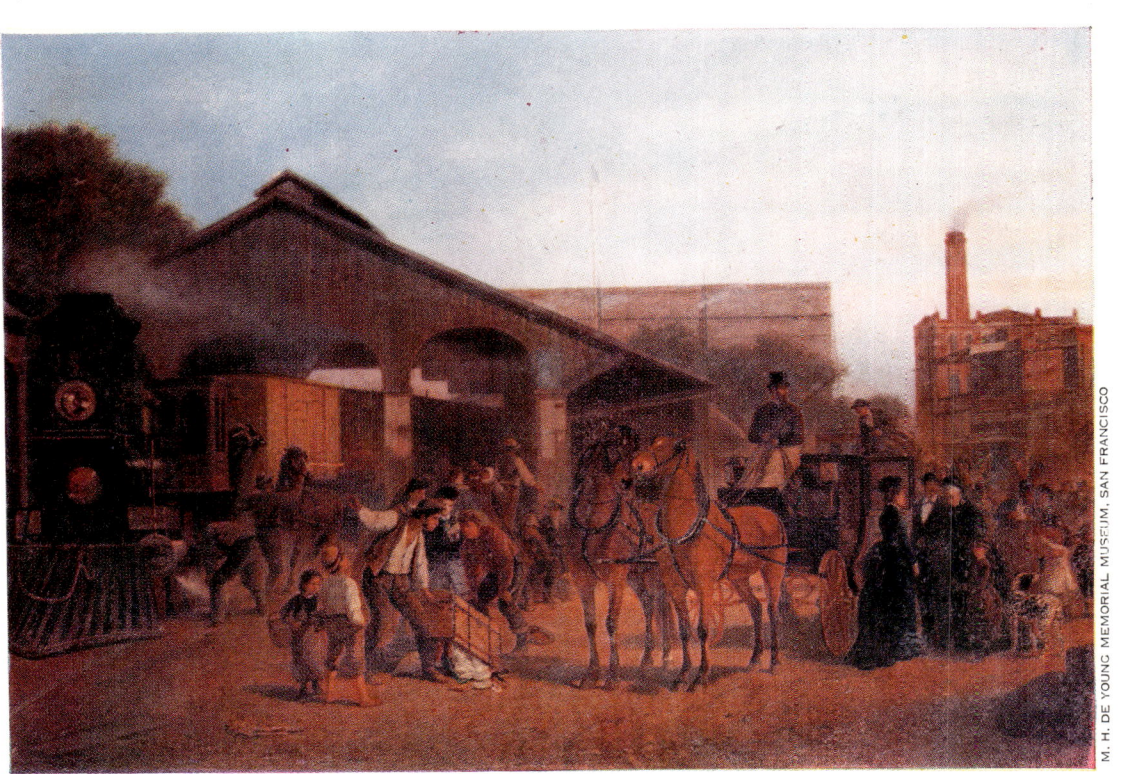

IN THE RAILROAD ERA coaches still met the trains and carried passengers to local hotels. This painting by William Hahn shows the Central Pacific (now Southern Pacific) station at Sacramento, 1870.

Heritage of

STATE OF ILLINOIS, DIVISION OF PARKS AND MEMORIALS

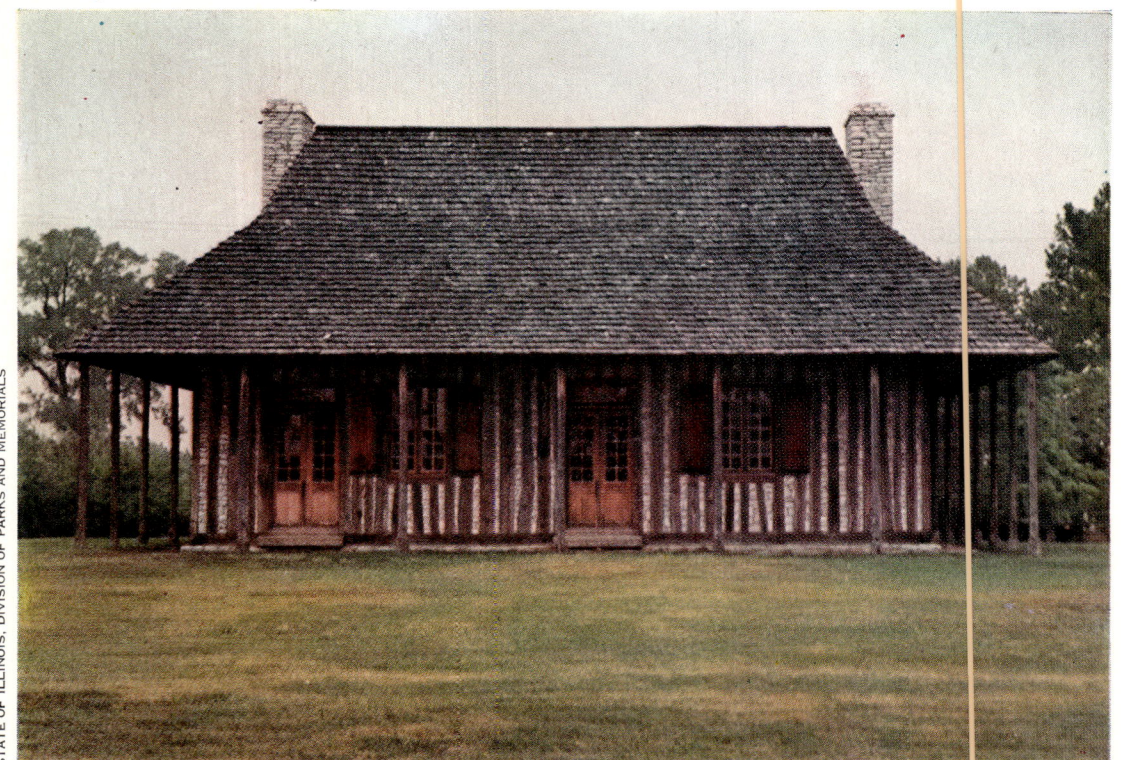

FRENCH DWELLING at Cahokia, Ill. was built about 1737, became the local courthouse in 1793. Built of upright posts with stone filling, it also boasted glass windows and wrought-iron hardware.

Cutting across the great east-west thrust of the American frontier, from Canada to the Gulf of Mexico, was the older frontier of the French. While English colonists were still cooped up behind the Appalachians, explorers, fur traders and Jesuit missionaries from French Canada circumnavigated the Great Lakes and sailed to the mouth of the Mississippi.

Other expeditions direct from France founded present-day Biloxi (*below*) and the great port of New Orleans. Detroit, Mobile, Natchez and St. Louis began as French towns; for more than 100 years the French colonial way of life ruled the Mississippi Valley.

Like the pioneer Americans, French frontier dwellers built their houses of logs. But they stood the logs on end instead of laying them on their sides. The most primitive technique was called *poteaux-en-terre*, or posts stuck in the ground. Substantial buildings were made of *poteaux-sur-sole*, or posts on foundations of stones. Spaces between the posts were filled with clay mixed with grass or small stones.

NEWBERRY LIBRARY, CHICAGO

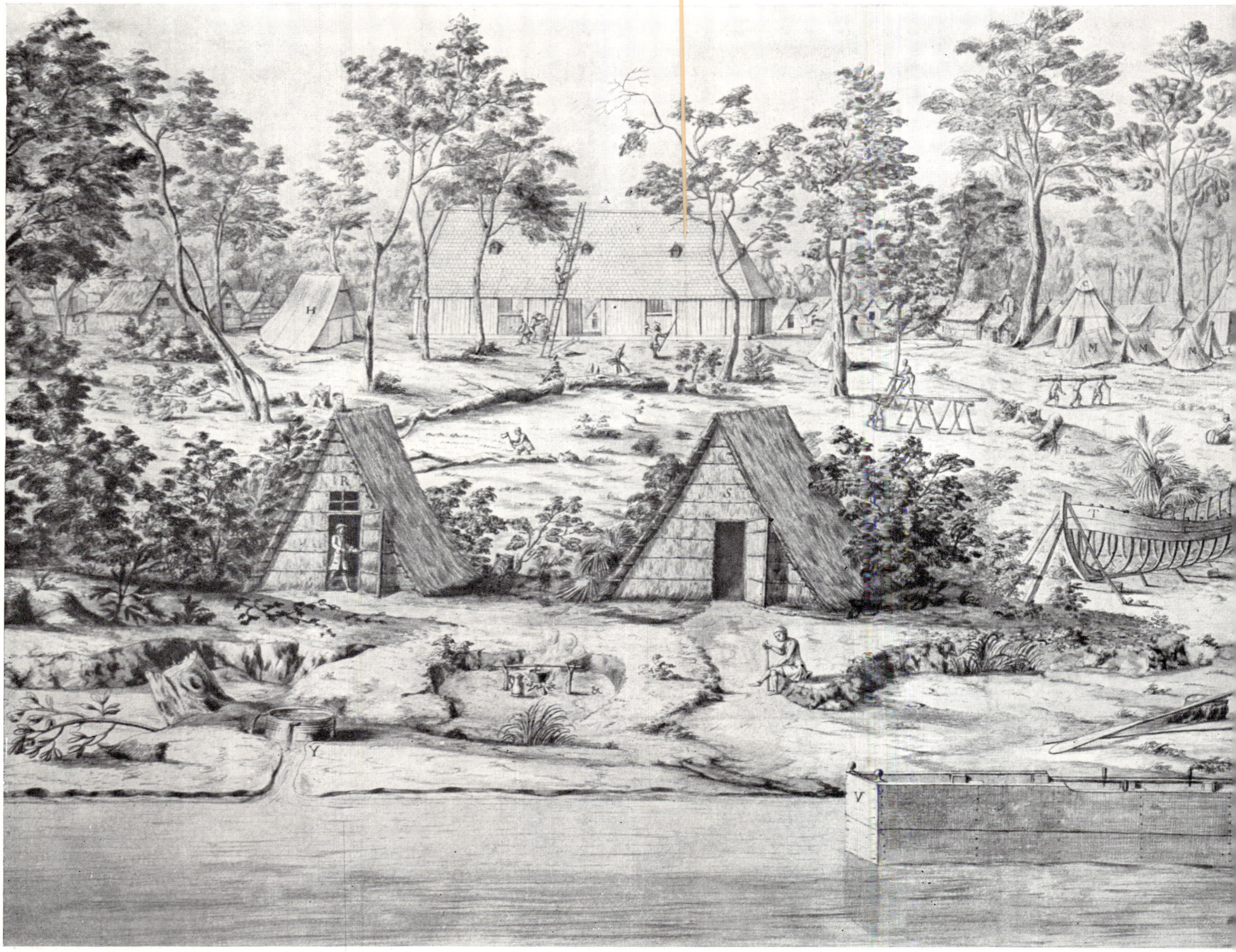

FRENCH COLONISTS busily go about their tasks at Biloxi, Miss. in December 1720. The main building (*upper left*) is made of upright posts like the one at top of this page. The colonists lived in tents and bark huts along the shore. Cross at right bears official title of the French concessionaire. This

the French

One of the finest survivors of this style is the old courthouse at Cahokia, Ill. (*left*) whose low, sweeping roof and gallery running around four sides are characteristic of French design. Here is an 18th Century Midwestern building with the same rugged structural beauty and unadorned simplicity as the colonial houses of New England.

Inside French homes the rooms were large and airy, with beamed or boarded ceilings, plastered walls and floors of earth or polished hardwood. The best furniture was imported from France, but French colonials also made decorative use of Indian mats and bearskin rugs. The most important feature of a French home was the gallery, or porch, which shaded and ventilated all the rooms. The French style did not greatly affect the main stream of American architecture. But along the Mississippi and especially at New Orleans—where the French porch was expanded to a graceful two-story balcony, richly ornamented with iron grillwork (*right*)—it has left a heritage of lasting beauty.

spirited drawing was made by Jean Baptiste Le Bouteux, who shows himself in the boat at lower right.

ORNATE CULMINATION of French style is seen in the handsome balcony and iron railings of this American-built New Orleans mansion, which also shows Creole and late Greek Revival influences.

DELICATE DESIGNS in wrought iron adorn a New Orleans grave. French excelled in such art.

CAST-IRON PATTERN on later Creole grave is heavier, more complicated and cheaper to make.

HARD-RIDING COWBOYS followed fast behind miners on the Far West frontier. This painting *In Without Knocking* is by Montana's Charlie Russell.

Dramatic survivals of the old mining era

Just behind the fur traders and ahead of the cattlemen and farmers came the miners and prospectors, lured by raw gold and silver to build their boom towns and extend the American frontier. The first arrivals in a mining camp cared nothing for appearances. Their homes were in caves, log huts or tents made of flour sacks and worn-out shirts. The most ambitious buildings in their towns were the board saloons and gambling halls. If the strike was rich, wooden sidewalks were added, with an assay office, a Wells Fargo depot for shipping sacks of bullion, grocery stores and blacksmiths' shops for repairing the miners' tools.

Mining town architecture was flimsy and cheap because the miners spent most of their energy and engineering skills underground, and a mining town rarely lasted long anyway. Wood was the principal material, with sometimes a front of brick or prefabricated cast iron. Such buildings were highly inflammable and, as a result, most of the earlier ones have disappeared. The photograph at the right shows almost all that is left of Bodie, Calif., a gold camp in the lower Sierras which in the 1870s had 30 mines and a floating population of about 12,000.

The false wooden fronts shown here were an American innovation used all along the frontier. Translated into brick or stone they are seen today on many a Midwest street. Presumably they were intended to give a one-story shack a two-story look. But they fooled nobody and satisfied only the ego of the owner, who acquired some extra space on which to paint his name and business. The false front was neither beautiful nor useful, and critics have seized on it as a mark of frontier crudity. But in such starkly patterned survivors as those at Bodie and in other towns which are still very much alive, the false front is a dramatic symbol of the fast-moving, hard-living, get-rich-quick Western mining frontier.

GOLD FLAKES imbedded in quartz were common decorations in frontier saloons, where miners often swapped nuggets for drinks.

BUILDINGS OF BODIE, once a teeming mining center, stand silent and forgotten in the California sunshine. At the far left is a former saloon built in

1872; adjoining it is the 1873 Odd Fellows Hall. The center building belonged to the Miners' Union, established in 1877. At right is the 1874 assay office. Bodie was founded in 1859 by William S. Body, a "Dutchman from Poughkeepsie" who found gold while chasing a wounded rabbit and died soon after in a blizzard.

Balloon frame houses and Chicago's big boom

The tremendous expansion of America's urban frontier was summed up best by Chicago where, as shown in the two prints below, a lonely fur traders' post became a metropolis in approximately 30 years. This phenomenal growth was made possible by a Chicago invention, the "balloon" frame house, which was cheaper, faster and easier to build than any carpenter-made house in history.

Most balloon frames followed the low simple lines of the ever-popular colonial Cape Cod house. But instead of being shaped on the job and mortised or bolted at the corners, the basic parts of a balloon frame were cut with a handsaw from lumber of standardized shapes (mostly 2x4s) and hammered together with machine-made nails. Traditional builders sneered that such structures would blow away like balloons in a prairie wind. This actually did happen, but when it did the frames hung together and were easily re-erected. The lightness and efficiency of the balloon frame made it a favorite in all frontier towns. With some added features it is the standard technique for building wood houses today.

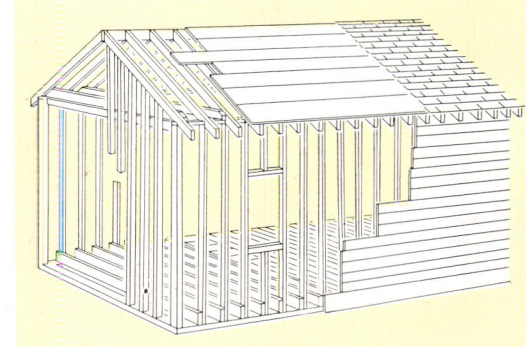

BALLOON FRAME diagram shows three stages: light wood skeleton, board siding, shingled roof.

CHICAGO IN 1820 (*left*) was the home of a few fur traders whose Indian clients arrived by canoe.

CHICAGO IN 1857 had a population of 87,600. Railroad trains and side-wheeled steamers arrived side by side on its lakefront. Most of the buildings shown above were balloon frame houses and were burned in 1871 when according to legend, a cow kicked over a lantern, setting fire to Patrick O'Leary's barn.

Part VII

THE TIMELESS SOUTHWEST

The Timeless Southwest

A BLENDING OF OLD CULTURES HAS SHAPED ITS UNIQUE STYLE

CLIFF HOUSE, ancestor of pueblo, was built of adobe about 1100 A.D. in natural cave near Flagstaff, Ariz. It has five stories, housed 50 Indians.

The first architects in what is now the U.S. were the pueblo-dwelling Indians of the Southwest. They were building multifamily apartment houses more than 800 years ago, and when the first Spanish colonists arrived in 1598 they found the Indians living in permanent towns and possessed of an advanced culture. Unlike the English then settling the Atlantic Coast—Santa Fe was founded in 1609, two years after Jamestown—the Spaniards did not destroy the Indian way of life. Instead they adopted it, using their own tools and techniques to create a blend of Indian and Spanish that became the unique style of the Southwest.

The blend produced a striking and timeless design in architecture, as valid today as it was a millennium ago. The Spaniards took over the Indians' favorite material, adobe, which is mud mixed from the clay-and-gypsum desert soil and hardened by the desert sun. The Indians piled up layers of adobe by hand to make their homes, and then they piled their homes in layers (*below*) to make a pueblo, or town. The Spaniards improved the method, mixing adobe with straw and baking it in portable bricks. On their cattle ranches they built low, wide, adobe houses which developed into the contemporary U.S. ranch house style.

The old Spanish Southwest was a vast area including present New Mexico and Arizona, plus parts of Utah, Colorado and Texas. California was a separate and later part of the Spanish empire. There the local Indians had no building tradition and the Franciscan padres followed the ornate religious architecture of Spain and Mexico. This style, executed in adobe and other native materials, flowered fully at San Juan Capistrano (*opposite page*), one of the 21 California missions. The open-air patio around which the mission buildings were grouped was adopted in many parts of the U.S. It is especially useful in the arid Southwest, providing airy coolness by day and radiating stored sunlight from its paving at night.

← MISSION GARDEN in San Juan Capistrano near San Gabriel, Calif., where doves flutter around the pool, is flanked by bell wall. Behind the wall is a 1777 chapel. At upper right are ruins of a large church destroyed by 1812 earthquake.

ADOBE PUEBLO at Taos, N. Mex. is still populated by 500 Indians who use ladders because they have no inside stairs. This five-story "North House" pueblo was built about 1700 to replace a much older structure which burned.

MISSION CHURCH of San Esteban Rey built in 1640s stands atop a steep mesa at Acoma, a 1,000-year-old New Mexico pueblo. The adobe, the huge timbers, even the soil for the priest's garden were carried up 357 feet by Indian laborers.

Builders of churches, workers in wood

Unarmed and often on foot, across hundreds of miles of dangerous desert, came the hardy Spanish friars who won the Southwest for Christianity. In New Mexico, where Indian architecture was well established, and where a local priest was outnumbered by his congregation by as much as 1,000 to one, the Spanish church builders followed the low and massive pueblo style, enlarging it a little to accommodate square bell towers (*above*).

Inside, the New Mexico churches were often lavishly decorated by Indian artists who combined religious themes of the Renaissance with age-old Indian symbols and exuberant Indian colors which had been developed in their ancient ceremonial paintings. These native American folk artists were known as *santeros*, or makers of saints, and their great masterpiece is the sanctuary of San Jose (*right*). The *santeros* also carved and sold many small images, or *santos*, which are now eagerly sought by collectors. From tin cans discarded by American soldiers in the 1840s and '50s, the ingenious New Mexican craftsmen fashioned dainty wall shrines to hold their family saints, like the one which hangs in the dining room at far right.

WOOD FURNISHINGS of churches are 1640 stairs of San Esteban (*left*), a crude copy of European design, 1760 pulpit of Las Trampas (*right*), with refined carving of a local mountain wildflower. Priest still climbs ladder to enter pulpit.

MISSION ALTARPIECE of San Jose at Laguna, N. Mex. is richly adorned with native *santero* paintings of Holy Trinity and three patron saints—San Juan Nepomuceno, San Jose, Santa Barbara. Above hangs a canopy of buffalo or elk

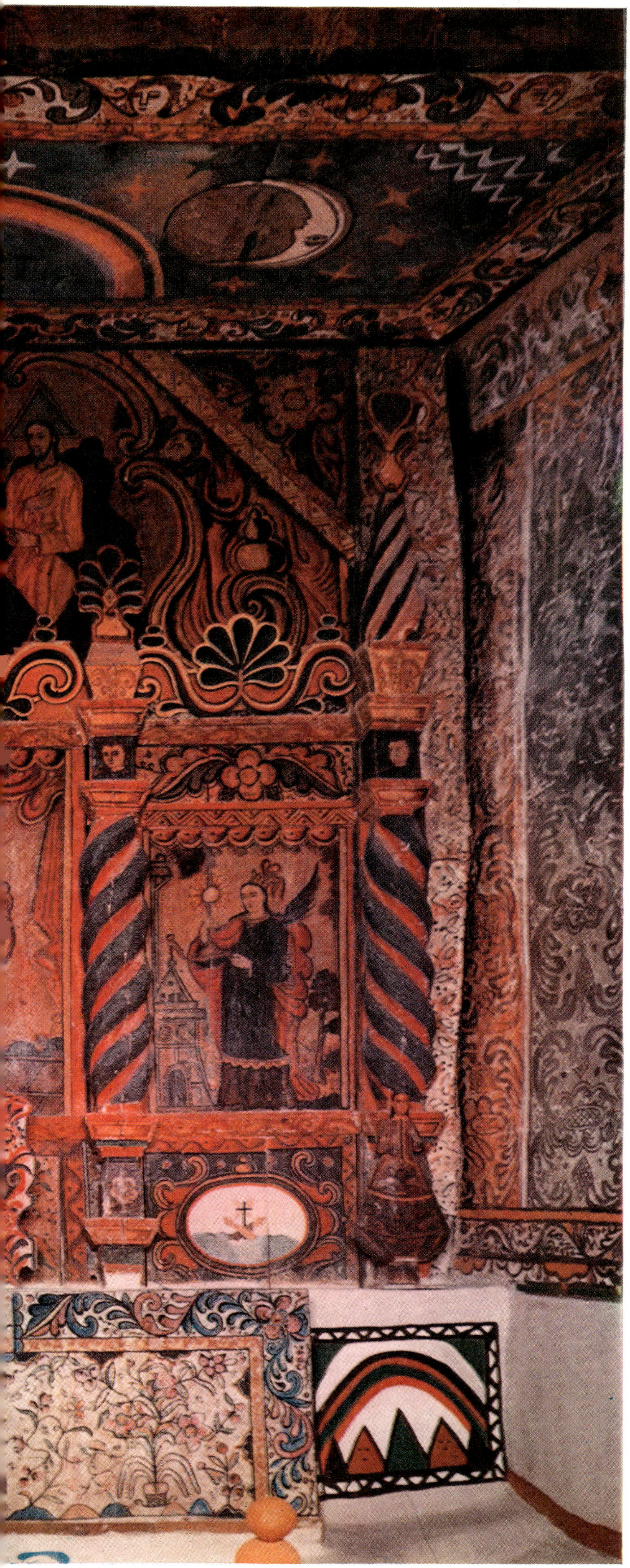

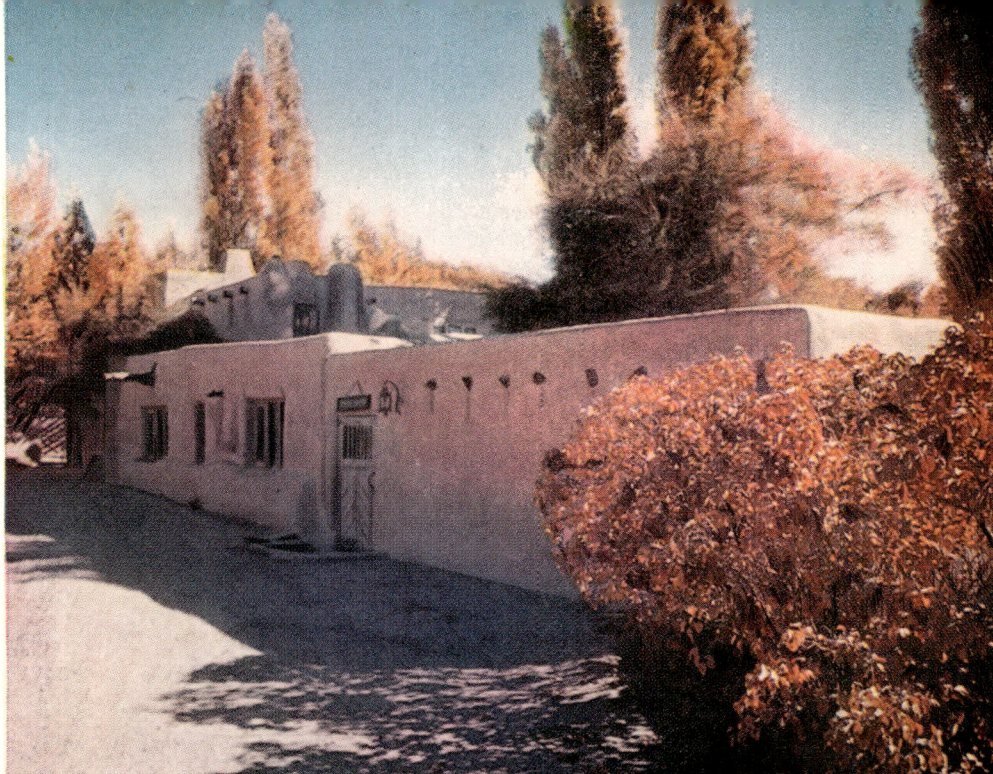

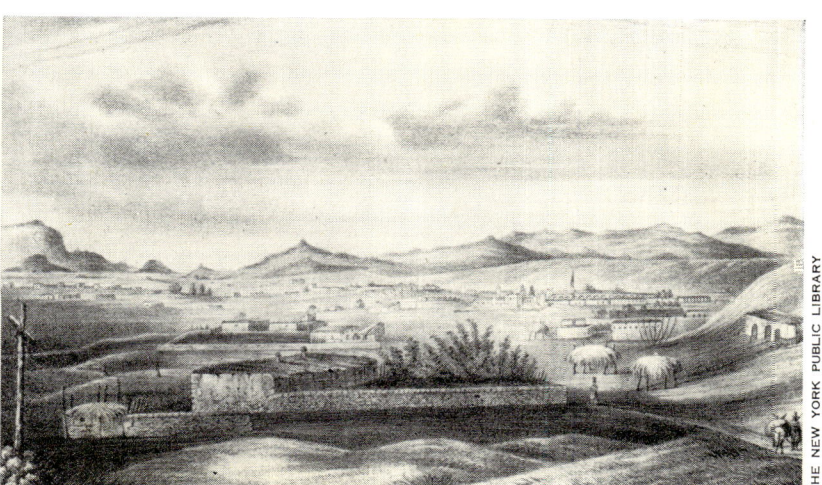

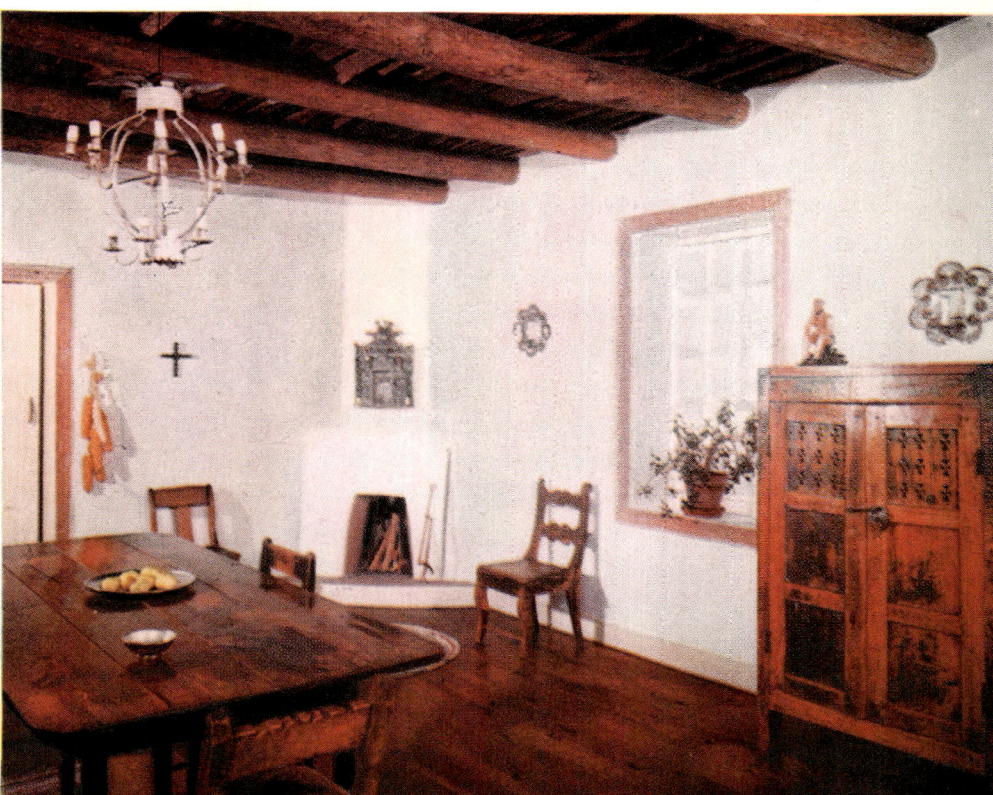

skin painted in tempera with Indian symbols of sun, moon, rainbow and stars bordered by cherubs. Below, center, is a buckskin antependium painted in European floral patterns and flanked by two small panels with vivid Indian designs.

LIVABLE EPITOME of Southwest adobe style is this Spanish Sante Fe home of 1800, with two-story American addition in rear. The Indian vigas, or roof beams, project through the walls, following the design of the early pueblos.

THE NEW YORK PUBLIC LIBRARY

BUSY CAPITAL of Spanish colony, shown in 1849 lithograph, was Santa Fe, with adobe corral (*foreground*), cathedral and Governor's Palace at right rear. Yankee invaders seized Santa Fe in 1846, annexed the whole Southwest in 1848.

TASTEFUL SIMPLICITY of Spanish colonial interiors is reproduced in modern New Mexico home above. Roof beams are split cedar, graceful chandelier and sconces are made of tin. On *trastero* cupboard (*right*) is small wood *santo*.

LADY'S SADDLE used in California about 1830 is embroidered with colored hemp, has platform for feet.
LOS ANGELES COUNTY MUSEUM

RANCHER'S SADDLE sold for $200 when made in 1855. It has carved leather flowers and lions breathing fire.
LOS ANGELES COUNTY MUSEUM

OFFICER'S SADDLE presented to Col. Jesse Leavenworth in 1862 has pistol holsters, picture of Washington.
COLORADO STATE MUSEUM

TEXAS SADDLE of about 1880 has high horn, two cinches, several leather strings to secure ropes and blankets.
PANHANDLE-PLAINS HISTORICAL MUSEUM

Elegant products of the saddler's craft

The Spaniards brought the first horses to America and on their ranches in old Mexico they developed the roomy Western stock saddle. Their saddles were richly decorated with finely tooled leather and embroidery in imported designs like the Mediterranean acanthus leaf (*top far left*). Ornamental silver on saddles was a later Mexican idea which reached its peak after 1900.

The saddle's basic design changed in many practical ways as it moved north into the U.S. The old California saddle shown second from left, top, for instance, still has the *mochila*, a separate leather cover that fitted over the saddle tree. This Spanish survival was too cumbersome for the U.S. open range, so it was replaced by a short leather skirt sewed under the saddle (*upper right*). A distinct American improvement was the swelled fork saddle shown directly below, which is traditional in its lavish decoration but modern in its workmanlike design. Here the oval swelling just under the horn gives the cowboy extra leg grip when his steed bucks or rears.

PARADE SADDLE owned by Los Angeles' mayor has *tapaderos* (foot coverings), silver horn, goat's hair plumes.
LOS ANGELES COUNTY MUSEUM

DENVER SADDLE of 1875 has a bucking roll lashed behind its horn to help cowboy stay on a bucking pony.
COLORADO STATE MUSEUM

FANCY SADDLE has swelled fork under its horn, round silver *conchas*, carved leather oak leaves and acorns.
MR. & MRS. GODWIN PELISSERO, GOLETA, CALIF.

Handmade tools and trappings of the cattle kingdom

All of the gadgets in the picture above were used by Texas cowboys in their daily work of tending cattle, the great economic product of the American Southwest. Here they are displayed against an expanse of the Texas Panhandle plains, a region so dry and desolate that it was not conquered until the 1880s by the tough Texas longhorn steer.

Many of these objects were made by the cowboy himself to suit his personal needs and ideas of decoration. They are museum pieces today because their functional design illustrates the use they were put to. The silver-mounted bronc-buster's belt which hangs on the fence, at left of the longhorn skull, was made by a cowboy on the Texas Matador Ranch. It supported his back and abdomen while he was breaking a fractious

PANHANDLE-PLAINS HISTORICAL MUSEUM, CANYON, TEXAS

horse. To the right of the skull is more of the cowboy's leather armor— a pair of straight "shotgun" chaps which protected his legs from thorny brush or cactus. Next are some wider and fancier "bat-wing" chaps which appeared in Texas in the 1890s and are still widely used. Cowboys like them because they snap on, and can be removed without pulling off spurs. Next to the chaps is a hand-plaited leather quirt. Attached to the gatepost is a saddle holster with a Winchester Model 73 rifle, used to exterminate coyotes. On the gap are a silver-decorated leather bridle and (*right*) an older bridle of hand-woven horsehair.

On the ground, at left rear, are a cowboy's Stetson hat with four-inch brim, a pair of leather gauntlets and an array of historic branding irons. The corkscrew objects at far left and front right are picket pins, which were screwed into the earth to tether a horse. The spurs at front left include handmade and shopmade varieties with round and star-shaped rowels. The rowels with long spikes were called "Chihuahua rowels" in Texas, where the shorter, less punishing spikes were preferred.

In the center are American types of stirrups and bits, grouped around an ivory-handled Colt revolver. The very heavy bit at far front was called a "jawbreaker," and was only used on a dangerous horse. At far right is a wire cutter, and behind it strands of barbed wire, an American invention which was patented in 1874 by Joseph F. Glidden of Illinois. Behind the wire are a bull whip and lariats of plaited rawhide (*right*) and horsehair.

121

NAVAHO BLANKETS USE NATIVE WOOL, RICH COLORS, TRADITIONAL INDIAN PATTERNS. THE OLDEST, DATED 1850, IS AT FAR LEFT

Indian arts which persist

For at least 2,000 years the Southwest has been inhabited by the same Indian peoples who live there now and practice their ancient skills. The earliest tribes wove baskets from fiber and twigs and used them to gather food. Primitive Indian potters perfected a marvelously ornamental art without the aid of the European's potter's wheel. The Spaniards brought in sheep and taught the Indians to use wool in weaving their handsome blankets. About 1860 some captured Navahos learned silversmithing from the Mexicans, and began making fine silver jewelry in a blend of Mexican and Indian designs based on stylized leaves and blossoms.

BASKETS FOR NUTS AND CORN

DESIGNS OF MEN AND ANIMALS

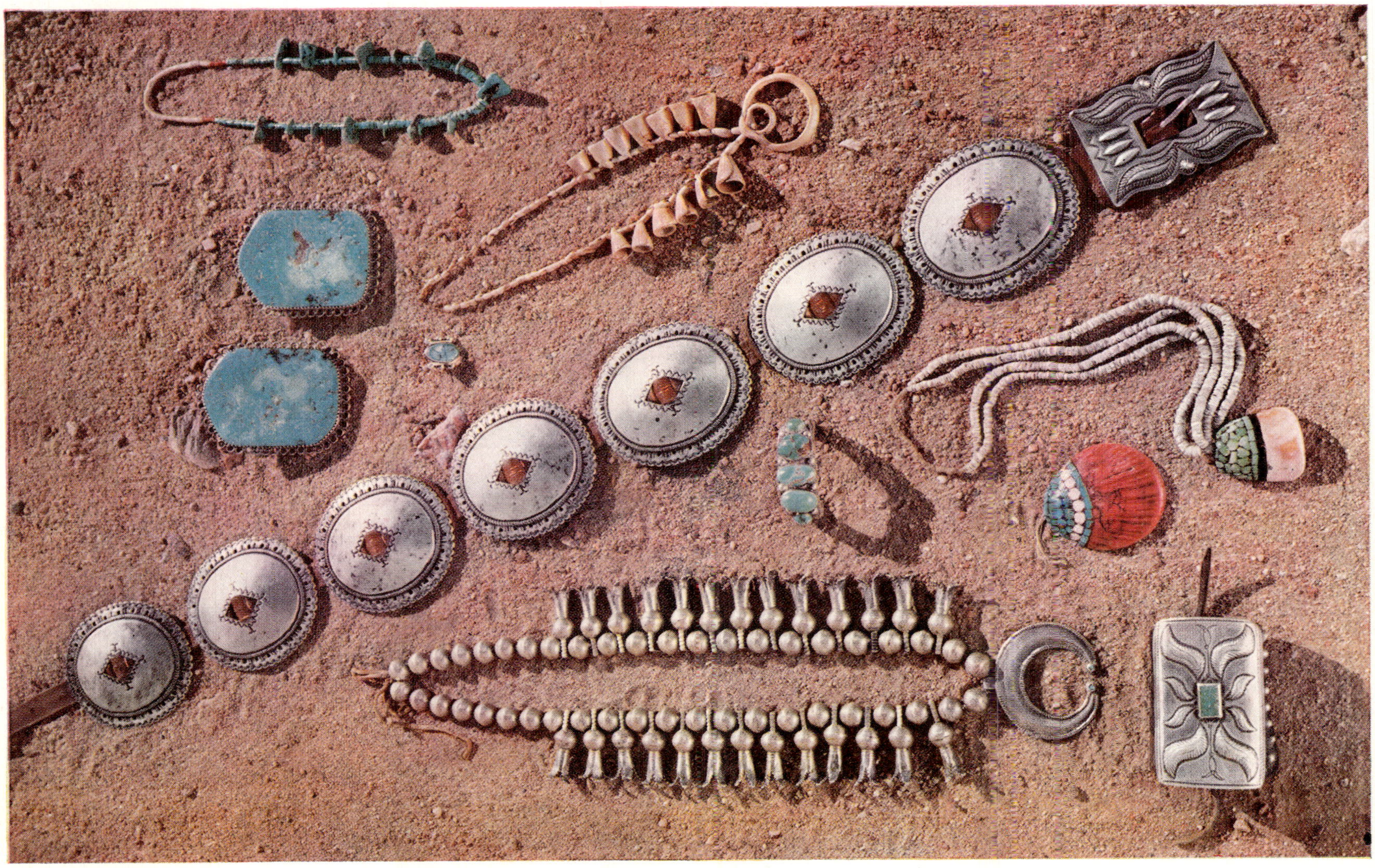

INDIAN JEWELRY array includes (top, left) Navaho necklace of turquoise, a Southwest gem stone which Indians used before they worked in silver. Next to it is prehistoric shell necklace. Below this are a small ring and large ornaments of turquoise and silver. Long belt across center was hammered from silver coins. Under it (right) are bracelet, necklace, pendant with red shell. At bottom is silver necklace in popular squash-blossom design, archer's wrist guard (far right).

122

INDIAN POTTERY in this display was shaped by hand and fired in primitive kilns. Rare Mimbres bowl (*lower left*) was made about 1100 A.D. and painted with lifelike fish. Others listed clockwise: Tewa polychrome water jar; Acoma bowl for dough; small black-on-black pot of modern make; flared-rim water jar and large jar from Santa Clara; large pot in Zuni colors (*top*); Zia water jar; Santo Domingo bowl; Zuni jar; ancient Socorro jar; modern Hopi bowl (*front, right*).

123

CARVED DOORS at San Juan Capistrano are made of native woods. "River of life" pattern at left with wavy lines symbolizing the four Gospels

Phases of the

In colonial California, Spanish ideas, Mexican additions, Indians' work combined to produce the "California Mission" style. The origins of this style are traced on these pages in details from the original missions, all of which were built between 1769 and 1823.

The rounded arch, used for mission windows and doorways and repeated in the long arcades, was inherited by the Spaniards from the Romans. From the Moors of North Africa came the decorative and cooling patio and

BELL TOWER of San Carlos Borromeo at Carmel shows original Moorish influence on Spanish design. This famous church was the headquarters of Father Serra, who built nine of the missions. Small round objects on facade are mud swallows' nests.

WOOD SCULPTURE of Saint Benedict was carved by an Indian neophyte and stood in an outdoor niche at San Carlos Borromeo. Its basic design is European but the boldly cut cowl, symbolized by curved loop over head, is a primitive touch.

FRESCOED WALLS of the governor's room at San Fernando mission were discovered under a coat of whitewash in 1935. These Indian paintings were

is still used on many California doors. Abstract geometric design at right has no religious meaning, resembles the pattern on old Spanish doors.

mission style

the Oriental shapes of the prominent bell towers. The principal building material of the missions was native adobe brick, usually covered with stucco, and this accounts for the missions' thick walls.

The early missions were roofed with tule thatch. But after many fires the first fireproof roof tiles were made at San Luis Obispo in 1786. These bright red overlapping roof coverings became standard at all the missions and they are still used on many California houses.

copied from designs imported by the Franciscan friars. Though less imaginative than the altar work of New Mexico, they have a fresh charm of their own.

OPEN "CORREDOR" at San Fernando mission is 243 feet long with 19 arches. This long arcade followed the design of old Spanish convents and provided a shady place to walk and meditate. The stuccoed pillars are built of kiln-fired brick.

IRON CROSS used to stand atop the bell tower at San Carlos Borromeo (upper left). It was made by Indians trained by artisans from Mexico. The decorative scroll design is Christian and Spanish in origin and was often seen in mission grillwork.

FORTIFIED OUTPOST of Spanish power in California was San Francisco, shown above in an 1816 lithograph. The presidio at upper left was built in 1776 around a large square patio. The Indians in loincloths are bringing in firewood.

From the rancho, a contemporary style

After the Mexican revolution of 1821 the great land and cattle holdings of the California missions were broken up by the government, and private ranchers moved in. The houses which they built retained the mission patio and *corredor* as basic features. But because the ranchers lived outdoor lives and felt no need for complicated architecture, their houses took on the low, horizontal shape that was typical of the New Mexican adobe. The ranch house patio became a garden and courtyard, around which the wings of the house were grouped. The *corredor* became a long veranda, with graceful wood posts and railings instead of thick pillars and arches. Chairs and benches were set along it to make a shady resting place for the ranch owner and the *vaqueros*—his cowboys.

Because of its great versatility, the California ranch house style has lately become a universal favorite with U.S. home designers. Its clean, functional lines can be expanded almost indefinitely without damaging its proportions, and this is especially true in the wide-open Southwest. No one knows who cut the first "picture window" in a ranch house. But the use of large glass areas was a natural development where sunlight is often the main source of heat, and where beautiful gardens and patios deserve to be seen. In the modern ranch house at right below, wide windows and a magnificent mountain setting have been combined with traditional design to make an inviting sample of Southwest living today.

MISSION STYLE was adopted in many California houses before the ranch house became more popular. In this San Marino home the missions' red tile roofs, thick stuccoed walls and small windows have been duplicated almost exactly.

RANCH HOUSE development is illustrated by these two examples, built 88 years apart. The 1865 Las Flores ranch house above, near Oceanside, Calif., is made of adobe with a covered veranda along its whole length. The veranda was

also a hallway to the rooms, which had no inside doors. Below is a 1953 ranch house at Montecito, Calif. designed by Cliff May, considered the dean of modern ranch house architects. Its Y-shaped wings enclose an open patio, and in the rear, facing the mountain, are three more patios with walls. The veranda itself has become an outdoor room, with furniture groupings and plants moved against the walls. Large glass windows give a feeling of extra space to the one-story interior.

MISSION STYLE at its peak is seen in 1900 photograph of Roycroft Inn at East Aurora, N.Y. The Morris chairs (*left foreground*), tables and sofas were handmade by craftsmen in shops adjoining inn. Here they are shown with Southwest Indian rugs, beamed ceiling, "art glass" hanging lamps.

Mission in the home

The sturdy "mission" furniture which stocked thousands of U.S. parlors at the turn of the century was inspired in part by the design and materials—usually fumed or natural oak—of Spanish mission furniture in the Southwest. The mission style as it appeared in eastern homes was developed by Gustave Stickley, a Syracuse, N.Y. craftsman and editor who believed that U.S. family life should be simple, durable and devoid of needless luxury. He tried to make his furniture patterns reflect those wholesome virtues. Stickley's designs became a national craze under the sponsorship of Elbert Hubbard, a supersalesman of culture and soap—he invented the coupon system. At the famous Roycrofters shops in East Aurora, N.Y., Hubbard's employes turned out handmade mission tables, sofas and benches which still give solid service after many decades of wear.

An especially popular mission piece was the Morris chair named after the English poet and handicraft teacher, William Morris. Morris chairs had adjustable backs, upholstery pads which were easy to remove and clean, and thick, four-square arms and legs (*above*). Mission parlor tables often had built-in bookshelves at each end and mission sofas were sometimes made with magazine racks attached. In such designs and in their clean rectangular lines mission pieces clearly foreshadowed the functional "modern" furniture of the present day.

Part VIII

AN AGE OF GILDED OPULENCE

An Age of Gilded Opulence

VIGOR EXPANDED VICTORIAN TASTE

In the half century that followed the Civil War the U.S. economy expanded with dazzling speed. Enormous fortunes were made by building railroads, founding new industries and exploiting natural resources. Important inventions followed one another thick and fast as the nation moved through a technological revolution which landed it, at the end of this period, in the age of the steel skeleton skyscraper and the mass-produced family automobile.

The vigorous Victorians who made money during these years could afford to live lavishly and to entertain expensively—and they were expected to do so in the burgeoning society of America's Gilded Age. The houses which they built were big and pretentious, elaborately decorated outside and in. The Victorian style in domestic architecture was never a clear-cut single pattern like the Colonial Cape Cod or the Greek Revival. Rather it was a boisterous medley of several styles blended into something distinctively American. It included the American Gothic, with peaked gables, towers and profusion of carving; the French Renaissance, with mansard roofs and colored stonework; and the English Tudor, with its casement windows and half-timbered walls covered with stucco or shingles. A full-blown house of the General Grant era might have all these showy features, plus some more ideas borrowed from Italy, Japan and the 18th Century U.S.

Inside, the Victorian style at its peak was marked by baronial "living halls" with massive staircases which cascaded down through the central bulk of the house, unifying it and giving an impression of dignity and power. A magnificent example is shown in the photo at right. This is the staircase at Chateau-sur-Mer, in Newport, R.I., which was built by George Wetmore, a China trader, and rated Newport's finest in the 1850s. Twenty years later it was being outclassed by the mansions of new millionaires, so Wetmore's son, recently graduated from Yale (and later to become governor of Rhode Island), engaged Richard Morris Hunt, the most fashionable architect of the day, to give the house more grandeur.

Hunt added a French ballroom (which was Newport's first), an Eastlake library, an Italian dining room, a stone porte-cochere. The central feature of his plan was the broad three-story oak stairway shown here, with its lofty bronze lamp standards and stained-glass windows. The stair risers (*upper center in photo*) are painted in a design of latticework, birds and branches which create the illusion of a skylight looking out to a well-tamed garden. This cozy domestic effect, which was sought for in even the most spacious Victorian interiors, is enhanced by the foliage pattern of the dark green wallpaper.

A great house like this required more rooms and services (such as bathrooms, closets and pantries) than American homes ever had before. Architects expanded their designs to meet this demand: unlike the builders of Cape Cod cottages and Greek Revival temple-homes who tailored their houses to established forms, the Victorians allowed the enlarged interior plan of the house to determine its general shape and size. Victorian architecture, though it continued to borrow widely in its decorative effects, was in the end an indigenous American style, more flamboyant and more inventive than the English style from which it took its name.

BRONZE NYMPH, patterned after French sculpture and electrically wired, adorned Victorian drawing room.

GRAND STAIRCASE at Newport is lit by tall bronze candelabra on which torch-bearing cupids cling and climb.

VICTORIAN GRANDEUR at its gaudiest is seen in the Eureka, Calif. mansion above, built in 1886 by a lumberman. The ornate carvings, balconies and "candle-snuffer" peaks are a mixture of Gothic and Renaissance designs.

VICTORIAN COMFORT (*opposite*) is shown in bedroom of a fur trader at Prairie du Chien, Wis. It is furnished in typical fashion with marble-topped table, washstand and bureau, kerosene lamps, carved walnut bed made in New Orleans.

SLEEPY HOLLOW RESTORATIONS, PHILIPSE CASTLE, TARRYTOWN, N.Y.

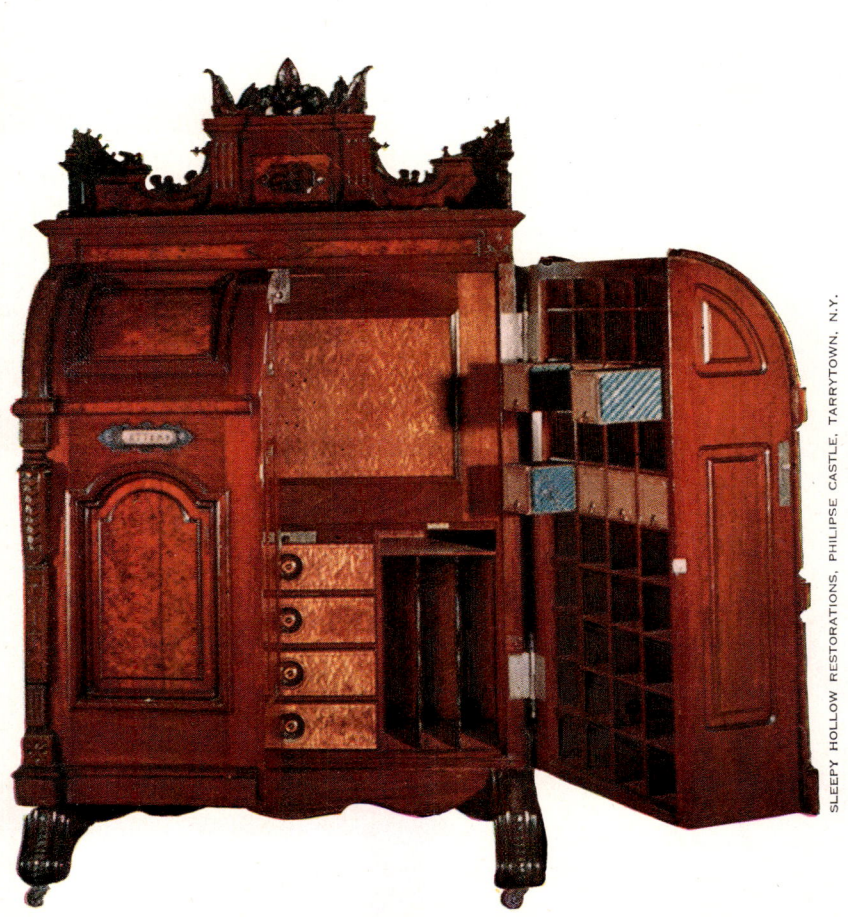

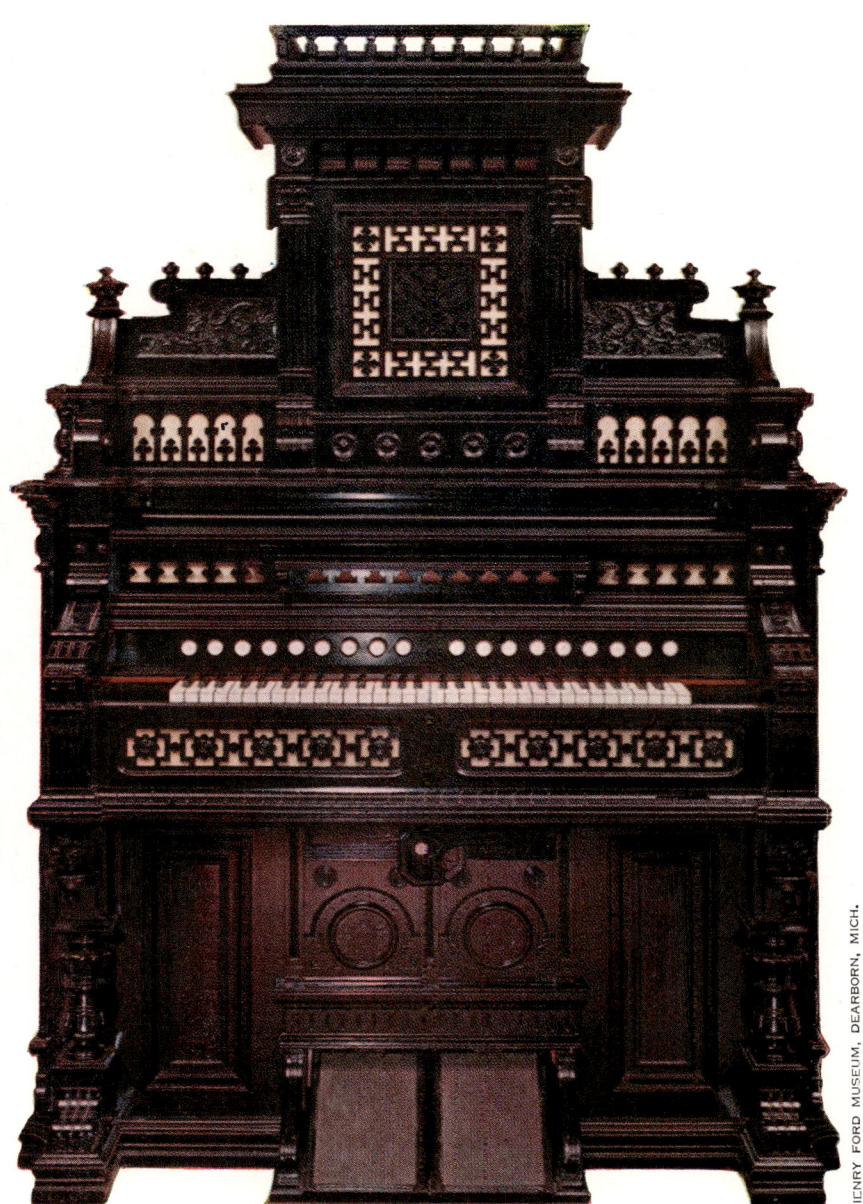

PATENT DESK invented by W. S. Wooten of Indianapolis in 1874 combined Victorian love for gadgetry and fine cabinetwork. This desk was used by John D. Rockefeller at the time the world's biggest oil firm was being organized.

HENRY FORD MUSEUM, DEARBORN, MICH.

COTTAGE ORGAN (*right*) made by Jacob Estey of Brattleboro in the 1870s was owned by Henry Ford. Its geometric openwork designs were cut by machinery and follow the patterns of Charles L. Eastlake, an English taste maker.

VILLA LOUIS, WISCONSIN STATE HISTORICAL SOCIETY, PRAIRIE DU CHIEN

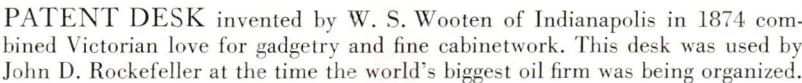

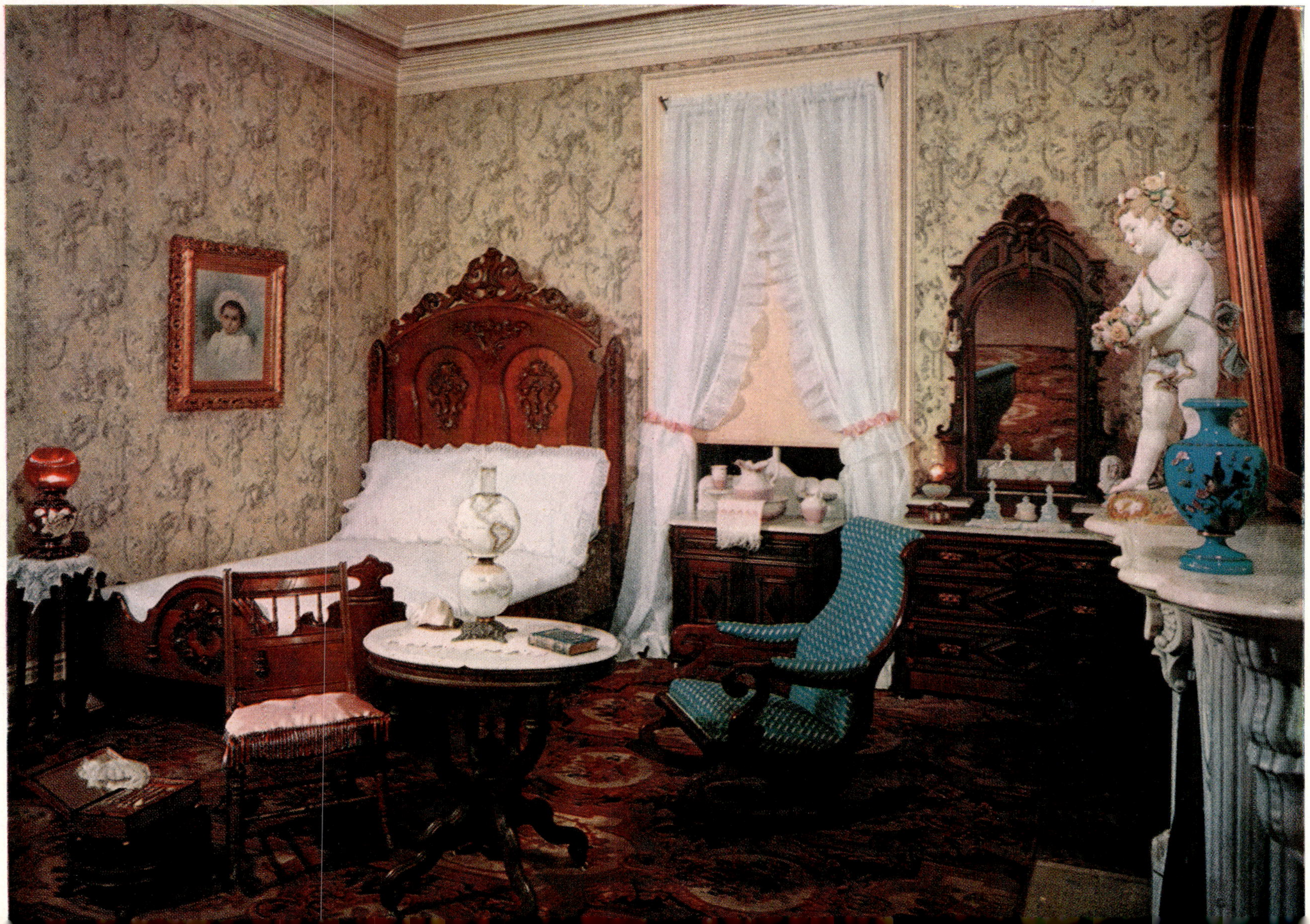

BABY CARRIAGE OF RATTAN IS GAILY ADORNED WITH EMBROIDERY-LIKE SCROLLS

A feeling for fancy furniture

Victorian furniture, like the houses, was a mingling of many styles. Its ornamentation was rich and strongly stressed to please a robust taste. Sometimes it became so fussy as to be garish and vulgar. But collectors now appreciate the appeal of this complex furniture which in its lighter moods could be as charming as a dainty wedding cake.

This was also the period when Americans, typically, made furniture a mass-production item. From 1840 to 1880 U.S.-made furniture rose in value from $7.5 to $78 million, and factories in Grand Rapids, Jamestown and elsewhere took over the job of making it.

UTILITY CHAIRS of the era are (*left*) walnut child's high chair whose curved legs folded down to form rockers. At the right is a cast-iron swivel and spring chair with red velvet seat and ornamental pierced scrolls. This basic design became the ancestor of the modern office chair.

BRIC-A-BRAC was dear to the hearts of all true Victorians. Pieces above on spool-turned "whatnot" include from top: porcelain hands holding vases, souvenir phone

bell, dolphin dish, glass shoe and boots, fancy Easter egg, copper luster pitcher, bisque statuette, glass swan, ear-of-corn vase, dogwood-trimmed vases and milk glass hands.

CIRCULAR SOFA with purple seat and potted palm in center furnished in elegant drawing room. Derived from French and Oriental designs, this piece had a well-known cruder counterpart with board seats surrounding a radiator in waiting rooms of U.S. railroad stations of the period.

ELABORATE CHAIRS show how widely the Victorians roamed to borrow designs and materials. The gilded corner chair has a rendering of Duncan Phyfe's famed lyre-back design. Ladder-back design of tall chair is Colonial. Rattan used to make these pieces came from Pacific islands.

135

TIFFANY GLASS above includes, top left, a domed lamp shade with stained glass pansies shaped to resemble the convolutions of the flower. Next is a leaded green glass shade with band of fruit design. The center shade with dripping wisteria clusters was one of Tiffany's favorite and most admired designs. Be-

Eye-filling creations in colored glass

The Victorian fondness for glowing color and densely textured materials led to a widespread use of stained glass in private homes. The pioneer American artist in this medium was Louis Comfort Tiffany, son of the famous New York jeweler, who designed or manufactured all of the objects shown above. At his Corona, Long Island furnaces Tiffany experimented with the chemistry of colored glass and produced new types which he pieced together in intricate mosaics of flowers, fruits and

NEW YORK HISTORICAL SOC., PETER LINDAMOOD ANTIQUES, AND PRIVATE COLLECTORS

side it are small lily-shaped lamp shades and at upper right a shade of roughly textured chunks of glass fitted together to resemble uncut gems. Smaller objects, all made of Tiffany favrile glass, are, from left: bulb-shaped vase, three-handled vase, ribbed bowl, compote with *retourné* rim, frilled footed vase, lily-pad vase.

abstract gems. Five of the examples above are glass shades for electric lamps, which began to illuminate U.S. homes in the 1880s. Such shades, and the many cheaper imitations that followed, became set pieces in the American parlor.

Tiffany also invented an iridescent glass of softly changing colors and uneven thickness which he called favrile glass, after the Latin word *faber*, for artisan. This he used for shaping vases and dishes in delicate patterns based on flowers and leaves. Toward the end of the century Tiffany became a leader in the *art nouveau* movement which sought to break away from the heavy ornamentation of the mid-Victorian and use less ornate, more natural designs. This is illustrated in the bronze standards of the Tiffany lamps shown above. Those at the left and center are cast in writhing, complicated masses of roots and branches, while the plain and fluted examples at the right are lean and simple in their design.

Shapes of the

During this period's industrial boom the American nation of craftsmen and tinkerers became a nation of mechanics and engineers. Henry Ford, a child of his times, mastered the old American skill of watchmaking before he was 15, then went on to become an expert operator of steam traction engines, chief engineer of the Detroit electric company, and, in 1896, the builder of his historic gasoline buggy. The engine alone was novel in this first Ford car; its body was merely a box with a seat on top, the wheels were like a bicycle's, the steering lever was like an electric trolley's.

Other U.S. automakers of the 1890s designed them as expensive, handbuilt vehicles whose body styling imitated fine carriages. Gradually a distinctive automobile design developed out

FUN OF MOTORING is the theme of this picture from a 1907 child's book. Actually there were few roads as smooth as this and fewer teen-age drivers. The car shown here has a body designed like an oldtime stagecoach, with emergency brake and gear shift realistically set on the running board.

VINTAGE MOTOR CARS from the Henry Ford Museum at Dearborn, all in running condition, are displayed above against a village blacksmith shop where early autoists went for repairs. At left is a luxurious Oldsmobile Limited of 1910, which sold for $5,000 when new and can still do 75 mph. Its 43 x 5 tires are the largest ever used on a U.S. pleasure car. In front is a three-wheeled Duryea gasoline trap of 1896, with a slipper-shaped body lacquered and finished like a fine

new auto age

of the new materials used (metal instead of wood), the engineering problem of accommodating a motor and transmission, and practical driving needs. Early American autos generally had high wheels to lift them above muddy roads, flared bodies to hold several passengers, detachable leather sides and top to keep out the rain, brass-trimmed acetylene lamps for decoration and light.

In 1908 Ford brought out his four-cylinder Model T, whose severely plain design was determined by the assembly-line techniques which produced it. There was not much conventional beauty in the puddle-straddling Model T. But its sturdy frame and magneto-fired engine along with its rock-bottom price sold 15 million cars before the type was discontinued in 1927.

FORD MODEL T of 1908, photographed fore and aft, had crank for starting the four-cylinder, 20 hp engine, elliptic springs over axles to give flexibility on rough roads. Differential is enclosed midway on rear axle. Most cars had steering wheel on right. Model T popularized the wheel on left.

carriage. In doorway is a 1909 Chalmers Detroit speed roadster, a forerunner of today's sports cars. The bright red car with one wheel lifted for a tire change is a 1910 Stanley Steamer, which was powered by a small steam boiler and two-cylinder sliding valve engine. At the right is the "Old Pacific," a one-cylinder Packard roadster with a maroon-painted wooden body and a chain drive which sped from New York to San Francisco in 52 days in a 1903 transcontinental road test.

139

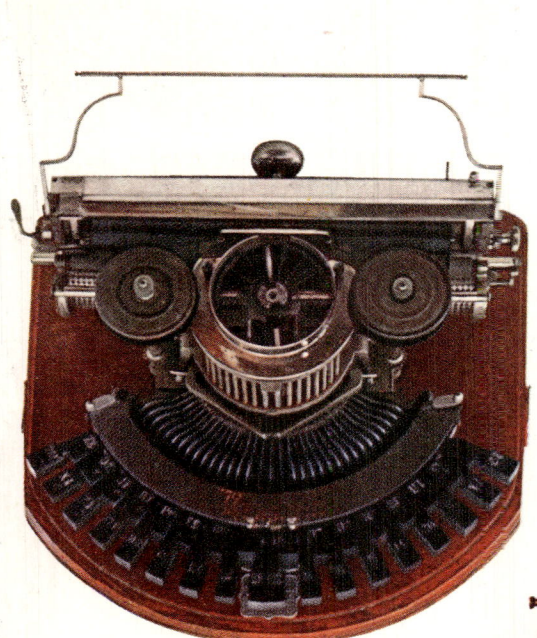

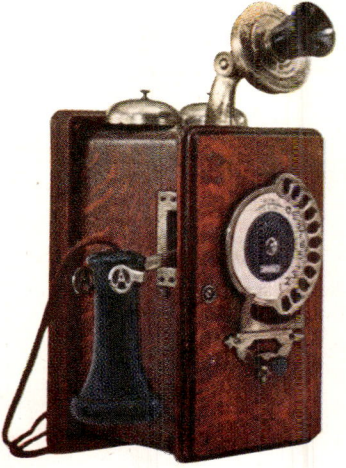

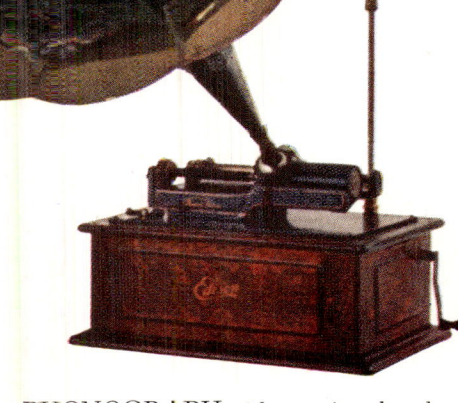

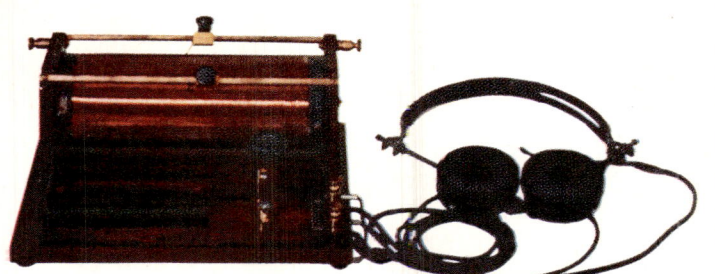

TYPEWRITER, an 1880 Hammond, has wood keys. Type is on a revolving metal ring.

TELEPHONE was patented first in 1876. This wall type with dial was made about 1904.

RADIO SET (*right*) used crystal detector of type invented by G. W. Pickard in 1906.

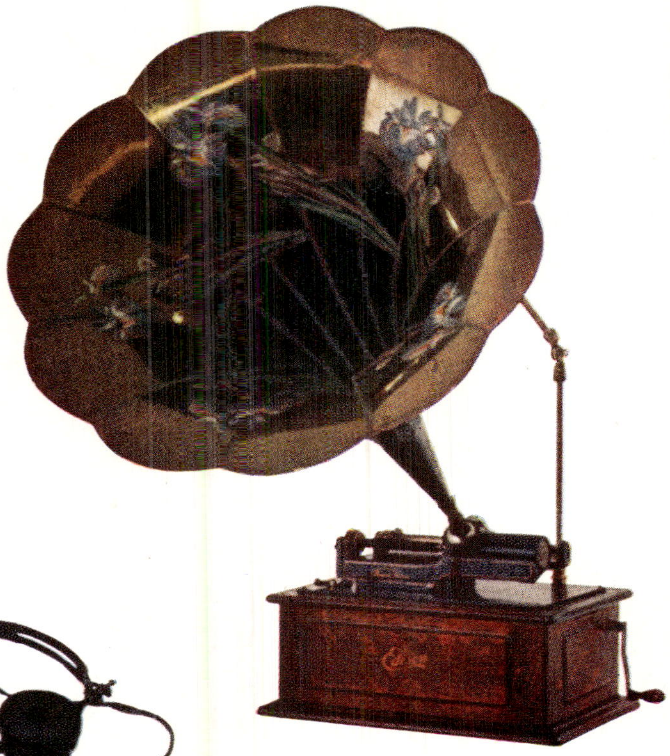

PHONOGRAPH with morning-glory horn was the Edison Model D, made about 1908.

Inventions for livelier living

These were the years when Thomas A. Edison invented his electric bulb and recited "Mary Had a Little Lamb" to a tin-foil cylinder that became the first phonograph record. Alexander Graham Bell studied the human ear in a Boston hospital and then invented the telephone. George Westinghouse Sr. designed threshing machines (*below*) and his son George Jr. invented the air brake. The typewriter made the stenographer possible.

These inventions stepped up the pace of daily work and living of the American people. The gargantuan wheel of George Washington Gales Ferris, shown opposite in an advertising poster, was designed for their pleasure at the Chicago world's fair of 1893. Constructed of new, tough bridge-building steel—which also made the skyscraper possible—the Ferris wheel weighed 2.8 million pounds, turned on 140,000-pound axle.

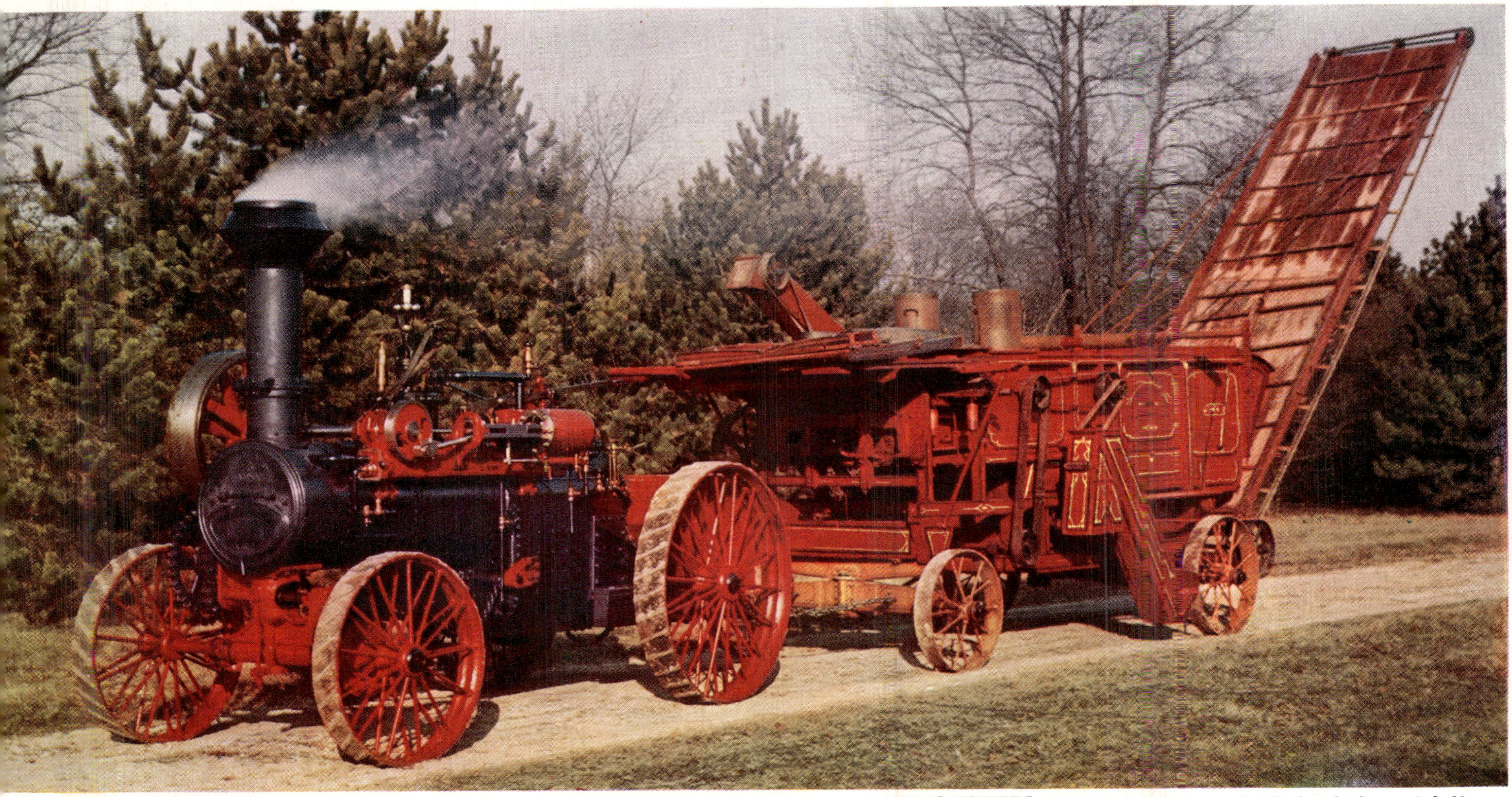

ENTIRE PAGE: HENRY FORD MUSEUM, DEARBORN, MICH.

THRESHING RIG of 1880s was powered by a "Rubicon" steam traction engine which hauled the Westinghouse separator (*right*), drove it by belts and wheels. Grain came from chute at side of separator, straw was stacked in rear.

FERRIS WHEEL of 1893 (*opposite*) stood 264 feet high, carried 60 passengers per ride in each of its 36 cars. The wheel took in $1 million at Chicago fair, $250,000 more at St. Louis fair in 1904. Then it was dynamited into scrap.

TRADITIONAL TUDOR STYLE was massively enlarged in this 1874 Newport mansion designed by H. H. Richardson for William Watts Sherman, a New York millionaire. The pretentious Victorian facade is a mixture of shingle, stone, pink stucco, obtrusive brick chimneys and half-timber decoration. But in widening the bulk of the house to accommodate his client's way of life the architect has given it a horizontal silhouette that foreshadows modern treatment.

AMERICAN SHINGLE STYLE flourished at New England seaside resorts and westward as far as Colorado Springs. This attractive example at Bristol, R.I. was designed in 1887 by the fashionable firm of McKim, Mead & (Stanford) White. Clean-cut and commodious in its triangular lines, this is essentially a very wide, flattened-out Cape Cod cottage covered with rough-textured shingles. It is now the summer home of Paul C. Nicholson Jr., a Providence file manufacturer.

HORIZONTAL STYLE of this 1903 house at Springfield, Ill. was the creation of Frank Lloyd Wright, who began his career as a draftsman for Louis Sullivan at Chicago in 1887. Wright's "prairie houses," of which this is an early example, were designed for the wide open landscape of the Midwest, with low ground-hugging lines and ample expanses of windows. Arched doorway and leaded glass decorations in this house, however, still follow traditional patterns.

TACOMA BUILDING at LaSalle and Madison Streets, Chicago was first skyscraper in which outer walls were supported by the riveted steel skeleton.

Spreading out, stretching up

The steel frame skyscraper was the crowning glory of Victorian inventiveness and engineering skill. When business offices jammed the downtown districts of cities, every foot of real estate became precious and multistory buildings became a necessity. The safety elevator, invented in 1852, made such buildings practical. New methods of heating, lighting and sanitation and new materials—mass-produced steel, reinforced concrete, ceramics and glass—were developed for their construction.

In Chicago, a new generation of architect-engineers broke brilliantly with the past to design the world's first skyscrapers. The 10-story Home Insurance Building designed by William Jenney in 1885 had a steel and iron frame which required some support from surrounding masonry. In 1887 William Holabird and Martin Roche designed the 14-story Tacoma Building (*above*) in which, for the first time, the steel skeleton supported the brick and terra cotta outer walls, which thus served only as a curtain. The projecting cornice on the Tacoma Building and the rusticated stonework of the Flatiron Building (*right*), designed by Chicago's Daniel Burnham, are transitional decorative features which had no structural function. But buildings like these began the soaring skylines which are the pride and chief adornment of U.S. cities today.

As commercial buildings climbed higher and higher, Victorian domestic architecture spread out wider and developed eventually into the modern horizontal home style (*opposite page*).

FLATIRON BUILDING at Fifth Avenue and ➤ Broadway, New York, built in 1902, crowds 200,000 square feet of floors on a triangular 10,000-foot plot.

The wonderful vertical railway car

The convenience that every skyscraper had to have was a passenger elevator or, as it was often called, a vertical railway car. The first safety elevator for human cargo was installed in a Manhattan store in 1857 by Elisha Graves Otis, a farm-born Vermonter who went on to improve the invention and establish a famous business. The earliest elevators were steam-powered and lifted by ropes which wound around steel drums. After 1878 the hydraulic cylinder of Cyrus Baldwin of Boston (*lower rt.*) provided more even flow of power and extra safety.

SAFETY ELEVATOR of 1853, used for freight, had upright racks with slanting teeth lining both sides of shaft and pawls or "dogs" attached to the car. Here Inventor Otis is shown crying "All safe" as rope is cut and "dogs" engage the ratchet-like teeth to stop the car's fall.

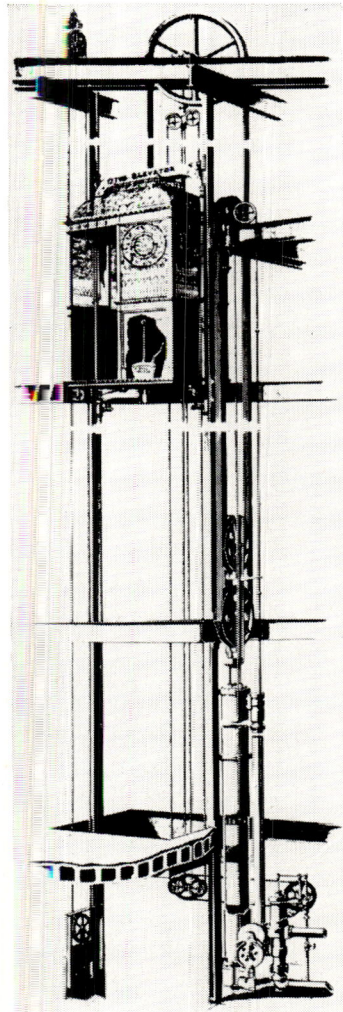

HYDRAULIC LIFT in use after 1878 is shown above. Wire ropes supporting elevator are attached to piston inside tall water-filled cylinder at lower right. As the valves shift water under pressure from bottom of cylinder to top, the piston moves down and the car goes up—or vice versa.

ELEGANT ELEVATOR car of 1881 was lit by gas through a flexible tube and furnished with mirrors, ventilators, a sofa bench for ladies and much carved and gilded woodwork. The operator pulled the rope up or down to start flow of water through the valves below and move the car.

Part IX

BEAUTY IN THE TOOLS OF TODAY

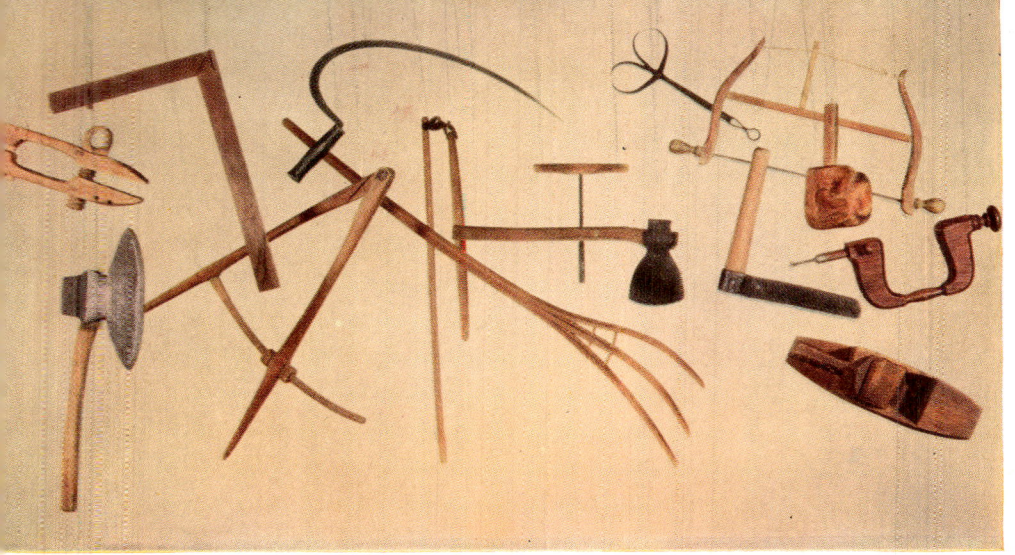

HAND TOOLS of the colonists required direct muscle power for piecemeal production.

Beauty in

Today, as in colonial times, Americans are attacking a new frontier. With powerful tools—the atomic reactor, the jet engine, the electronic "brain" —they seek to master some of the ultimate secrets of nature and put them to work for man. Out of this drive come exciting shapes of precision and speed, gleaming new materials, designs of useful, unpremeditated beauty which are creating a distinctive, contemporary American style.

the Tools of Today

To appreciate these new forms of American creation let us look at some of these contemporary tools and designs. Among them are simple shapes, like the rocket, and abstractions made for a purpose, like the control panel of the automated oil refinery below. Unlike the old Industrial Revolution the new revolution in technology pays attention to the human hunger for beauty. Its architecture is resplendently bright, clean and functional; its consumer products are packaged for eye appeal. Its style is not self-consciously conceived or adapted from older styles, like the Greek and Gothic revivals. Rather it springs spontaneously from new needs and new techniques for control of power, and today it is seen everywhere—in automobiles, household gadgets, modern paintings—as well as in laboratories and factories where most of the following photographs were taken.

THREE MEN TENDING DIALS AT McMURREY OIL REFINERY IN TYLER, TEXAS CONTROL PROCESSES USED IN HANDLING 20,000 BARRELS A DAY

BRASS CARVING, resembling a modern sculpture by Brancusi, was made by an automatic milling machine at the Massachusetts Institute of Technology as part of its research program. Strips of punched tape are fed into machine and regulate its action far more precisely than human fingers. The piece is a stage in the manufacture of a master die used to make automobile transmissions and it represents the most efficient flow of liquid through a vaned impeller wheel.

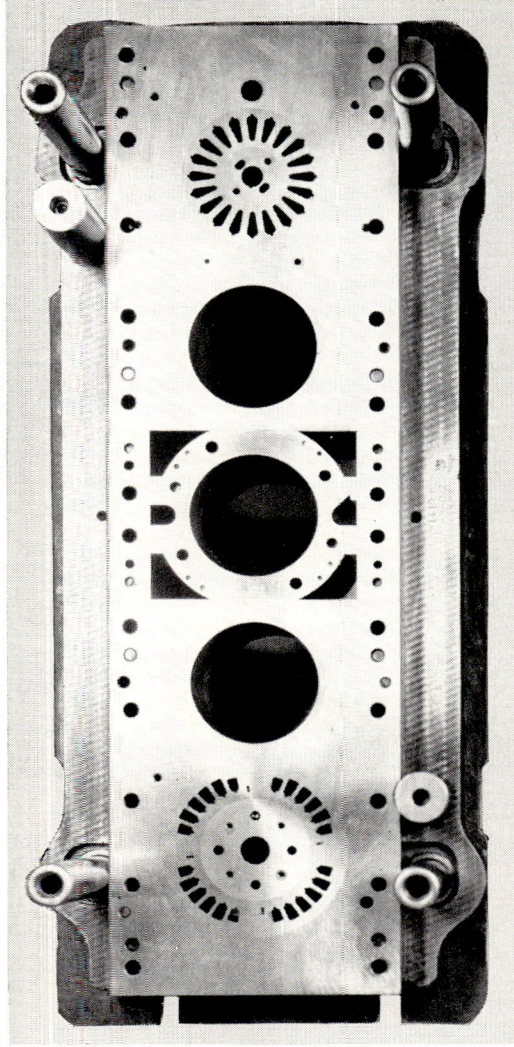

STENCILED DIE with flowerlike patterns is used with the punch below in an automatic machine which stamps out parts for air-conditioner motors.

TOOTHED PUNCH fits exactly into die above. The basis for modern mass production, finely made parts like these are still shaped by hand craftsmen.

PURPOSEFUL COMPLEXITY of the automatic age is examined in this photo looking down into a Transfer-matic machine which performs 688 separate jobs in manufacturing cylinder blocks with only one man as operator. Tubes at left exhaust dust from drills driven by the cylindrical motors at right.

Across the land, silhouettes of strength

Among the familiar symbols of contemporary America are the engineered symmetry of its great bridges and highways, and the steep skylines of its cities. Americans see so much of these things that they overlook their real beauty, taking it for granted. Yet there is no more masterful combination of modern art and skill—comparable in its perfection to the Parthenon of Athens or the paintings of the Renaissance—than the long-span suspension bridge which was made possible by the invention of an immensely strong cable spun of parallel wires by the American, John A. Roebling, during the last century. Shown above is a recent (1951) example, the Delaware Memorial Bridge linking New Jersey and Delaware, whose basic components—towers, roadbed and two 20-inch suspension cables—stand magnificently free of needless ornament or complication.

Below is the skyline of Houston, one of several U.S. cities which have been building in a hurry since the end of World War II. (In 1955 the population of Metropolitan Houston passed the one million mark.) Poised here against a wide-open landscape, the peaks of America's favorite art form, the skyscraper, take on an extra, symbolic beauty, as though rising to express the fabulous vitality of the fast-growing heart of the nation.

VIEW ACROSS LAKE of the GM center looks toward low, wide Styling buildings and the aluminum-covered dome of the Styling Auditorium (*right*) where full-size plastic models of new automobiles are exhibited and studied.

SPECTACULAR STAIRCASE (*opposite*) in the Styling Administration Building rises above a pool lined with creamy travertine. Stair treads are white terrazzo suspended on pencil-thin stainless steel rods. Handrail is polished teak.

Architecture for the future
GM CONSTRUCTS A 'VERSAILLES OF INDUSTRY'

In the $100 million General Motors Technical Center, dedicated May 1956, at Warren, Mich., a versatile U.S. corporation and a gifted U.S. architect—Eero Saarinen—joined to create a combined showplace and workshop which has already been hailed as a model for tomorrow's advanced factory design.

Like the automobile itself the 25 buildings of GM's new center are constructed mainly of steel, glass and aluminum, with occasional walls of bright glazed brick to provide contrasts in color. Also like the automobile, the buildings are all mass-produced products, put together from prefabricated parts made in shops and factories all over the U.S. In their long low geometric shapes the buildings follow—and enrich—the horizontal trend in factory planning which was established in Detroit by the early automobile plants of the late, great Albert Kahn. Interiors like the stone and steel staircase on the opposite page are handsomely fin-

ished yet stylistically simple and clean, efficient for use and pleasing to the eye. Since none of the buildings is over three stories high there is no need to wait for elevators.

Because the center was planned as a unit, its associated architects and engineers were able to group their buildings in a campuslike setting of 320 landscaped acres around an artificial lake, embellished with islands of weeping willow trees and a fountain designed by Sculptor Alexander Calder. The gleaming dome of the Styling Auditorium (*right, above*), 65 feet high and 188 feet across, provides another focal point of interest. Eventually the whole center, with its 11 miles of roads and 85 acres of parking lots, will be enclosed in a green belt of forest trees, of which more than 13,000 have been planted. Today more than 4,000 technicians, designers, engineers and executives of five GM central staff organizations are employed here in planning and styling the company's future products.

FESTIVELY FLOODLIT, the buildings of the General Motors Technical Center stand over an artificial lake, which covers 22 acres and provides a restful, cooling central point for grouping its 25 units. The colored end walls shown above are those of the Process Development Administration Building (*left, blue*), the Engineering Staff Administration Building (*center, red*) and the Engineering Shop (*right, blue*). Concealed mercury vapor lamps shed a mantle of misty green

HARMONIOUS PATTERN in shadow, reflection and sundrenched color is made by intersecting walls at GM's Technical Center. Such beauty spots were deliberately planned by Architect Saarinen to make the most of novel materials. The glazed orange bricks are a special color created for the center with minute variations in shade and texture. They contrast pleasingly with greenish windows and gray enameled steel panels of "sandwich" wall which intersects at right.

over the winter bare trees. Designed as a single big lighting unit, the center gleams at night with an orchestration of varicolored lights whose 56 miles of fluorescent tubing are serviced by 378 miles of wires and 12 miles of floor ducts.

GLOWING WALL of yellow brick is the only decorative feature of this shop where GM tests engines. As in other center buildings, its simple rectangular shape is determined by its steel framework and the efficient use of interior space.

Brilliant coloring and techniques

Not since the fabulous palaces of the Assyrian kings has color been used for architectural effect as it has in the new General Motors Technical Center. The richly varied yet stylistically simple combinations of color and form shown on these pages are made possible by specially glazed bricks and permanent enamels developed by the center's designers and engineers. These are now on the market and could spark a color revolution in U.S. building practice.

Even more important are the center's many innovations in techniques and materials. Here is the first use of a uniquely thin "sandwich panel" wall whose enameled steel sides enclosing two inches of insulation give as much protection as a thick masonry wall while effecting great savings in space. From experience in designing windshields for buses and autos, GM engineers with the architects developed a neoprene gasket seal for holding glass windows and solid wall panels in frames, replacing the less efficient (and messier) calking method. These and many other new ideas have gone into the building of a unified environment in which men at work on tomorrow's technical problems can give free rein to their imagination and skill.

UNDER SHADOWLESS LIGHTS in an engineering building draftsmen work at twilight. Continuous luminous ceiling was designed for center.

POWERFUL PROPELLERS of steel, adjusted as precisely as a delicate watch, are used at GM's Technical Center to create artificial windstorms. Such simple, clean-cut, streamlined forms dominate much American interior decoration today, are often seen in lamps, tableware, kitchen utensils.

POWERHOUSE EQUIPMENT at GM center is sparklingly clean, brightly lighted, cheerfully colored. Such modern factory design is a far cry from the "dark, Satanic mills" of the 19th Century and it reflects the growing tendency of U.S. industry to provide an attractive environment for work.

MECHANICAL MAZE of Technical Center's powerhouse generates 320,000 pounds of steam per hour from five huge boilers like the one

at center above. Designed for efficiency and economy of space, the whole assembly resembles a complex creation of Painter Fernand Léger. Gay colors carry out Architect Saarinen's desire to brighten usually drab areas and here they help to identify the intricate network of pipes (*blue*), valves and motors (*red*), catwalks and stairways (*lemon yellow*). Steam created here is used for heating all the buildings of the center and cleaning machinery.

157

NETWORK OF COLORED WIRES looks like a modern fabric design. This is part of the "arithmetical and logical unit" of IBM's new 705 Electronic Data Processing Machine, which performs up to 720,000 calculations a minute.

Electronic intricacy in compact design

The basic tool of electronics is the vacuum tube (*below*) whose principle —that electric current will jump from a heated filament to a cold metal plate within an empty space—was noted by Thomas Edison. Two other Americans, Lee DeForest and E. H. Armstrong, enormously strengthened the tube by inserting a tiny metal "grid." They also created the regenerative circuit or feedback which gives the tube an uncanny power to record and regulate its own actions—*i.e.*, to "think" for itself—and out of this have come many of the wonders of today's age of automation.

The use of the tubes in today's computers and electronic brains requires the control of repeated, precise impulses of power and the compact arrangement of thousands of tiny parts. This produces the tightly packed, purposeful patterns shown on these pages, whose intricate designs are reflected in modern textiles, wallpapers and even in men's ties.

SOLID RANKS OF TUBES form another section of the IBM 705 machine. Tubes glow softly as information is fed into machine by magnetic tapes and electronic impulses process the data for storage in "memory bank" (*opposite page*).

TIGHT PATTERN of main memory bank (*upper part of photo*) in the IBM 705 machine is formed by 140,000 tiny magnetic ferrite cores, each one storing an essential "bit" of information. The orange objects are switching devices.

◀— RANDOM DESIGN of printed circuit board for Admiral TV set is made by solder covering thin copper foil which replaces wires. Electric connections are inserted on the board by automatic machinery, then soldered together in seconds.

EERIE BEAUTY of the supersonic age is explored in this impressionistic photo by Eliot Elisofon, whose camera is placed where the 2,000°F. blast of a jet engine would emerge if it were running. The corrugated metal with slitlike holes is the sheathing of the afterburner. The round red rings are the flame holder. (A pie-shaped section at top has been cut away for exhibition purposes.) The protruding objects like eyeballs are spark plugs set in yellow dome of afterburner.

TREMENDOUS THRUST of jet engine is created by bullet-shaped design and powerful mechanism, shown here by removing sides of a General Electric J-47. Its linear pattern, without the interruption of reciprocating parts, accounts for engine's beautiful efficiency, both in design and operation.

Exciting look of speed

In the jet aircraft engine and the space-hurdling rocket Americans are building machines which must—by their very purpose—combine pure functional form with the utmost in the management of power. The jet engine which is pictured above and on the opposite page is essentially a hollow projectile with its power plant packed around its inside surface. Its penetrating, straightforward design is dictated by the great change which came with the jet engine: the switch from push-and-pull power —human and animal legs—or the reciprocating pistons of internal combustion engines to the direct thrust of the jet stream which flows steadily in one direction.

The probing shape of the rocket at right suggests even more dramatically man's ancient dream of soaring through seas of space and landing on other worlds. Both these designs—the finned rocket and the bullet-nosed jet—are symbols of speed and efficiency which strongly appeal to the taste of our time. As decorative motifs they are found in automobile radiator ornaments, fenders and tail lamps, in household fixtures and fountain pens, even when they serve no direct functional purpose.

GARGANTUAN TUBES of world's largest supersonic wind tunnel at Moffett Field, California control 200,000 hp in simulated speeds to 2,500 mph.

TAPERED TIP and thin metal skin of rocket at Wallops Island, Virginia, civilian research center, conceal engine which lifts it 100,000 feet into sky.

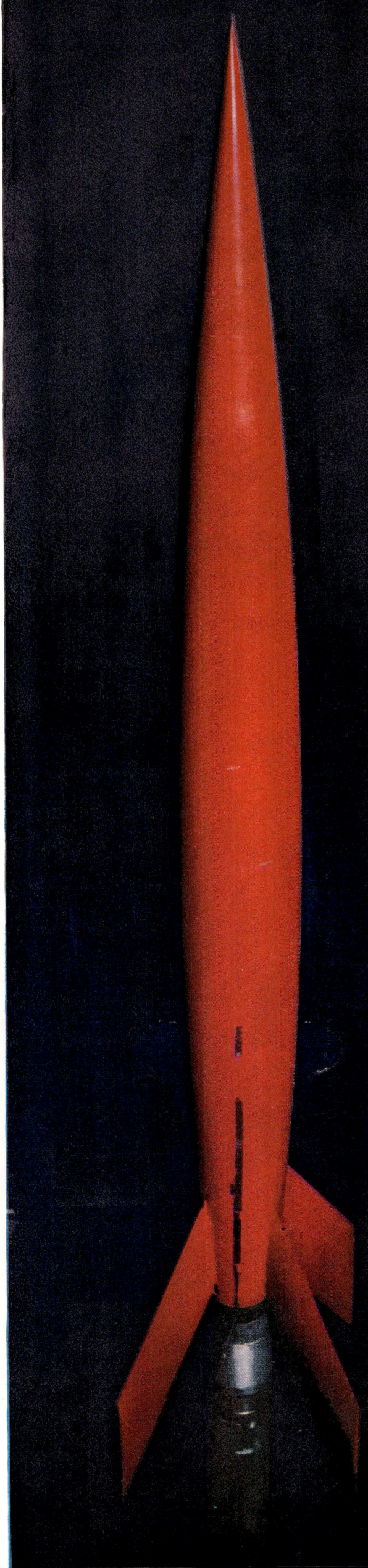

CHEMICAL EQUIPMENT at the new Oakland plant of the Liquid Carbonic Company suggests clean-cut industrial paintings of Charles Sheeler.

From applied science, significant beauty

The tools of modern technology often bear a striking resemblance to the expressions of modern art. The Oak Ridge atom splitter at the left might be an abstract sculptor's version of a whirling dancer or a totem pole. The other photographs on these pages were made in factories and laboratories, yet each suggests the work of a distinctive modern painter.

These analogies are important because they foreshadow an ever closer and more fruitful union between art and skill, between the old American pride of craftsmanship—represented by the engineer and tool-builder—and the inspiration to create new designs of lasting appeal and significance. Modern art in all its variety is moved by the ancient teaching of Plato: that out of "straight lines and circles, and the plane or solid figures which are formed out of them by turning lathes and rulers and measures of angles" comes the true beauty which overrides time.

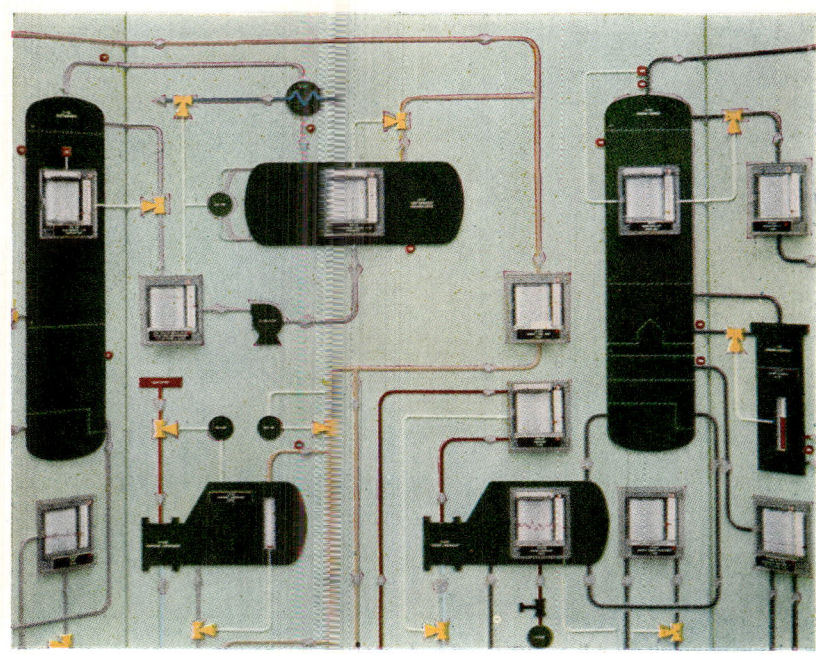

ELECTRONIC CONTROLS at Esso refinery in Linden, New Jersey resemble colored lines and forms in abstract paintings of I. Rice Pereira.

←OAK RIDGE ATOMIC ACCELERATOR CREATES HELIUM IONS

ATOMIC FUEL elements mounted on metal grid and submerged in water at Atomic Energy Commission's center in Idaho Falls resemble in their diffused colors fanciful paintings of Loren MacIver.

163

THE PERFECT PARABOLA which forms the antenna of a Harvard University radio telescope straddles an observatory and strains toward space like an enormous ear. In form it resembles the intricate wire and metal sculpture which modern artists have created. Radio telescopes, new since 1932, detect signals from matter in outer space far beyond the reach of any optical telescope. Streaks in photo are visible stars whose position changed during half-hour exposure.

PICTURE SOURCES

Pictures are listed by pages and position on page — center, left, right, top, bottom.

ABBREVIATIONS: B–Bottom, ©–Copyright, C–Center, L–Left, R–Right, T–Top

I THE PRACTICAL WORLD OF THE COLONISTS

Photographs by Eliot Elisofon *except where otherwise noted*

Frontispiece	Frigate's Figurehead	
	Courtesy The Mariners Museum, Newport News, Va.	
12, 13	Early American Tools	
	Courtesy Old Sturbridge Village, Mass.	
14	Studded Door	
	Courtesy Topsfield, Mass., Historical Society	
15	Young Puritans	
	Courtesy Major Nathaniel Hamlen	
16, 17 T	Old New York	
	Courtesy New York Historical Society	
B	Newer New York	
	Courtesy New York Historical Society	
18 T	New York Shipyard	
	Courtesy New York Historical Society	
B	Ferry Landing in Brooklyn	
	Courtesy New York Historical Society	
19	Girl With Red Shoes	
	Courtesy Du Pont Museum, Winterthur, Del.	
20 T–L	Gold Pap Spoon with Bells	
20, 21	Earliest American Silver	
	All Courtesy Yale University Art Gallery, Mabel Brady Garvan Collection	
22 T–L	"Sacred Cod" Cut from Wood	
T–R	Bull's Head Sign	
	Courtesy Wadsworth Atheneum, Morgan B. Brainard Collection	
B–L	Tin Chandelier	
	Courtesy Du Pont Museum, Winterthur, Del.	
23	Wooden Utensils	
	Courtesy Old Sturbridge Village, Mass.	
24	Needlework	
	Courtesy Wadsworth Atheneum, Hartford, Conn.	
25 T–L	Weather Vane	
	Courtesy Mass. Historical Society, Boston	
T–R	Sculptured Gravestone	
B–L	Weather Vane	
	Courtesy Du Pont Museum, Winterthur, Del.	
B–R	Puritan Portrait	
	Courtesy Mass. Historical Society, Boston	
26 T–L	Garden of Eden	
T–R	Cain Killing Abel	
	Courtesy Bucks County Historical Society, Doylestown, Pa.	
B–L	The Franklin Stove	
	Drawing by Adolph E. Brotman	
B–R	Franklin's Design for Stove	
	Courtesy Historical Society of Pennsylvania, Philadelphia	
27	Fieldstone Hearth	
28, 29	Parson Capen House	
	Courtesy Topsfield, Mass., Historical Society	
	Richard Jackson House	
	Courtesy Society for the Preservation of New England Antiquities	
30 T–L	Pottery Jug	
	Gilbert Ask	
C	17th Century Parlor	
	Courtesy Du Pont Museum, Winterthur, Del.	
B–L	Spice Cabinet	
	Courtesy Du Pont Museum, Winterthur, Del.	
30, 31 C	Trestle Table	
31 T–R	Carved Box	
	Courtesy Museum of Fine Arts, Boston	
C	18th Century Kitchen	
	Courtesy Du Pont Museum, Winterthur, Del.	
B–C	Brewster Chair	
	Courtesy Metropolitan Museum of Art	
B–R	Dower Chest	
	Courtesy Museum of Fine Arts, Boston	
32 L	Old Ship Meeting House	
32, 33 C	Interior	
33 T–R	Pendill of Wood	
	Courtesy Topsfield, Mass., Historical Society	
C	Wall of Stone	
	Courtesy Miss Ruth Waterbury	
B–R	Design of Brick	
	Courtesy William Edmund Sterling	
34	Chimney of Cape Cod House	
	Courtesy Daniel Osborne Earle	
35 T	Diagram Construction Cape Cod House	
	Drawings by Gerald Watland	
B	Shingled Cape Cod House	
	Courtesy Library of Congress	
36	Ancient Ironworks	
	Courtesy First Ironworks Assn., Inc., Saugus, Mass.	

II THE LOOK OF LIBERTY IN CRAFTSMANSHIP

Photographs by Arnold Newman *except where otherwise noted*

38	Paul Revere	
	Courtesy Museum of Fine Arts, Boston	
39 T	Bowl	
	Courtesy Museum of Fine Arts, Boston	
B	Revere's Rattlesnake	
	Courtesy Clarence S. Brigham, American Antiquarian Society	
40, 41, 42	"The most fatal widow and orphan makers in the world"	
	Courtesy Joe Kindig, Jr.; Harold L. Peterson, Fort Ticonderoga Museum, National Park Service; Pennsylvania Farm Museum of Landis Valley	
43, 44 L	Carter's Grove	
	Courtesy Mrs. Archibald McCrea	
44 T	Ceiling at Kenmore	
	Courtesy Kenmore Association	
B	Staircase of Peirce House	
	Courtesy Essex Institute, Salem, Mass.	
45 T–L	Wood Carving	
	Courtesy Du Pont Museum, Winterthur, Del.	
T–C	Medallion	
	Courtesy Essex Institute, Salem, Mass.	
T–R	Cornucopia	
	Courtesy Du Pont Museum, Winterthur, Del.	
C	Peirce House	
	Courtesy Essex Institute, Salem, Mass.	
B–L	Eagle	
	Courtesy Du Pont Museum, Winterthur, Del.	
B–C	Arms of Massachusetts	
	Courtesy Essex Institute, Salem, Mass.	
B–R	Eagle	
	Courtesy Essex Institute, Salem, Mass.	
46 T–L	Portrait of Roger Sherman	
	Courtesy Yale University Art Gallery	
B–L	Queen Anne Style Chairs	
	Courtesy Du Pont Museum, Winterthur, Del.	
46, 47	Varied Windsor Forms	
	All Chairs: Courtesy Du Pont Museum, Winterthur, Del.	
48 T–L	Tilt-top Tea Table	
	Courtesy Museum of Fine Arts, Boston	
B–L	Elliptical Commode	
	Courtesy Museum of Fine Arts, Boston	
49 T–L	Tambour Secretary	
	Courtesy Du Pont Museum, Winterthur, Del.	
B–L	"Bombé" Desk	
	Courtesy Museum of Fine Arts, Boston	

165

48, 49 T Block-front Secretary
Courtesy Rhode Island Historical Society, Providence

50 T–L Philadelphia East Indiaman
Herbert Orth

B–L Salem Square-rigger, *The George*
Courtesy Peabody Museum, Salem, Mass.

50, 51 Chinese Parlor
Courtesy Du Pont Museum, Winterthur, Del.

52 Rare, Historic Playing Cards
Arnold Newman. *Courtesy Guy De Lagerbert, Westport, Conn.*

53 T Card Table Top

B Card Table
Courtesy Museum of Fine Arts, Boston

54 Proposed Designs for Great Seal of U. S.
Courtesy National Archives and Records Service

III THE STURDY AGE OF HOMESPUN

Photographs by Arnold Newman *except where otherwise noted*

56 Farmhouse Kitchen
Courtesy Farmers' Museum, Cooperstown, N. Y.

57 Farmhouse Portrait

58 T–L Tin Pitcher

C–L Earthenware Plate

B–L Stoneware Jug

T–R Toleware Box

58, 59 C Array of Pewter
Courtesy Du Pont Museum, Winterthur, Del.

59 T–L Tole "Coffin Tray"

T–R Tin Teapot

C–R Slipware Plate

B–R Sgraffito Jug

60, 61 Early American Glass
Courtesy Corning Museum of Glass, Corning Glass Center

61 T–R Glass Blowers
Courtesy New York Public Library

62 T–L Hotel Kitchen

C–L A Self Portrait of Lewis Miller

B–L York Brewhouse

62, 63 T "An Accident"

B Carpenter Miller

63 T–R Tavern Keeper

C–R Bootmaker

B–R Old Lutheran Church
All Courtesy York County Historical Society, York, Pa.

64 T–L Street Lamp

B–L Elliptical Shape of American Stagecoach

64, 65 Common Room of the Red Lion Inn
Courtesy Du Pont Museum, Winterthur, Del

66 L Tall Clock
Courtesy Drexel Institute of Technology

C Shelf Clock

R Banjo Clock
Courtesy Metropolitan Museum of Art

67 Wooden 30-Hour Clock Movement
Arnold Newman. *Courtesy Brooks Palmer*

68 T How Mill Worked
Arnold Newman. *Courtesy Eleutherian Mills—Hagley Foundation, Wilmington, Del.*

B–R Fulton Self-portrait
Arnold Newman. *Courtesy N. Y. Public Library*

IV THE MAGNIFICENT GREEK REVIVAL

Photographs by Fritz Goro *except where otherwise noted*

70, 71 Stately Façade of Andalusia

71 T–R Banker-Romantic Nicholas Biddle
Both Courtesy Mr. and Mrs. Charles J. Biddle, Andalusia, Pa.

B Classic Vase
Courtesy Philadelphia Museum of Art

72 T Phyfe Headquarters
Courtesy The Metropolitan Museum of Art

B–L Phyfe Chair
Courtesy Du Pont Museum, Winterthur, Del.

B–C Phyfe Table
Courtesy Yale University Art Gallery

B–R Phyfe Sofa
Courtesy Henry Ford Museum, Dearborn, Mich.

72, 73 T–R Ideal Interior
Herbert Orth. *Courtesy The New York Historical Society*

73 B–L Tambour Sewing Table
Courtesy Henry Ford Museum, Dearborn, Mich.

B–R Lyre-back Chair
Courtesy Du Pont Museum, Winterthur, Del.

74 T–L Acorn Clock
Courtesy Henry Ford Museum, Dearborn, Mich.

B–L "Fourth of July"
Courtesy Pennsylvania Academy of the Fine Arts

74, 75 C Hand-Pumped Fire Engine
Courtesy Henry Ford Museum, Dearborn, Mich.

T–R Dunce-Cap Stove
Courtesy Henry Ford Museum, Dearborn, Mich.

B–R Richardson Memorial
Courtesy New York State Historical Association, Cooperstown, N. Y.

76 T–L Tobacco Flowers

76, 77 B–L–R Enduring Beauty

77 T–R Corn Columns

78 L Whitney Workshop with Gin from The Atlanta Museum, Georgia
Courtesy J. M. Griggs, Washington, Ga., and J H. Elliott, Atlanta, Ga.
Whitney's Portrait
Courtesy Yale University Art Gallery

79 "Rattle and Snap"
Courtesy Mr. and Mrs. Oliver M. Babcock, Columbia, Tenn.

80 T Papered Bandboxes
Courtesy Cooper Union Museum

B–L Greek Revival Bathroom
Courtesy Museum of the City of New York

V THE ROMANTIC DECADES

Photographs by Bradley Smith *except where otherwise noted*

82 Swiss Gothic House
Courtesy Mrs. R. H. Reilly, Jr. and Miss Edith Lockwood

83 T–R Tuscan Villa

84 T–L Trim Church

B–L Quaint Homestead
Courtesy Sunnyside Restoration

B–R Snug Clubhouse
Courtesy Marine Historical Assoc., Mystic, Conn.

85 Scrollsaw Gothic

86 John Belter's Victorian Parlor
Courtesy Museum of the City of New York

87 The Shakers' Gathering Room
Courtesy Mr. and Mrs. Edward D. Andrews

88 B 1850 Wagon Shop
Eileen Tweedy and Thames & Hudson Publishers, Inc.
Courtesy Mr. and Mrs. Edwin Grabhorn

88, 89, 90 T Carriages
Courtesy of Suffolk Museum, Stony Brook, L. I.

90 B–R 1858 Trotting Match

91 T–L Clipper Builder Donald McKay
Courtesy Metropolitan Museum of Art, New York

B–L Poster advertising the *Galatea*
Courtesy Marine Historical Assoc., Mystic, Conn.

91, 92, 93 T Clipper's Hull
Courtesy Marine Historical Assoc., Mystic, Conn.

92 B The *Galatea*
Courtesy Marine Historical Assoc., Mystic, Conn.

93 C Whalers' Harpoon
Courtesy Marine Historical Assoc., Mystic, Conn.

B Whalers' Art
Courtesy Marine Historical Assoc., Mystic, Conn.

94 T–L Grater
Courtesy Bucks Co. Historical Soc., Doylestown, Pa.

	c	Sewing Machine
		Courtesy Singer Sewing Machine Co.
94	b-l	Mousetrap
		Courtesy Bucks Co. Historical Society, Doylestown, Pa.
	b-c	Apple Parer
		Courtesy Bucks Co. Historical Society, Doylestown, Pa.
	b-r	Milk Warmer
		Courtesy Bucks Co. Historical Society, Doylestown, Pa.
95		Gatling Gun
		Courtesy Bucks Co. Historical Society, Doylestown, Pa.
96	t	Eight-sided House
		Bradley Smith
	b	Floor Plan for Eight-sided House

VI THE FABULOUS FRONTIER

Photographs by Gjon Mili except where otherwise noted

98	l	"Ships of the Plains"
		Herbert Orth. *Courtesy Union League Club, New York*
98, 99		Conestoga Wagon
		Courtesy Pennsylvania Farm Museum of Landis Valley
100	t-l	Fur Trade Outpost
		Fernand Bourges. *Courtesy Mrs. Clyde Porter, Taos, N. Mex.*
	b-l	Frontier Firearms
		Herman Leonard. *Courtesy Robert Abels, New York*
100, 101		Fur Trade Goods
		Courtesy Missouri Historical Society, St. Louis
102	t	Well Built Cabin of Squared Oak Logs
		Courtesy Norwegian-American Historical Museum, Decorah, Iowa
	b	Cozy Interior
103	t-r	"Singing Plow"
		Courtesy Henry Ford Museum, Dearborn, Mich.
	r-c	Mechanized Rakes
		Courtesy Henry Ford Museum, Dearborn, Mich.
	b-r	McCormick's Reaper
		Courtesy Henry Ford Museum, Dearborn, Mich.
104, 105	t	Old River Steamboat
		Gjon Mili. *Courtesy U. S. Corps of Engineers, Memphis District*
104	b	Keelboat and Flatboat
		Courtesy City Art Museum of St. Louis
105	l	Mississippi Steamboat
		Courtesy City Art Museum of St. Louis
105, 106	t	Frontier's Locomotive
		Gjon Mili. *Courtesy Railway and Locomotive Historical Society and Western Pacific Railroad Company*
106	b	Concord Coach
		Gjon Mili. *Courtesy Wells Fargo Bank History Room, San Francisco*
107	b	Central Pacific Station at Sacramento
		Harry Baskerville. *Courtesy M. H. De Young Memorial Museum, San Francisco*
108	t-l	French Dwelling
		Gjon Mili. *Courtesy State of Illinois, Division of Parks and Memorials*
	b	French Colonists
		Courtesy Newberry Library, Chicago
109	t-r	Balcony and Iron Railings of New Orleans Mansion
		Gjon Mili. *Courtesy Mr. and Mrs. Alfred Jay Moran, New Orleans*
	b-l	Delicate Designs in Wrought Iron
		Gjon Mili
	b-r	Cast-Iron Pattern
		Gjon Mili
110	t-l	Hard-Riding Cowboys
		©Brown & Bigelow
	b-l	Gold Flakes Imbedded in Quartz
		Gjon Mili
110, 111		Buildings of Bodie
		Gjon Mili
112	t-l	Chicago in 1820
		Courtesy Chicago Historical Society
	t-r	Balloon Frame Diagram
		Drawing by Matt Greene
112	b	Chicago in 1857
		Courtesy Chicago Historical Society

VII THE TIMELESS SOUTHWEST

Photographs by Eliot Elisofon except where otherwise noted

114		Mission Garden of San Juan Capistrano
115	t-r	Cliff House
	b	Adobe Pueblo at Taos, N. Mex.
116	t-l	Mission Church of San Esteban Rey
	b-l	Wooden Stairs of San Esteban
	b-c	Pulpit of Las Trampas
116, 117	c	Mission Altarpiece of San Jose
117	t-r	Livable Epitome of Southwest Abode
		Courtesy Mrs. Lois Field
	c-r	Lithograph of Busy Capital of Spanish Colony
		Courtesy New York Public Library
	b-r	Spanish Colonial Interior Reproduced in Modern New Mexico Home
		Courtesy Cornelia Gieed Thompson
118	t-l	Lady's Saddle
		Courtesy Los Angeles County Museum
	b-l	Officer's Saddle
		Courtesy Colorado State Museum
	t-r	Rancher's Saddle
		Courtesy Los Angeles County Museum
	b-r	Texas Saddle
		Courtesy Panhandle-Plains Historical Museum, Canyon, Texas
119	t-l	Parade Saddle
		Courtesy Los Angeles County Museum
	b-l	Denver Saddle
		Courtesy Colorado State Museum
	b-r	Fancy Saddle
		Courtesy Mr. and Mrs. Godwin Pelissero, Goleta, Calif.
120, 121		Handmade Tools and Trappings of the Cattle Kingdom
		Courtesy Panhandle-Plains Historical Museum, Canyon, Texas
122	t-l	Navaho Blankets
	c-l	Baskets for Nuts and Corn
	c-r	Designs of Men and Animals
	b	Indian Jewelry
123		Indian Pottery
		All Courtesy of The Museum of New Mexico
124	t-l	Bell Tower of San Carlos
	b-r	Carved Door at San Juan Capistrano
124, 125	b-c	Frescoed Walls, Governor's Room at San Fernando
125	t-l	Carved Door at San Juan Capistrano
	t-r	Open "Corredor" at San Fernando Mission
	b-r	Iron Cross
126	t-l	Fortified Outpost
		Courtesy The New York Public Library
	b-l	Mission Style House
126, 127	t-r	Ranch House, 1865
		Courtesy Mr. and Mrs. Louis Magee
	b-r	Ranch House
		Courtesy Mr. and Mrs. Arthur Marquette
128		Roycroft Inn, Mission Style
		Courtesy Roycroft Inn

VIII AN AGE OF GILDED OPULENCE

130	l	Bronze Nymph
130, 131		Grand Staircase
		All Courtesy Miss Edith Wetmore
132		Victorian Grandeur
		Courtesy The Ingomar Club
133	t-l	Patent Desk
		Courtesy Sleepy Hollow Restorations, Philipse Castle, Tarrytown, N. Y.
	t-r	Cottage Organ
		Courtesy Henry Ford Museum, Dearborn, Mich.
	b	Victorian Comfort
		Courtesy Villa Louis, Wisconsin State Historical Society, Prairie Du Chien, Wis.

167

134 T–L	Baby Carriage of Rattan	146, 147	Men Tending Dies at McMurrey Oil Refinery in Tyler, Texas
B–L	Child's High Chair *Courtesy Staten Island Historical Society*		William Vandivert for *Time*
B–R	Spring Chair *Courtesy Peter Lindamood Antiques, New York*	148	Brass Carving Eliot Elisofon
134, 135	Bric-A-Brac "Whatnot" *Courtesy New York Historical Society and Private Collections*	149 T–L	Stenciled Die
		B–L	Toothed Punch Both by Ehrhardt Tool and Machine Co. for *Wagner Electric Co.*
135 T–R	Circular Sofa *Courtesy Peter Lindamood Antiques, New York*	R	Transfer-matic Machine Gordon Tenney *Courtesy The Cross Co.*
B	Elaborate Chairs *Courtesy Peter Lindamood Antiques, New York*	150, 151 T	Delaware Memorial Bridge Ralph Morse
136, 137	Tiffany Glass *Courtesy New York Historical Society, Peter Lindamood Antiques, and Private Collections* *Background courtesy U. S. Plywood Corp.*	B	Skyline of Houston Joe Scherschel
		152	View Across Lake of the GM Center Andreas Feininger
138 T–L	Fun of Motoring Robert S. Crandall from *Around the World In an Automobile* © 1907 by McLoughlin Bros., N.Y.	153	Spectacular Staircase Andreas Feininger
		154, 155 T–L	Floodlit Buildings of the General Motors Technical Center Andreas Feininger
138, 139 B	Vintage Motor Cars *Courtesy Henry Ford Museum, Dearborn, Mich.*	B–L	Harmonious Pattern Andreas Feininger
139 T	Ford Model T *Courtesy Henry Ford Museum, Dearborn, Mich.*	155, T–R	Glowing Wall Andreas Feininger
140 T–L	Typewriter, 1880 *Courtesy Henry Ford Museum, Dearborn, Mich.*	B–R	Under Shadowless Lights Andreas Feininger
T–C	Telephone, 1904 *Courtesy Henry Ford Museum, Dearborn, Mich.*	156 T–L	Powerful Propellers Andreas Feininger
T–C	Radio Set, 1906 *Courtesy Henry Ford Museum, Dearborn, Mich.*	B–L	Powerhouse Equipment Andreas Feininger
T–R	Phonograph, 1908 *Courtesy Henry Ford Museum, Dearborn, Mich.*	155, 156	Mechanical Maze Andreas Feininger
B	Threshing Rig of 1880's *Courtesy Henry Ford Museum, Dearborn, Mich.*	158 T–L	Network of Colored Wires Andreas Feininger
141	Ferris Wheel of 1893 Walter W. Krutz. *Courtesy Chicago Historical Society*	B–L	Solid Ranks of Tubes Eliot Elisofon
142 T	Traditional Tudor Style Mansion, 1874 *Courtesy Baptist Home of Rhode Island*	158, 159 C	Random Design Printed Circuit Board for Admiral TV Eliot Elisofon
C	American Shingle Style House *Courtesy Paul C. Nicholson, Jr.*	159 T	Tight Pattern of Main Memory Bank in the IBM Eliot Elisofon
B	Horizontal Style House *Courtesy Charles C. Thomas, Publisher*	160	Eerie Beauty Eliot Elisofon
143 T–L	Tacoma Building, Chicago *Courtesy Museum of Modern Art*	161 T–L	Jet Engine Eliot Elisofon
R	Flatiron Building, New York	B–L	Wind Tunnel at Moffett Field, Calif. Eliot Elisofon
144 L	Hydraulic Lift, 1878 *Courtesy Otis Elevator Co.*	R	Rocket at Wallops Island, Va. Eliot Elisofon
T–R	Elegant Elevator Car, 1881 *Courtesy Otis Elevator Co.*	162 L	Oak Ridge Atomic Accelerator Eliot Elisofon
B–R	Safety Elevator, 1853 *Courtesy Otis Elevator Co.*	T–R	Chemical Equipment Eliot Elisofon
R–C	Sullivan and Adler's Guaranty Building, Buffalo Wilder Photo Copy Co. *Courtesy owners of Prudential Building*	B–R	Electronic Controls Andreas Feininger
		163	Atomic Fuel R. G. Larsen for *Phillips Petroleum Co., Atomic Energy Division*
B–R	Louis Sullivan Chicago Architectural Photographing Co.	164	The Perfect Parabola Eliot Elisofon

IX BEAUTY IN THE TOOLS OF TODAY

146 T–L	Hand Tools of the Colonists	Eliot Elisofon. *Courtesy of Old Sturbridge Village, Mass.*

INDEX

* This symbol in front of a page number indicates that an illustration as well as mention of the subject is to be found on the page thus marked.

Abels, Robert, 100
accelerator, atomic, Oak Ridge, *162
acorn clock, *74
Adler, Dankmar, architect, 144
adobe home, Santa Fe, N. Mex., *117
adobe pueblo, Taos, N. Mex., *115
Age, Gilded, *130–137
Age of Homespun, 57
Albany cutter, *90
amateur art, 25
Amelung, John Frederick, 61
American Gothic, 127
American Shingle style architecture, *142
Andalusia, in Greek style, *70–71, 78
Andrew Jackson, clipper ship, 91
Andrews, Mr. and Mrs. Edward D., 87
architecture; American Shingle style, *142
    Bulfinch, *45
    early, *28–*29
    federal style, *45
    for the future, *152–157
    form and function, *144
    Georgian, *43
    Gothic variations, *84–85
    Greek; revival of, *71–77
    Horizontal style, *142
    "Hudson River" Bracketed, *83
    Mission, *124–125, *126
    styles, romantic, 83
    Tudor style, *142
Armstrong, E. H., inventor, 158
art; amateur, and the artisan, 25
    definition of, 13
    Mission, *124–125
    nouveau, 137
artisan, art of, 25
artisans and artists, early, 15
arts, Indian, *122–123
Atlanta Museum, 78
atomic accelerator, Oak Ridge, *162
Atomic Energy Commission, atomic fuel elements, *163
atomic fuel elements, AEC center, *163
automation, *149, 158
    early; signs of, 68
automobiles, early, *138–139

baby carriage, *134
Baldwin, Cyrus, inventor, 144
Baldwin, Mathias, locomotive builder, 107
balloon-frame houses, *112
bandbox boom, *80
Barton, William 54
bathroom, Greek revival, 80
    Latrobe design, 77
Battle of Saratoga, 41
beauty from applied science, *162
Bell, Alexander Graham, 140
Belter, John, cabinetmaker, 86
Biddle, Nicholas, *71
Biloxi, Miss. (in 1720), *108
blankets, Navajo, *122
blast from jet engine, *160
block-front secretary, *48–49
Bodie, Calif., *110, 111
Body, William S., 111
"bombé" desk, *49
Boston Museum of Fine Arts, 31,38,39,49,53

bowl, punch, by Paul Revere, *39
box, carved, *31
bracket, carved, *14–15
brass carving, *148
bric-a-brac, *134
brick design, "Make Peace," Somerset County, Md., *33
bridges and highways, *150–151
Bristol, R. I.; Richardson mansion, *142
Brown, Jonathan, clock maker, *75
Brown, Joseph, 49
Bucks County Historical Society, 94
Buffalo, N. Y.; Guaranty (now Prudential) Building, *144
Bulfinch, Charles, 45
Burwell, Carter, 43

cabin, Iowa, *102
cabinetmakers, American, 48
cabins, log, 29
Cahokia, Ill.; courthouse, *108–109
    French dwelling, *108
Calder, Alexander, sculptor, 152
California Mission style, *124–125
Cape Cod house, 29, *34, *35
Capen, Parson, house, Topsfield, Mass., *28, *29
Capitol, United States, 71, *76, *77
card games, 53
cards, historic playing, and table, *52–53
Carmel, Calif.; San Carlos Borromeo Mission, *124
Carmer, Carl, 96
carriage, baby, *134
carriages, horse-drawn, *88–90
Carter's Grove, Virginia, *43
cartoon, rattlesnake, by Paul Revere, *39
carving, brass, *148
    wood, *45
cattlemen's tools and trappings, *120–121
chairs, hoop-and-stick, *46–47
    Victorian, 135
    Windsor, *46–47
chaise, Boston, *88
chalets, Swiss, 83
Chalmers Detroit car (1909), *138
chandelier, tin, *22
Chateau-sur-Mer, Newport, R. I., 130, *131
chemical equipment, Liquid Carbonic Co., *162
Chicago Fair (1893); World's Columbian Exposition, 141
Chicago Historical Society, 112, 141
Chicago in 1829 and in 1857, *112
Chinese style; vogue of, *50–51
Chippendale, Thomas, 48, 50
Chippendale style, *50–51
churches of the Southwest, *116
cities' sky outlines, *150–151
City Art Museum of Saint Louis, 104, 105
clapboarded house, *29
clay, tin, and pewter, *58–59
cliff house, Indian, *115
clipper ships, 83, *91–93
clock, acorn, *74
clocks, *66–67

Cod, Sacred, in the Massachusetts State House, *22
"coffin tray," 59
Colman, Samuel, painter, 98
colonists, early, *15
color, use of, in the General Motors Technical Center, *154–155
Colorado State Museum, 118, 119
commode, elliptical, *49
common room, Red Lion Inn, Delaware, *64–65
Concord coach, *106
Conestoga wagon, *98–99
Coney, John, silversmith, 21
Cooper Union Museum, 80
Cooperstown, N. Y., Farmers' Museum, 57
controls, electronic, Esso refinery, *162
Copley, John Singleton, 38
Corning Museum of Glass, 61
cottage, Flemish, Topsfield, Mass., *29
cottage organ, Estey, *133
Cotton, King, the gin, and Eli Whitney, *78–79
covered wagon, *98–99
Currier & Ives print, *75
cutter, Albany, *90

Data Processing Machine, International Business Machines Corp., *158
Davis, A. J., 72
Davis, Phineas, inventor, 63
Dearborn, Mich.; Henry Ford Museum, 72, 73, 74, 75, 103, 133, *138, 139, 140
decades, romantic, 82–96
Decatur, Stephen, 53
Deere plow, *103
DeForest, Lee, 158
Delaware Memorial Bridge, *150–151
Delaware Valley kitchen, seventeenth-century, *31
design; development of, 15
    factory, *152–157
designs for travelers, *64–65
desk, "bombé," *49
desk, patent; used by John D. Rockefeller, *133
DeYoung Memorial Museum, 107
distributing, selling, and mass production, 66
door, nail-studded, *14–15
Douw, Magdalena, *19
dower chest, *31
drawings by Lewis Miller, *62–63
Drexel Institute of Technology, 66
Drowne, Shem, 25
drum, Revolutionary War, *40
Dummer, Governor William, 53
dunce-cap stove, *75
Du Pont Museum, Winterthur, Del., 19, 22, 25,30,31,45,46,49,50,59,*64–65,72,73
Duryea car (1896), *138
dyestuffs, 57

eagle, American, 54
Earl, Ralph, painter, 46
East Aurora, N. Y., 128
East Indiaman, *50
Eastlake, Charles L., 133
Eastlake Library, 130

169

Edison, Thomas A., 140, 158
  Model D phonograph, *140
electronic controls, Esso refinery, *162
electronic intricacy in compact designs, *158, 159
elevators; car, elegant (1881), *144
  lift, hydraulic (1878), *144
  Otis, *144
  safety; invention of, 143
Elisofon, Eliot, photographer, 15, 160
embroidery, Richardson memorial, *75
engine, jet, *160–161
engines, steam, first, 68
English cottage, Topsfield, Mass., *28
equipment, chemical; Liquid Carbonic Co., *162
equipment, soldiers', Revolutionary War, *41
Essex Institute, Salem, Mass., 45
Esso refinery; electronic controls, *162
Estey cottage organ, *133
Ethan Allen; trotter, *90
Eureka, Calif., mansion, *132
Evans, Oliver, inventions, 68
  mill, *68

factory, planning, *152–157
falso-front buildings, *110–111
Faneuil Hall; grasshopper vane, 25
farmers' home and tools, *102–103
Farmers' Museum, Cooperstown, N. Y., 57
farmhouse portrait, Leeds, N. Y., *57
favrile glass, *137
federal style architecture, *45
Feininger, Andreas, photographer, 152
Ferris, George Washington Gales, 140
Ferris Wheel, Chicago World's Fair, 140, *141
fieldstone hearth, Hyland House, Guilford, Conn., *27
fire engine, hand-pumped (1843), *74–75
firearms, frontier, *100
Flatiron (Fuller) Building, New York, *143
Flemish cottage, Portsmouth, N. H., *29
Flying Cloud; clipper ship, 91
Ford, Henry, 138
  organ owned by him, *133
Ford, Henry, Museum, Dearborn, Mich., 72, 73, 74, 75, 103, 133, *138, 139, 140
Ford, Jazaniah, 53
Ford car, first, 138
  Model T, *139
form and function, *144
Foster, John, first maker of woodcut, *25
Fourth of July in Philadelphia (1812), *74
Fowler, Orson W., 96
France; heritage from, *108–109
Franklin, Benjamin, 39, 54, 64
  stove, *26, *75
French Renaissance, 130
French Tudor, 130
Frontier, Fabulous, *98–101
fuel; atomic element, A.E.C. Center, *163
Fuller (Flatiron) Building, New York, *143
Fulton, Robert, and inventions, *68
function and form, *144
fur traders, *100
furniture, fancy, *134–135
  fine, *48–49
  Grand Rapids, 134
  mass production, 134
  "modern," 128
  Old World, *30, *31
future; architecture for, *152–157

gadgets and guns, *94–95
Galatea; clipper ship, *91–92
games, card, 53

Gansvoort, Mrs. Harmon; portrait, *19
Garvan, Mabel Brady, Collection, Yale, 20
Gatling, Richard, and the Gatling Gun, 94, *95
General Electric J-47; thrust of, *161
General Motors Technical Center, Warren, Mich., *152–157
George III, 46
Georgian architecture, *43
Gilded Age, *130–137
glass, colored (stained), *136–137
  favrile, *136–137
  pressed, 61
glassware, Early American, *60–61
glassworks, first, *51
Goddard, John, cabinetmaker, 48, 49
gold, *110
Gothic architecture, 83
  variations, *84–85
Grabhorn, Mr. and Mrs. Edwin, 88
Grand Rapids furniture, 134
Grant, General, Era, 130
gravestone, sculptured, Dorchester, Mass., *25
Great Seal of the United States; proposed designs, *54
Greek Revival, *70–77
  bathroom, *80
  home in New York; interior, *72–73
Guaranty (now Prudential) Building, Buffalo, N. Y., *144
Guilford, Conn.; Hyland House fieldstone hearth, *27
guns and gadgets, *94–95

Hammond typewriter (1880), *140
harpoon, whaler's, *93
Harrison, Peter, architect, 18
Harvard University radio telescope, *164
hearth, fieldstone; Hyland House, Guilford, Conn., *27
heating, house, *26, *27
Henry Ford Museum, Dearborn, Mich., 72, 73, 74, 75, 103, 133, *138, 139, 140
Hepplewhite, George, 48
highways and bridges, *150–151
Hingham, Mass.; Old Ship Meeting House, *52
Historical Society of Pennsylvania, 26
Hoboken, N. J.; New York Yacht Club house, *84
Holabird, William, architect, 143
Holmes, Oliver Wendell, "Wonderful One-Horse Shay," *88
Home Insurance Building, Chicago, *143
homes, early, *28, *29
  French, *109
homes and tools, farmers', *102–103
Homespun, Age of, 57
hoop-and-stick chairs, *46–47
horse-drawn age; equipment, *88–90
horse-racing, Union Course, L. I. (1858), *90
"horses, iron," *106–107
Houston, Texas, skyline, *150–151
Hubbard, Elbert, 128
"Hudson River Bracketed Style," *83
Hull, John, silversmith, 21
Humphreys, J. Y., 53
Hunt, Richard Morris, architect, 130
Hurley, N. Y.; Van Deusen House; wall of stone, *33
hydraulic lift (elevator) (1878), *144
Hyland House field-stone hearth, Guilford, Conn., *27

Idaho Falls Center, A.E.C.; atomic fuel elements, *163

Illinois Division of Parks and Memorials, 108
Indian art, *122–123
Industrial Revolution, 47
inns, *54–55
interchangeability of parts (standardization), 26, 66, 78
International Business Machines Corp.; electronic intricacy, *158–159
intricacy, electronic, in compact design, *158–159
inventors; gadgets and guns, *94–95
inventors for livelier living, *140
inventor, first American; Joseph Jenks, *36
Iowa log cabin, *102
"iron horses," *106–107
iron making, *36
iron work, ornamental, of New Orleans, *109
Irving, Washington; Sunnyside, Tarrytown, N. Y., and Corporation, *84

Jackson, Richard House, Portsmouth, N. H., *29
Jefferson, Thomas, 71
Jenks, Joseph; first American inventor, 36
Jenney, William, architect, 143
Jerome, Chauncey; clockmaker, 66
Jervis, John B., engineer, 106
jet engine; blast of, *160
  thrust of, *161

Kahn, Albert, architect, 152
Kenmore, Va., *44
kitchen, early, *27
  farmhouse (1820); Farmers' Museum, Cooperstown, N.Y., *56
  seventeenth-century; Delaware Valley, *31
Krimmel, John Lewis, painter, 74

Laguna, N. Mex.; Church of San Jose, *116
lampshades, glass, *136–137
lamps, Tiffany, *137
Las Trampas, Church of, *116
Latrobe, Benjamin, architect, 76–77
Leavenworth, Colonel Jesse, 118
Leeds, N. Y.; farmhouse portrait, *57
Le Roux, Bartholomew, silversmith, 21
lift (elevator) hydraulic (1878), *144
Lindamood, Peter, 136
Lippitt House, Cooperstown, N. Y., *56
Liquid Carbonic Co.; chemical equipment, *162
living standard, 39
Lockwood, Miss Edith, 82
Lockwood, William E.; Swiss Gothic house, *82
locomotive, early, *106–107
log cabin, Iowa, *102
log cabins, *102
Los Angeles County Museum, 118, 119

"Make Peace," Somerset County, Md.; brick design, *33
Manheim, Pa.; glass, 61
Marine Historical Association, Mystic, Conn., 84, *85, 93
Massachusetts Historical Society, 25
Massachusetts Institute of Technology; research program, *148
mass production, distributing and selling, 66
Matador Ranch, 120
materials, common; craftsmen in, *22, *23
Mather, Richard; first woodcut, *25
May, Cliff, architect, 127
McCormick reaper, *103
McIntire, Samuel, wood carver and architect, 45

McKay, Donald; clipper-ship builder, *91
McKim, Mead & White, architects, 142
McMurrey Oil Refinery, Tyler, Texas, *147
meetinghouses, old, *32
memorial embroidery, Richardson, *75
Metropolitan Museum of Art, 31, 66, 72, 91
mid-Victorian taste, *86
Mill, Evans', *68
Miller, Alfred Jacob, painter, 100
Miller, Joaquin, poet, 106
Miller, Lewis; drawings, *62–63
Mills, Robert, architect, 77
mining era survival, *110–111
Mission architecture, *124–125, *126
    art. *124–125
    furniture and furnishings, *128
Missions. See names of missions under "San"
Missions, California, style, *124–125
    Southwest, 115, 116
Mississippi Valley, 108
Missouri Historical Society, 100
"modern" furniture, 128
modern tools, 146
Montecito, Calif., 127
Moore, Harriet, 75
Morris, William, and the Morris chair, 128
Morse, Samuel F. B., inventor and painter, 78
motor cars, early, *138–139
Murphy, Tim, 41
Museum of Art, Metropolitan, 31, 66, 72, 91
Museum of Art, Philadelphia, 71, *76–77
Museum of Fine Arts, Boston, 31, 38, 39, 49, 53
Museum of the City of New York, 80, 86
Mystic, Conn.; house with Gothic ornaments, 84, *85
Mystic Marine Historical Association, 93

Navajo blankets, *122
    silverware, *122
navigation, space; rockets for, *161
needlework, early, *24, 25
New Mexico; modern home, *117
New Orleans houses; iron work, *109
New York City, early; architecture, *16–17
New York Historical Society, 73, 134, 136
New York Public Library, 117
New York State Historical Association, 75
New York Yacht Club house, Hoboken, N. J., *84
Newberry Library, 108
Newcomen's steam engine, 68
Newport, R. I.; staircase of Chateau-sur-Mer, 130, *131
    William Watts Sherman mansion, *142
Nicholson, Paul C., Jr., 142
Norman mansions, 83
Norwegian-American Historical Museum, 102
nouveau, art, 137

Oak Ridge atomic accelerator, *162
Oceanside, Calif., 126
octagonal houses, *96
oil refinery, McMurrey, Tyler, Texas, *147
"Old Pacific" (Packard car, 1903), *139
Old Ship Meeting House, Hingham, Mass., *32
Old Sturbridge Village, Mass., 12
Oldsmobile Limited (1910), *138
organ, Estey cottage, *133
"Oroktor Amphibolos," 68
Otis, Elisha Graves, inventor, 144
outlines, sky, of cities, *150–151

Packard car (1903; "Old Pacific"), *139
painters, portrait, early, 18
Panhandle, Texas, 120

Panhandle-Plains Historical Museum, Canyon, Texas, 118, 121
parlor, seventeenth-century, Oyster Bay, N. Y., *30
    Victorian, John Belter's, *86
Parson Capen House, Topsfield, Mass., *28, *29
    pendill of wood, *33
parts, punching out, *149
parts; standardization of, 26, 66, 78
patterns that caught the eye, *74–75
Peabody, Joseph, 50
Peabody Museum, Salem, Mass., 50
Peirce House, Salem, Mass., *45
    staircase, *44
Pelissero, Mr. and Mrs. Goodwin, 119
pendill, wooden, *33
Pennsylvania Academy of the Fine Arts, 74
Pennsylvania Farm Museum of Landis Valley, 98
Pennsylvania Historical Society, 26
Pennsylvania rifle, *40, *41
perambulator, baby, *134
period rooms, *30, *31
pewter, tin, and clay, *58–59
Philadelphia Fourth of July (1812), *74
    Greek Revival in, 71
    water-system buildings, *76–77
Philadelphia Museum of Art, 71, *76–77
phonograph, Edison, Model D (1908), *140
Phyfe, Duncan, 135
    headquarters in New York, *72
    styles, *72–73
Pickard, G. W., inventor, 140
pioneers; arts of, *98–99
planning, factory, *152–157
playing cards, historic, and table, *52–53
plow, Deere, *103
Polk, James K., 78
portrait painters, early, 18
Portsmouth, N. H.; Richard Jackson House, *29
pottery, early, *30
    Indian, *123
pottery, tin, and clay, *58–59
Prairie du Chien, Wis., 132, *133
pressed glass, 61
Prudential (formerly Guaranty) Building, Buffalo, N. Y., *144
pueblo, adobe, Taos, N. Mex., *115
punch bowl, Revere, *39
punching out of parts, *148
"Puritans, Young"; painting, *15

racing, horse; Union Course, L. I. (1858), *90
radio set (1906), *140
radio telescope, Harvard University, *164
railroad, transcontinental, 107
railroads, early, *106–107
railway car, vertical, 144
ranch-house style, *126–127
"Rattle and Snap", Columbia, Tenn., 78, *79
reaper, McCormick, *103
Red Lion Inn, Del.; common room, *64–65
Regency, English, style, 73
Reilly, Mrs. R. H., Jr., 82
Renaissance, French, 130
research program, M.I.T., *148
Revere, Paul, *38, 39
    punch bowl, *39
    rattlesnake cartoon, *39
    silversmith, *39
    versatility, 39
Rhode Island Historical Society, 49
Richardson, H. H., architect, 142
Richardson memorial, embroidery, *75
rifle, Pennsylvania, *40, *41
Rittenhouse, David; clock, *66
river travel, *104–105

Roche, Martin, architect, 143
Rockaway carriage, *89
Rockefeller, John D.; desk, *133
rockets for space navigation, *161
Roebling, John A., inventor, 151
romantic decades, 82–96
rooms, period, *30, *31
Roycroft Inn, East Aurora, N. Y., *128
Russell, Charlie, artist, 110

Saarinen, Eero, architect, 152, 154
saddles, *118–119
safety elevator; invention of, 143
Saint Alban's Episcopal Church, Staten Island, N. Y., *84
Saint Louis City Art Museum, 104, 105
saint makers, 116
Salem, Mass.; Essex Institute, 45
    Peabody Museum, 50
    Peirce House, *45; staircase, *44
Salem square-rigger, *The George*, *50
San Capistrano, Mission of, *114–115
San Carlos Borromeo, Mission of, Carmel, Calif., *124, *125
Sanderson, Robert, silversmith, 21
San Esteban Rey, Mission of, *116
San Fernando, Mission of, *124, 125
San Francisco (in 1816), *126
San Jose, Church of, Laguna, N. Mex., *116
San Juan Capistrano, Mission of, *114–115, *124
San Luis Obispo, Mission of, 125
Sandwich glass, 61
Santa Fe, N. Mex.; adobe home, *117
Santa Fe, N. Mex., early, *117
santeros, 116
Saratoga, Battle of, 41
Sarven, James D., inventor, 89
Saugus, Mass.; iron works, *36
Savage, Thomas, silversmith, 21
sawmill, first in New England, 29
science, applied, and beauty, *162–163
scrimshaw work, whalers', *93
sculptor, first American professional (William Rush), 74
Seal, Great, of the United States; proposed designs, *54
secretary, block-front, *48–49
    tambour, *49
selling, distributing, and mass production, 66
sewing machine; invention of, *94
Seymour, Thomas, cabinetmaker, 49
sgraffito jug, *59
shades, glass, for lamps, *136–137
Shakers' gathering room, *87
"Shay, the Wonderful One-Hoss," *88
Sheraton, Thomas, 48
Sherman, Roger, *46
Shingle Style architecture, *143
ships, clipper, 83, *91–93
"ships of the plains," *98
Shryock, Gideon, architect, 77
sign, tavern, *22
silversmiths, early, 18
silversmiths, *20, *21
silverware, Navajo, *122
    Revere, *38, *39
Singer Sewing Machine Co., 94
sketches by Lewis Miller, *62–63
sky outlines of cities, *150–151
skyscrapers, 143
sleigh, horse-drawn, *90
slipware, *59
sofa, circular, *135
Somerset County, Md.; "Make Peace" brick design, *33
South Orleans, Mass.; Cape Cod house, *35
Southwest, timeless, *115
    churches, *116

171

space navigation; rockets for, *161
speed; exciting look of, *161
spice cabinet, 30
spinning and weaving, *56–57
Springfield, Ill.; Horizontal Style house, *142
square-rigger, *The George*, *50
stagecoaches, *64–65, *106
staircase, Peirce House, Salem, Mass., *44
standard of living (1730), 39
standardization of units (parts), 26, 66, 78
Stanley Steamer (1910), *139
Staten Island, N. Y.; Saint Alban's Episcopal Church, *84
steam engines, first, 68
steamboats, river, *104–105
steel skeleton frame building, first (Tacoma Building, Chicago), *143
Stickley, Gustave, 128
Stiegel, William Henry; glassware, 61
stone wall, Van Deusen House, Hurley, N. Y., *33
stove, dunce-cap, *75
  Franklin, *26, *75
stoves, early, decorated, *26
Strickland, William, architect, 77
Suffolk Museum, Stony Brook, L. I., 90
Sullivan, Louis, architect, *144
Sully, Thomas, artist, 71
Sunnyside; home of Washington Irving, Tarrytown, N. Y.; and Corporation, *84
supersonic age, *160
suspension bridges, *150–151
Swiss chalets, 83
Swiss Gothic house, Lockwood's, *82

table, tilt-top, *48
trestle, *30
table, card, and historic playing cards, *52–53
Tacoma Building, Chicago, *143
Taliaferro, Richard, architect, 18
tambour secretary, *49
Taos, N. Mex.; adobe pueblo, *115
Tarrytown, N. Y.; Sunnyside, home of Washington Irving; and Corporation, *84
taste; development of, 15
  mid-Victorian, *86
tavern sign, *22
taverns, *64–65
Technical Center; General Motors; Warren, Mich., 152–157
telephone, wall-type (1904), *140
telescope, radio; Harvard University, *164
television city circuit board, *159
Temple, Lewis, whaler and inventor, 93

Terry, Eli, clockmaker, *66–67
Texas Panhandle, 120
Thomas, Seth, clockmaker, 66–67
Thomas Fitch; clipper ship; model, *92
Thomson, Charles, 54
Thornton, William, architect, 76
Tiffany, Louis Comfort, and Tiffany glass, *136–137
Tiffany & Co., 54
timbers, house, *35
tin, clay, and pewter, *58–59
Titcomb, May Sarah, 24, 25
toleware, *58
tools and homes, farmers', *102–103
tools and trappings, cattlemen's, *120–121
tools, early American, *12–13
tools, hand, *146
tools of today, *146–149
Topsfield, Mass.; Parson Capen House, *28, *29
  pendill of wood, *33
towns, mining, *110–111
trades, early, 15
Trampas, Las, Church of, *116
transcontinental railroad, 107
Transfer-matic machine, *149
trappings and tools, cattlemen's, *120–121
travel on inland waters, *104–105
travelers; designs for, *64–65
trestle table, *30
trotting match (1858), *90
trotting wagon, 83, *89
tube, vacuum, *158–159
Tudor cottages, 83
Tudor style architecture, *142
Tudor, French, 130
tunnel, wind, largest, *161
Tuscan Villa, 83
typewriter, Hammond (1880), *140

Union Course, Long Island (1858), *90
Union League Club, 98
units, parts, standardization of, 26, 66, 78

vacuum tube, *158
Van Bergen, Marten, 57
van der Spiegel, Jacobus, silversmith, 20
Van Deusen House, Hurley, N. Y.; wall of stone, *33
van Dyck, Pieter, silversmith, 21
vanes, weather, of metal, *25
van Inburgh, Peter, silversmith, 21
vehicles, horse-drawn, *88–90
"Versailles of Industry," *152–157
vertical railway car, 144
Victorian Era, *130–137

Victorian parlor, John Belter's, *86
Villa Louis, *133

Wadsworth, Atheneum, 22, 24
wagon, covered, *98–99
  trotting, 83
wagons, horse-drawn, *88–90
wall of stone; Van Deusen House; Hurley, N. Y., *33
Walter, Thomas U., architect, 76, 77
Washington, George, 51
wealth along the waterways, *18
weather vanes of metal, *25
weaving and spinning, *56–57
Webster, Daniel; definition of art, 13
Wells, Fargo & Co.; Overland Stage, *106, 116
West, winning of the, *98–101
West Chester, Pa.; Swiss Gothic House, Lockwood's, *82
Westinghouse, George, Sr., and Jr., 140
Wetmore, Miss Edith, 130
Wetmore, George, 130
  mansion, Chateau-sur-Mer, Newport, R. I., 130, *131
whalers, 91, *93
  art; scrimshaw, *93
White, Stanford, architect, 142
Whitney, Eli, and the Cotton Kingdom, *78–79
  invention of the interchangeability of parts, 78
  workshop, *78
Willard, Aaron, clockmaker and clocks, *66
Wilson, James, inventor, 75
wind tunnel, largest, *161
Windsor chairs, *46–47
Winslow, Edward, silversmith, 21
Winterthur, Du Pont Museum, Winterthur, Del., 19, 22, 25, 30, 31, 45, 46, 49, 50, 59, *64–65, 72, 73
Wisconsin State Historical Society, 133
Wistar, Caspar, 61
"Wisterberg" glass, *60, 61
"Wonderful One-Hoss Shay," *88
wood; early use of, *22–23
wood carving, *45
woodcut, first, *25
Wooten, W. S., inventor, 133
Wren, Sir Christopher, 43
Wright, Frank Lloyd, architect, 142

Yale University Art Gallery, 46, 72, 78
  Mabel Brady Garvan Collection, *20–21
York County, Pa., Historical Society, 63
"Young Puritans," painting, *15